Madame Song

Pi Li

Madame Song

A Life in Art and Fashion

Thames &Hudson M+

With over 300 illustrations

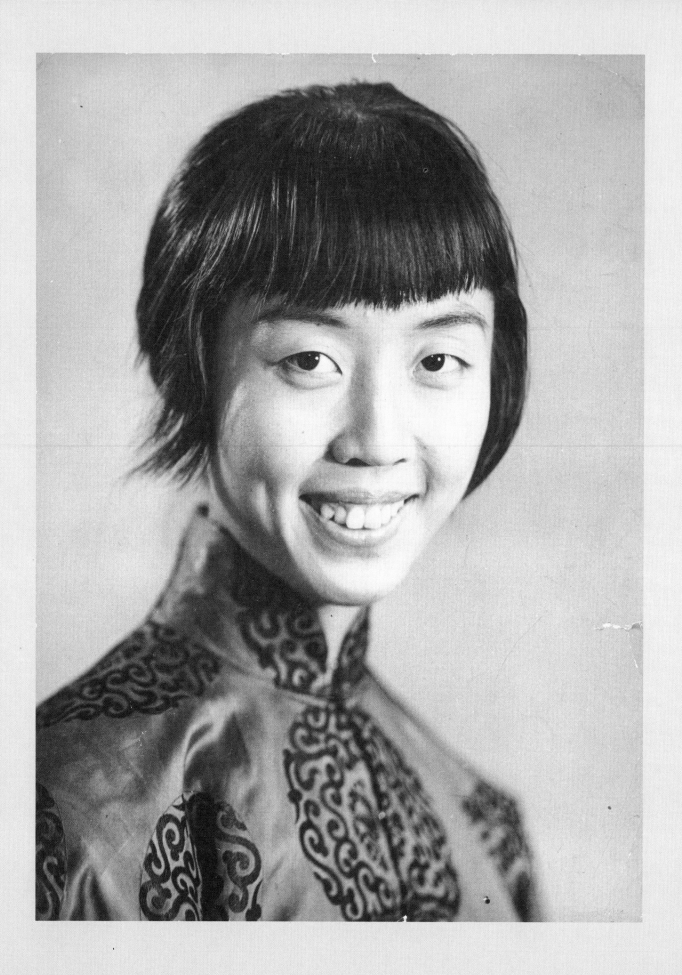

Song Huai-Kuei

Née à Pékin en 7. 12 (DEC) 1939

1954 - 1958 : Etudes à l'Académie Centrale
des Beaux-Arts à Pékin.

1959 - 1962 : Etudes à l'Académie des
Beaux-Arts de Sofia.

1962 - 1970 : A Participé à des expositions Collectives à Sofia, VARSOVIE,
Berlin Prague, TOKYO, San Francisco. ECT

1971 - 1973 : Participe à la Ve et VIe
Biennales internationales de la
Tapisserie à lausanne.

1974, Participe à des expositions de
groupe à la Galerie La Demeure
et à la Galerie Etienne de Causans
à PARis.

1975 : Participe à une exposition internationale à la galerie Jacques
Baruch à Chicago.

Dr Pi Li is Head of Art at Tai Kwun Contemporary in Hong Kong. He was previously at M+, Hong Kong, where he served as Sigg Senior Curator (2012–2023) and Head of Curatorial Affairs (2020–2023).

Front cover: Song Huai-Kuei, 1985. Garments: Pierre Cardin archives. Photo: © Yonfan.
Back cover: Song Huai-Kuei and her artwork *Composition in Rose*, mid-1980s. Photo: © Yonfan.
Page 2: Song Huai-Kuei and models at the Forbidden City. Garments: Pierre Cardin archives. Photo: © Yonfan.
Page 4: Song Huai-Kuei, early 1960s. © Boryana Varbanov and Phénix Varbanov.
Page 5: Song Huai-Kuei's handwritten biography in French, 1975. © M+, Hong Kong.
Page 9: Song Huai-Kuei, *Dream of Zhuangzi*, 1970s (see page 103).

First published in the United Kingdom in 2023 by
Thames & Hudson Ltd, 181A High Holborn, London WC1V 7QX,
in collaboration with M+, West Kowloon Cultural District,
38 Museum Drive, Kowloon, Hong Kong

Madame Song: A Life in Art and Fashion © 2023 Thames & Hudson
Ltd, London, and M+, West Kowloon Cultural District, Hong Kong

Text and illustrations © 2023 M+, Hong Kong, unless otherwise
stated on pages 283–284
Design © 2023 Thames & Hudson Ltd, London

Assistant editors: Wu Mo, Tanja Cunz
Editorial assistant: Tin Ping Yeung
English editing: William Smith, Jacqueline Leung
Chinese editing: Lam Lap-wai, Zhong Yuling, Or Ka Uen
Translations: Piera Chen, Grace Lam, Amy Li, Alvin Li,
Andrea D. Lingenfelter
Publishing manager: Dustin Cosentino
Rights and reproductions: Jacqueline Chan, Crystal Yu, Mankit Lai
Design: Roger Fawcett-Tang

British Library Cataloguing-in-Publication Data
A catalogue record for this book is available from the British Library

ISBN 978-0-500-48095-3

Printed in Malaysia by Papercraft

Be the first to know about our new releases,
exclusive content and author events by visiting
thamesandhudson.com
thamesandhudsonusa.com
thamesandhudson.com.au

Contents

Foreword

Suhanya Raffel

The extraordinary life story of Song Huai-Kuei, better known as Madame Song, follows the arc of twentieth-century history. Artist, entrepreneur, and impresario, Song broke cultural barriers for love, transcended Cold War borders for her art, and laid the foundations for a global fashion industry. Her epic tale, narrated from many perspectives in this publication, also embodies a spirit that resonates with the core mission of M+. With her cosmopolitan outlook, she defined an influential vision for Chinese culture on the world stage and asserted an Asian perspective in twenty-first-century art and design. Indeed, Madame Song is a name that everyone interested in the roots of contemporary visual culture needs to know.

In many ways, Song's tale could only be told at M+, the first global museum of visual culture in Asia. True to her wide-ranging life in visual art, design, and fashion, this publication is the work of an interdisciplinary team led by Dr Pi Li in his former role of M+'s Sigg Senior Curator and Head of Curatorial Affairs. It also serves as a companion volume to the exhibition *Madame Song: Pioneering Art and Fashion in China*, which highlights her iconic style in works of both art and fashion.

At the heart of this volume is a critical biography that explores Song's youth in revolutionary China, her cross-cultural marriage to Bulgarian fibre artist Maryn Varbanov, her success within avant-garde circles in Eastern and Western Europe during the Cold War, and finally her efforts within China to revive traditional aesthetics in tandem with the explosive rise of global couture. Throughout her life, she cultivated an aspirational image of what a modern Chinese woman could be within a changing and opening world. A consummate networker, Song built bridges between people, disciplines, and business interests, often in the elegant surroundings of Maxim's de Paris, Beijing, the restaurant she famously helped to open.

I am proud that M+ can spotlight the work of this exceptional figure. I would like to thank the members of the curatorial team at M+: Dr Wu Mo, De Ying Associate Curator, Visual Art; Tanja Cunz, Associate Curator; and Yeung Tin Ping, Curatorial Assistant. They have crafted a nuanced presentation of Madame Song's life and times. My sincere thanks to Cui Jian and Liu Heung Shing, who contributed their reflections to this book. Finally, gratitude goes out to Boryana Varbanov and the family of Song Huai-Kuei, who have entrusted her archives to M+ and supported this project from the start.

Who is Madame Song?

Introduction

The first question to arise as a reader opens this book may well be, 'Who is this Madame Song?' Even her full name—Song Huai-Kuei—is unlikely to ring a bell. Yet a mere twenty years ago, Madame Song was practically a household name in Chinese literary, artistic, film, and fashion circles. In early twentieth-century China, 'Madame' was commonly used to honour women with high social status.[1] Song Huai-Kuei, with her intellectual upbringing and extraordinary charm, doubtlessly merited the title. But in the socialist era in which she was active, this honourific was waning in popularity, the remnant of a bygone era. Its use for Song adds an alluring embellishment to her legendary life.

Song was born in 1937, in the shadow of the Japanese invasion of China. Her father worked for the Nationalist government, and the family was displaced during the war while Song was still an infant. They finally settled in Beijing in 1947. After graduating from high school, Song was admitted to the oil painting department of the Central Academy of Fine Arts, where she fell in love with Maryn Varbanov (1932–1989), a student from the People's Republic of Bulgaria. The pair managed to obtain a marriage licence with the blessing of Premier Zhou Enlai (1898–1976)—the first case of a Chinese citizen marrying a foreigner in the People's Republic of China (PRC). In 1958, Song, Varbanov, and their infant daughter moved to the Bulgarian capital, Sofia. There, the couple became artistic collaborators. They used tapestry—a traditional craft form with a rich history in the Balkans—as a medium for modernist experimentation, creating three-dimensional installations. Through serendipity, the two found ways to cross the Iron Curtain to participate in modern art exhibitions, including the Lausanne International Tapestry Biennial in Switzerland, before relocating to Paris in 1975.

In the French capital, the couple met Pierre Cardin (1922–2020), a fashion designer and pioneering business mogul eager to explore the Chinese market. This encounter was a turning point in Song's life. With little hesitation, she bid farewell to Paris and her identity as an artist and moved back to China to help Cardin expand his empire. At that time, in the early 1980s, China was starting to implement policies of reform and opening-up, transforming the economy and ushering in dramatic social change. In addition, the emergence of new art movements and the rise of fifth-generation filmmakers heralded a decade in which avant-garde art and popular culture flourished in China.[2]

It was upon this fertile ground that Song promoted Cardin's designs in Beijing, introducing vibrant colour to a capital city once saturated with dour greys and blues. In 1981, Song organised a watershed fashion show in the Beijing Hotel, then took Chinese models she had trained herself to Cardin's runway in Paris. She also collaborated with Cardin to open a Beijing branch of Maxim's, the renowned French restaurant. As the first Western dining establishment to open in China after the Cultural Revolution, Maxim's soon became the favourite gathering spot for local and international filmmakers, actors, musicians, artists, businessmen, and diplomats. Presiding over Maxim's, a symbol of the Western cosmopolitan lifestyle, Song became the salon hostess of Beijing's elite in the 1980s. The media dubbed her the 'Godmother of Fashion', reflecting the frequency with which she judged modelling competitions. Song spent much of the decade facilitating a growing exchange between cultural and artistic figures in China and abroad. She helped secure Dior's support for the comedy *The Troubleshooters* (1988) by fifth-generation director Mi Jiashan (b. 1947). She even appeared as Empress Dowager Longyu in *The Last Emperor* (1987), the epic film directed by Bernardo Bertolucci (1941–2018).

After the 1989 protests, with China's market economy entering a decade of exponential growth, Song weathered the pain of losing Varbanov to cancer. She recovered to oversee a series of international fashion shows and attend receptions with state leaders. At the inaugural Chinese International Clothing and Accessories Fair, in 1993, Song was involved in the production of large-scale runway presentations for Gianfranco Ferré (1944–2007) and Valentino (Valentino Clemente Ludovico Garavani, b. 1932), as well as Cardin. In the wake of her cameo in *The Last Emperor*, she organised *Five Dynasties*, a world-touring fashion show that portrayed the evolution of clothing from the Tang to the Qing dynasties and wove together performances of Chinese martial arts with ballet and modern dance. The culmination of Song's career, *Five Dynasties* was a world-class spectacle in which East and West converged.

Such artistic experimentation was part of a revolution in Chinese visual culture in the 1990s that included films by some of Song's friends, such as *Raise the Red Lantern* (Zhang Yimou, 1991), *Farewell My Concubine* (Chen Kaige, 1993), and *Peony Pavilion* (Yonfan, 2001). Traditional cultural touchstones—royal courts, gardens, kung fu, and Peking opera—had previously been dismissed by PRC leaders as the dregs of an old society. In the avant-garde cultural and artistic movements of the 1980s, 'tradition' was equally frowned upon by innovators eager to ditch everything old in favour of Western modernism. Song and those in her circle revived Chinese traditions for the newly globalised world emerging in the 1990s. As China regained international visibility, its cultural heritage became central to the identities of its artistic and economic elite. By the time the country was ready to welcome the world for the 2008 Olympic Games, traditional culture had become an accepted part of the national image. Having pioneered this wave, however, Song passed away shortly before its apotheosis in the opening ceremony of the games in Beijing, an extravaganza of fireworks, *fou* drumming, and myriad performers clad in costumes inspired by national dress.

In the eyes of the public, Song's role as the chief representative of Pierre Cardin in China and the manager of Maxim's made her eventful life inseparable from Cardin's fashion empire. In 1981, Peter Dunn Siu-Yue (b. 1951)—co-founder of *City Magazine*, Hong Kong's oldest lifestyle magazine—travelled to Beijing to attend the Cardin fashion show that Song had orchestrated in the Beijing Hotel. Two years later, the two met again when Song was passing through Hong Kong. Based on that encounter, Dunn published 'Woman in Transit: Song Huai-Kuei', the earliest known account of Song's life and work. The article vividly conveys her ambition to bring the world to China while presenting China to the world. The 1990s saw her gradually introduced to mainland readers as well. In 1991, *China Today* was the first magazine on the mainland to publish a profile covering her international marriage, career in fashion, and involvement with Maxim's. The story established the core elements of her professional life, which would be repeated in much of the ensuing coverage. Curiously, Song never mentioned her almost two-decade-long artistic career, even as her family background and social life were illuminated in the media spotlight.

Song and those in her circle revived Chinese traditions for the newly globalised world emerging in the 1990s.

After 2000, Song gradually disappeared from the public eye. It was not until the 2016 release of director Lixin Fan's *Craft a Destiny*, a documentary series focused on distinguished women, that Song's rich life was narrated in detail. Her story began to resurface on television, the internet, and social media along with the recollections of celebrities and members of the cultural elite. These accounts are always tinged with nostalgia, but understandably so: Song embodies a bygone era, a moment when China was under-developed economically, yet confident, open, and ready to embrace the world with hope and optimism.

There remains much to uncover about Song's life. When she was not acting as chief China representative of Pierre Cardin and the manager of Maxim's, who was she? Why did she give up art, and how should we understand the nature of her life's work? With the exception of a few paintings, garments, and documents, Song did not leave many personal records behind. But these fragments reveal a vibrant voice and a life far more exuberant than that portrayed in the standard accounts circulating in popular media. This is what prompted our decision to dedicate a publication to her story and produce an exhibition at M+ examining her diverse contributions to visual culture.

The present volume traces Song's steps through different cities during her lifetime, from Beijing in the early days of the PRC to Cold War Sofia in the 1960s, and then from 1970s Paris to a post-reform Beijing and Hangzhou. Interspersed throughout the book are essays and other texts that examine not only the trajectory of her life, but also the political, cultural, and artistic contexts behind her activities to better represent the motivations behind her vanguardism. The book also ties together a number of figures with whom Song was in close contact during different periods: her college professors Shen Congwen (1902–1988) and Dong Xiwen (1914–1973); her close circle of artist friends in Paris, including T'ang Haywen (1927–1991), Zao Wou-Ki (1920–2013), and Pierre Cardin; and a younger generation of fashionistas she met in Beijing, such as runway director Jerry Zhang (b. 1959) and model Chen Juanhong (b. 1969). By mapping Song's intersections with these figures, what emerges is an atlas of the art and culture of her time.

Two other essays examine different facets of Song's life. Wu Mo zooms in on Song's artistic identity, taking her key tapestry series *Dream of Zhuangzi* (or *Butterfly*) as a point of departure. Wu analyses the integration of traditional Chinese artistic languages into Song's work and discusses how she connected the art worlds of Europe and China through collaborations with her husband, a juxtaposition that fuelled the ensuing new art movements in China. Song acted as a sponsor in the founding of the Institute of Art Tapestry Varbanov in 1986 at Zhejiang Academy of Fine Arts (now China Academy of Art), a development that enabled Varbanov to establish the earliest courses on modernism in socialist China and cultivate a cohort of artists—notably Gu Wenda (b. 1955), Liang Shaoji (b. 1945), and Shi Hui (b. 1955). Meanwhile, with an understanding of how Madame Song used fashion as a means of self-expression in Paris and Beijing, Tanja Cunz examines how 'Chineseness' has become a contested topic in Western fashion and explores how youthful Chinese designers articulate their identities by interpreting the country's traditions in a contemporary way.

Our research into Madame Song—a figure who stands at the intersection of various streams of visual culture—has also pointed to further insights that can be gleaned from studying the biographies of women who lived in tumultuous times. In twentieth-century China, the lives of heroic women generally followed one of two distinct paths: the first dedicated entirely to the fight for ideals, lending willing devotion to the revolution even to the point of being swallowed and torn into shreds by politics, as in the notable cases of writer Ding Ling (1904–1986) and activist Zhang Zhixin (1930–1975); the second characterised by the tragic fates of highly talented individuals brought down by historical turmoil, such as actress Ruan Lingyu (1910–1935) and pianist Gu Shengying (1937–1967). Taking a path all her own, Song neither succumbed to nor revolted against the crushing weight of life; rather, she always looked for possibilities in the crevices, tirelessly adjusting and shaping her actions to let light through. A life like hers can be easily underestimated, especially given her later investment in fashion, which could be seen to lack the profundity of literature and art. But in a China where socialist ideology persists, investing oneself in fashion and grounding oneself in everyday life can also be revolutionary. Tragic sacrifices for political ideals are not the only actions worth eulogising: Song's way of life, at once open-ended and resilient, offers a uniquely relevant reference for today's increasingly divided, black-or-white reality.

While sorting through Song's archives, we were shocked to discover just how many memories of her have become blurred, almost to the point of vanishing, in little more than a decade. This constant battle between memory and amnesia has also, consequently, contributed to shaping her history. As historian Luo Xin once observed, 'Memories are like lone islands, surrounded by long-forgotten oceans … If collective memories are the shared memories of a society in a particular era, then to study such memories must require a survey of not only what is remembered, but also what is excluded from remembrance.'[3] If the mainstream narratives of Chinese cultural history during the second half of the twentieth century are our lone islands of memory, then Song must represent the body of water in between. To study Song is to study the linkages between the various cultural phenomena of her lifetime. What this volume seeks to portray is not only the story of Madame Song, but also the exchange, evolution, and transmutation of a visual culture invented by her and her friends. Only in this way can we fully perceive the dynamic flows of art and fashion over time.

To study Song is to study the linkages between the various cultural phenomena of her lifetime.

Song Huai-Kuei and
her daughter, Boryana
Varbanov, 1988.

1950s: A Window of Freedom in Beijing

Chapter One

n 30 April 1950, a plaque inscribed with the calligraphy of Mao Zedong was installed on the former Imperial Ancestral Temple, located on the eastern edge of Tiananmen Square. The plaque gave the site a new name appropriate to a new China: 'Beijing Working People's Cultural Palace'. It was less than a year since the establishment of the People's Republic of China (PRC), and Beijing was overflowing with the vibrant energy of spring. The next day was the first of May, International Workers' Day, and more than ten thousand people would visit the former Imperial Ancestral Temple to enjoy leisure activities. It was just as the well-known writer Guo Moruo (1892–1978) had exulted: 'Once the Emperor's Temple, now the Cultural Palace'. The temple was no longer the exclusive domain of the imperial family; it had become a cultural centre the proletariat could freely enter to make use of everything from a theatre, a library, and exhibition spaces to floodlit playing fields and entertainment halls. The Beijing Federation of Trade Unions and the Beijing Federation of Literary and Art Circles, along with other organisations, had only that year established the Beijing Amateur Art School, inviting Lao She, Zhao Shuli, Tian Han, Li Huanzhi, Ye Qianyu, and other artists and scholars to teach courses in culture and vocational education. Among this cohort of instructors was the eminent artist Gu Yuan (1919–1996), whose woodcut *Working People's Cultural Palace* (1951) depicts a lively scene of workers and peasants studying and playing chess outside the complex. The artist instructors came from a wide variety of backgrounds, but all responded enthusiastically to the Communist Party of China (CPC) slogan, 'Serve the People'. They regarded their teaching at the Working People's Cultural Palace as putting into practice the party's method of going 'to the masses': forsaking the privileged solitude of the studio to apply their skills building a new, classless society.

One of the many people taking part in activities at the Working People's Cultural Palace was the young Song Huai-Kuei, who studied painting there every weekend. Although Song was still in high school, she had already chosen a path in the arts. In those days, most young people dreamed of becoming soldiers, engineers, or doctors so that they could help rebuild the nation out of the post-war rubble. Song's choice was unusual. That she could develop such an independent and self-directed character had much to do with the quality of her education and her family's open-mindedness.

Born in 1937 in Beijing, Song was her parents' first child, and was followed by three siblings. Her father, Song Liquan (1903–1991), and mother, Li Jingfang (1904–1980), were both passionate about education, and both had taught in middle schools. Li Jingfang chose the name Huai-Kuei ('missing Kuei') in memory of her younger brother, Li Guifang. The name could also denote longing for the osmanthus flowers of South China, whose fragrance, according to local lore, could be smelled for miles around. Despite her elegant and genteel name, Song was born at a time of great turmoil. Following the Marco Polo Bridge Incident of July 1937, Beijing residents were living under Japanese occupation. Not wishing to be the subjugated citizen of a defeated nation, Song Liquan joined the National Revolutionary Army, working in a civilian capacity in the fight against Japan. Li Jingfang took the infant Song Huai-Kuei, still wrapped in swaddling clothes, and went with the troops to find refuge wherever she could. It was not until 1940 that she was reunited with

Song Liquan, who had been transferred to the tax bureau in Shangrao Gan Prefecture of Jiangxi province.

In 1947, after the end of the Second Sino-Japanese War, a ten-year-old Song and her family returned to Beijing. Her mother, a Christian, sent her daughter to Christian schools not far from the family home: Peiyuan Elementary School and Bridgman Girls' College. Founded by the American Episcopal missionary Eliza Jane Gillett Bridgman (1805–1871), these were the first schools in North China to offer Western-style education to girls, and the values of the teachers were notably progressive. Bridgman Girls' College was located in a mansion that had once been the residence of the family of the Kangxi Emperor's mother, Madame Tong. Although the mansion had suffered the ravages of time, traces remained of the original upward curving eaves, green tiles, and red pillars characteristic of traditional aristo-cratic architecture. By 1951, the year that Song Huai-Kuei entered high school, Bridgman Girls' College had been renamed Beijing No. 51 School. Because many of its teachers had joined the CPC before the Chinese Civil War, the institution became an 'elite school' in the PRC. The sons and daughters of many important people were students there, including Zhang Hanzhi (1935–2008), who was the stepdaughter of the prominent politician Zhang Shizhao (1881–1973), and who later became Mao Zedong's English tutor. Li Yingnan (b. 1943), the half-Russian daughter of early CPC leader Li Lisan (1899–1967), also attended the school. Decades later, when she returned to China to assist Pierre Cardin in introducing a modern lifestyle to the country, Song's network of friends from No. 51 School would prove instrumental.

This print shows workers and peasants enjoying their leisure time, reading and playing chess before the solemn-looking Imperial Ancestral Temple. Some are sitting on the stone railings or on the ground, as if to proclaim their status as new owners of the building. A plaque bearing the words 'Beijing Working People's Cultural Palace' inscribed by Mao Zedong is hung at the entrance the temple, denoting the reformation of tradition under a new political regime.

Opposite
Song Huai-Kuei (third from left) with her three younger siblings, early 1950s.

‡

Left
Song Huai-Kuei (top) with
her secondary-school
classmates, early 1950s.

Below
Song Huai-Kuei (front
row, first from left) with
her secondary-school
classmates, early 1950s.

Opposite
Song Huai-Kuei's father,
Song Liquan, and mother,
Li Jingfang.

In 1954, after three years spent diligently studying painting, Song was one of ten students from across China to be offered a place in the oil painting department of the Central Academy of Fine Arts (CAFA) in Beijing, the best art school in the country. By then, the government had completed its land reforms and had begun establishing agricultural communes. The government had also reformed business and industry through the policy of 'peaceful redemption', which gave capitalists an avenue to become workers who lived by their own labour. Decisive actions such as these had swept away the atmosphere of greed and corruption of the former Nationalist government. The progressive intellectuals and artists of the 1950s welcomed these huge social changes, enthusiastically abandoning pre-war pursuits and throwing themselves into the task of building a new nation.

Song was one of ten students from across China to be offered a place at the Central Academy of Fine Arts.

This wholehearted embrace of a new era spread to Song's instructors at CAFA, including the professor with whom she was closest as an undergraduate, Dong Xiwen. After graduating from the National College of Art (predecessor of the Zhejiang Academy of Fine Arts, now the China Academy of Art), Dong moved to Hanoi to study at the École des Beaux-Arts de l'Indochine (now the Vietnam University of Fine Arts). Dong had then intended to travel to Paris for further studies, but the rising threat of war had forced him to return to China. In 1942, he happened to see copies of the Dunhuang murals by Chang Shuhong (1904–1994) and was deeply impressed. The Buddhist frescoes, dating from the fourth to the twelfth centuries, cover more than fifty thousand square metres in a complex of grottoes in Gansu province. Two years later, Dong joined the National Dunhuang Art Institute (now the Dunhuang Academy), headed by Chang, and spent four years studying and copying the monumental paintings.

Ten years older than Dong, Chang had studied in France, staged a solo show in Paris, and received numerous gold and silver medals at French art salons. His works later entered the permanent collection of the Centre Pompidou. Chang was inspired to return to China by *Les Grottes de Touen-Houang*, a series of catalogues by Paul Eugène Pelliot (1878–1945) published between 1920 and 1924. Chang dedicated the rest of his life to researching and preserving the Dunhuang murals. Because of Dunhuang's location in China's northwest, it was relatively peaceful during the Second World War, and, for the most part, the only people who were interested in the murals were young artists such as Dong. After the war, Dong staged a highly successful exhibition of his copies of the Dunhuang murals and was offered the post of instructor at the National Beijing Art College—the institution that would become CAFA.

On 1 October 1949, Chang'an Avenue was thronged with people. Dong joined the crowd to watch the ceremonial founding of the PRC and excitedly sketched the scene. Three years later, the Central Revolution Museum (now the National Museum of China), in celebration of the thirtieth anniversary of the founding of the CPC, commissioned CAFA to create an oil painting depicting the founding ceremony. Dong gladly accepted the assignment, working day and

Song Huai-Kuei with her Central Academy of Fine Arts professor Dong Xiwen in Dayabao hutong, late 1950s.

night with the intention of using new artistic techniques to depict the scene of an ancient nation being given new life.

Dong's work, entitled *The Founding of the Nation* (1952), presents the key figures at the ceremony in an exquisite arrangement. The architectural details and decorations, such as red carpets and lanterns, white marble balustrades, and yellow chrysanthemums, add to a striking visual effect. The work eschews conventional three-point perspective, and the composition is rich with patterns and areas of pure colour. Taken as a whole, the painting evokes the style and feel of the Dunhuang murals despite the modern subject matter. In fact, Dong had already begun exploring a new style of national expression in an earlier painting, *Kazakh Shepherdess* (1948). As Dong remarked: 'When I began to paint *The Founding of the Nation*, my intention was to make an oil painting in a style that reflected the Chinese people, which would be different from the usual Western-style painting. This certainly does not mean that the painting in its current form is completely Chinese; if we are to achieve a thoroughly national style of oil painting, we must continue to engage in experimentation in the future.'[1] Dong's ambition to experiment reflects the confidence and hopes of the art world of the 1950s, with many cultural figures seeking ways to acknowledge a new national identity. When Mao saw *The Founding of the Nation*, he remarked excitedly: 'This is a great nation, this is China. If our paintings were placed among international artworks, no one else would be able to compete with us, because we have a unique national form.'[2]

Dong's painting was subsequently reproduced on the front page of *People's Daily* and was heralded as the first masterpiece of socialist China. From that point on, Dong threw himself with renewed vigour into exploring a style of oil painting with national characteristics, spearheading a new era of Chinese art. When the young Song saw Dong's exhibition of copies of the Dunhuang murals, she was deeply moved; she also later recalled feeling 'overwhelmed with admiration' by the study for *The Founding of the Nation*, which she had been fortunate enough to glimpse.[3] It is possible that Song may have had nothing more than a vague grasp of Dong's artistic intentions, but, forty years later, as an established figure in China's burgeoning fashion industry, she carried on her teacher's exploration of the national spirit in her own way.

Song was also close to another teacher at CAFA, Shen Congwen, who shared Dong's desire to leave the past behind and embrace the future. Shen, however, had a dramatically different experience from his colleague, enduring decades of both personal and professional struggle. When Song was studying painting at the Working People's Cultural Palace, Shen, always dressed in a long, Western Hunan–style robe, shuttled back and forth between the red walls, going to his office at the Beijing Museum of History (now the National Museum of China) next door. Starting in 1952, Song encountered him again when he taught the history of art and textiles at CAFA.

Shen was one of the greatest Chinese writers of the twentieth century, as prominent as Lu Xun. Shen's style was nimble and charming, full of yearning for the down-to-earth and unsophisticated vitality of rustic life, and his work exemplified the lyricism of the modern Chinese literature that evolved from the progressive May Fourth Movement of the early twentieth century. Shortly after the founding of the PRC, however, Shen's literary works became the target of fierce criticism. The doctrinaire Guo Moruo, who had praised the Working People's Cultural Palace, criticised Shen as a 'rosy' writer who wrote about nothing but decadent sexuality, a 'dissolute playboy watching clouds and picking stars', 'deliberately engaged in counterrevolutionary activities', 'harbouring evil intentions, motivated by the desire to poison his readers' minds and weaken the People's spirit of struggle'.[4] As Shen sought artistic breakthroughs in a nation that was undergoing radical transformation, his domestic life fell into turmoil. He teetered on the brink of a psychological breakdown. Eventually, the relentless criticism led him to make an attempt on his own life.

Following that suicide attempt, Shen was discharged from hospital in March 1949. Already an amateur collector of handicrafts and artworks, he applied for a research position at the Beijing Museum of History—a move that marked the beginning of his turn away from literary creation towards the study of historical costume and crafts. Over time, his name all but disappeared from Chinese literary circles. When the Nobel Prize for Literature committee contacted the Chinese embassy in Stockholm to enquire about Shen's whereabouts in 1988, the cultural attaché replied that they had no knowledge of him. For his part, Shen seemed to have concluded that the lyrical and moving literature he had championed had gone out of style, replaced by the literature of socialist China with its emphasis on revolutionary belief

Dong Xiwen

The Founding of the Nation
1952 (revised in 1954 and 1971),
replica 1972 (revised in 1972 and 1979)
Oil on canvas
229 × 400 cm
Collection of National Museum of China

Dong Xiwen painted *The Founding of the Nation* four years after *Kazakh Shepherdess*. Comparing the two paintings, one sees the changes in Dong's style after the founding of the People's Republic of China in 1949 as he, like other artists, embraced the 'new' China. While *Kazakh Shepherdess* features bold outlines and sheer blocks of colour, *The Founding of the Nation* goes beyond realistic composition to convey the grandeur of the inauguration. In the latter, Dong portrays the scene with soft light and subdued, less contrastive colours to accentuate the textures of the carpet and lanterns, creating an elegant and harmonious atmosphere. The work references the highly detailed *gongbi* style in Chinese painting as well as the colouring techniques of the Dunhuang murals.

and intense focus on drawing clear lessons from history. In 1952, he spent four months writing a very long letter to a young reader, 'Everything Starts with Love and Understanding', the conclusion of which reads:

> At closing time, there are usually a few people who want to linger, and after I have seen them off, I stand alone on the city wall at Meridian Gate Tower and gaze out over the courtyard compounds of Beijing in the dusk, a million households in serried rows, and dwelling within them all kinds of existences, all kinds of growth and transformation. I can hear the miscellaneous sounds of radio broadcast speakers in the distance, along with the warbling of a yellow oriole in the pines and cypresses by the nearby Imperial Ancestral Temple, [and it is then that] I realize that I am truly all alone in life. And thus, I have studied a great deal of history, an ordinary person in the history of an extraordinary age. This is quite significant. Because if you can understand that your life is separate, and recognize its hopelessness, then you can use this study to understand 'one's own inexplicability', and this is indeed a kind of understanding.[5]

Although Shen immersed himself in the ruins of history, he also sought to respond to the reality of the present. At the time, the history of costume belonged to an obscure and overlooked corner of art history. Because costume research often focused on clothing worn by emperors, ministers, and other high officials, it could sometimes be perceived as out of step with the spirit of the proletariat. For Shen, however, the patterns found in clothing were akin to the patterns of the written word (the character 文, for 'literature' or 'the written word', is the old form of the character 紋, for 'pattern').[6] The study of garments afforded Shen the opportunity to learn about the people who wore them, which, in turn, extended his research to include social structures and historical developments. One could say that Shen turned a writer's lyrical eye to the archaeology of clothing, so that the study of costume became a new literary form.

When the young Song sat in Shen's class, she could not have fully understood all the complexities hidden in the heart of this amiable elder. She was nonetheless inspired by his research into *kesi* silk tapestry weaving, which influenced the later wall hangings she made with her husband. In 1963, entrusted by Zhou Enlai with the task of compiling a volume on the history of Chinese textiles and costume to be used for diplomatic gifts, Shen began to write *A Study of Ancient Chinese Costumes*. The manuscript miraculously survived the upheavals of the Cultural Revolution and was finally published in 1981. That same year, Song was in China scouting for models on behalf of Pierre Cardin and building relationships within the fashion industry. A decade later, she produced the *Five Dynasties* fashion show, bringing the achievements of *A Study of Ancient Chinese Costumes* to the world stage.

‡

Dong Xiwen
Kazakh Shepherdess,
1948
Oil on canvas
163 × 128 cm
Collection of National Art Museum of China

Among Song's class at CAFA was a student from Bulgaria, Maryn Varbanov. Prior to his arrival in China, Varbanov had studied in the sculpture department at the National Academy of Art in Sofia. After completing a year of Chinese-language instruction in Beijing, he was admitted to CAFA. The school felt that his training in painting was average at best, so he enrolled in a two-year course of basic studies along with the newly entering students. Song was assigned to assist him because she knew some English. It was through this serendipitous coming-together that the two fell in love. At the time, relationships between people from different nations was forbidden in China, and their love had to blossom in secret. When Varbanov wanted to set up a meeting, he would leave a slip of paper in a previously agreed-upon location, and Song would signal her availability by wearing either a single braid or two. Despite their efforts at concealment, those around them soon worked out that they were in a relationship, and Song gained a reputation as a woman of unsavoury conduct.

To make matters worse, in 1955, the year Song and Varbanov first met, the CPC launched the Campaign to Eradicate Hidden Counter-Revolutionaries, also called the Sufan Movement. With the aim of consolidating power for the party, the campaign sought to locate, expose, and purge counter-revolutionaries hiding within government institutions. Song's father was identified as a former member of the Kuomintang (Nationalist Party, or KMT); moreover, a review of his dossier revealed that he had worked in the Jiangxi province tax office while the Nationalist government was in power. This information fuelled false accusations that, while in Jiangxi, he had worked alongside Chiang Ching-kuo, son of KMT leader Chiang Kai-shek. Song had only recently entered CAFA full of confidence, but now found herself vilified and shunned by her classmates. Rather than retreating into self-pity, however, she put her head down, worked hard, and applied herself to the study of painting. This commitment garnered the goodwill and praise of Dong Xiwen, who remarked, 'You may be a skinny little girl, but your paintings are quite substantial!'[7] Dong extended a special invitation to the visiting Soviet painter Konstantin Maximov (1913–1994) to view Song's work. At a time when she found herself in the throes of a great struggle, Dong's mentoring and approval were a precious source of comfort.

The turmoil swirling around Song seemed only to intensify during her years at CAFA. When her illicit relationship was discovered, academy officials demanded that Song sign a written pledge that she would never be in contact with Varbanov again. To further thwart the couple, the Chinese Foreign Ministry went so far as to inform the Bulgarian embassy of Song's unfavourable family circumstances. Song, however, was not the sort of person to meekly submit to fate. In 1956, she summoned her courage and wrote a letter to Premier Zhou Enlai. She was able to take such a step because of her connection to Rong Gaotang (1912–2006), Olympic medallist and former leader of the General Administration of Sport of the PRC. In 1920, when Rong was being pursued by the KMT, he had been rescued by Song's mother, Li Jingfang, then a teacher at a private high school. When Rong returned to Beijing in 1949, he kept in touch with Li and often visited the

People would speak of Song and Varbanov delightedly as 'the first international marriage after 1949'.

Shen Congwen at his
desk, 1980s.

family at weekends, treating Song like his own child. Rong even took her to visit Zhongnanhai, where the national leadership lived. It was there that he introduced her to Chen Yi (1901–1972), who would soon become minister of foreign affairs, and, perhaps most importantly, to Zhou.

Song's letter to Premier Zhou was a last-ditch attempt to stay with the person she loved, so the response she received must have come as a profound relief. Zhou wrote that under China's constitution, every citizen had the right to decide whom they would marry; however, since both parties were quite young, and because of the large cultural differences between them, he advised them to give the matter careful consideration. Song and Varbanov saw this letter as proof of the premier's 'blessing', and at the end of 1956 they obtained a marriage certificate. Later, people would speak of them delightedly as 'the first international marriage after 1949'. The international communist newlyweds had two wedding ceremonies: a Bulgarian-style wedding in the Bulgarian embassy, presided over by the ambassador; and a Chinese-style wedding at CAFA, presided over by the academy's interim director, Jiang Feng (1910–1983). Dong Xiwen's gift to the couple was a pair of seals with each of their names inscribed on them, nestled inside a Han Dynasty jade seal box. The Bulgarian ambassador gave the couple red and white Bulgarian wines, which were quite hard to come by, and which were happily consumed by the newlyweds' classmates.

‡

Maryn Varbanov with Zhu Hongxiu at the Central Academy of Fine Arts practising pattern design, 1954. After the Cultural Revolution began in 1966, many art forms with traditional elements were suppressed in China. However, decorative patterns that draw on traditional design in arts and crafts were preserved for their pragmatic nature.

Right
Maryn Varbanov (third from right) sketching at Beijing's Biyun Temple with fellow Central Academy of Fine Arts students, 1955.

Left
Song Huai-Kuei (third from left) and Maryn Varbanov (first from left) with the first cohort of overseas Central Academy of Fine Arts students in Beijing, mid-1950s.

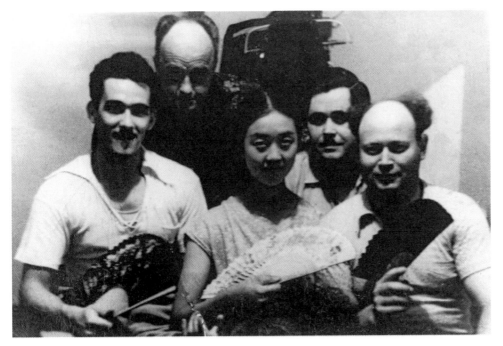

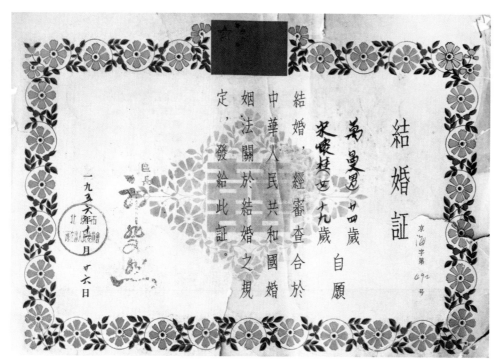

Song and Varbanov's union was inextricable from the cultural exchanges taking place between China and other countries during the 1950s. The fact that Varbanov had been recommended for study in China was a product of diplomacy. Although the United States and other Western countries had not yet established diplomatic relations with the PRC, the country was not completely cut off from the international community. On the contrary, Chinese diplomats attended such meetings as the Asian–African Conference in Bandung, Indonesia, and built relationships with counterparts from emerging nations, even making plans to establish contact with members of the European Left. Under a foreign policy guided by 'seeking common ground while reserving differences', a succession of modernist ideas trickled into China. The Chinese art world had yet to grasp the relationship between communism and artistic modernism, but political expediency allowed for a relatively open attitude for a time, even if it was subsequently suppressed by the blind criticism pervasive during the Cultural Revolution.

In 1952, the Chilean communist and artist José Venturelli (1924–1988) was sent to Beijing as vice-secretary of the Asia and Pacific Rim Peace Conference. Along with such political and cultural figures as Nobel laureate Pablo Neruda (1904–1973) and future Chilean president Salvador Allende (1908–1973), Venturelli co-founded the first Latin American non-governmental organisation aimed at promoting friendship with China, the Chile–China Cultural Association. During his time in Beijing, Venturelli also taught at CAFA and developed close friendships with such artists as Qi Baishi, Li Keran, Fu Baoshi, and Dong Xiwen. In 1956, Venturelli invited the Mexican muralist David Alfaro Siqueiros (1896–1974) to visit the academy. Siqueiros gave a slide presentation introducing the work of Mexican muralists, including José Clemente Orozco (1883–1949) and Diego Rivera (1886–1957). This was the second time that Chinese and Mexican artists

David Alfaro Siqueiros (front row, third from left) with artists at the *Second National Print Exhibition* held at the Gate of Divine Prowess of the Forbidden City during his visit to China, October 1956.

had found opportunities to share their work and exchange ideas since the 1930s, when Lu Xun introduced Rivera and Mexican mural art during the New Woodcut Movement. Dong Xiwen and other artists who had cast aside their admiration for modernist formal experimentation in pursuit of Socialist Realism were incredibly excited to hear Siqueiros describe the Cubist- and Primitivist-influenced style of Mexican murals as an entirely new kind of politicised art. Siqueiros urged Dong not to follow Soviet art, but to create his own style: 'The new realist painting that we're in favor of [Socialist Realism] requires more than new content, it also requires a new form, a new form that is nothing like the artistic forms of any era of the past ... This artistic form must be inclusive, integrated, complete, and all-embracing, in order to create a unique form of artistry.'[8] Siqueiros's slide-show had a profound effect on Dong and his students, including Song and Yuan Yunsheng (b. 1937). By the end of the 1950s, Song had already begun to pivot towards modernist abstraction. But Yuan was deeply influenced by Siqueiros's experimental approach to realism and began painting large-scale modernist murals, among them the mural commissioned for the Beijing Capital International Airport, *Water-Splashing Festival: Ode to Life* (1979), which many saw as a symbol of China's reform and opening-up.

In 1957, the year after Siqueiros's visit to China, French artist Jean Lurçat (1892–1966) was assigned by the French Communist Party to promote cultural exchange by staging an exhibition at CAFA. As the father of modern fibre arts, Lurçat revived the French tapestry industry and helped transform textiles into a medium of modern art. At his invitation, several modernist masters, including Fernand Léger (1881–1955), Henri Matisse (1869–1954), and Pablo Picasso (1881–1973), experimented with creating tapestries. Lurçat's exhibition introduced Varbanov to a rich artistic language. The presentation inspired him to combine modern fibre arts, traditional Balkan weaving, and Chinese textile arts, thereby setting him on his lifelong course of artistic innovation. Lurçat was also among the first cultural figures from Western Europe with whom Varbanov and Song established a professional relationship. When the couple eventually moved to France, in 1975, they participated in several editions of the Lausanne International Tapestry Biennial, directed by Lurçat.

‡

At the time of their marriage, Song and Varbanov were still students, and not yet twenty years old. CAFA arranged special housing for them, at A2 Dayabao hutong, at the foot of Dongcheng city wall in old Beijing, near the city moat. This traditional courtyard compound, formerly the home of a wealthy family, had been converted into housing for academy faculty. Between the 1950s and the Cultural Revolution, the most important artists in all of China gathered here: Dong Xiwen, Li Keran (1907–1989), Li Kuchan (1899–1983), Zhang Ding (1917–2010), Yan Han (1916–2011), and the painter Huang Yongyu (b. 1924), who was Shen Congwen's nephew. Song and Varbanov were the youngest residents of this convivial community. In July 1957, their daughter, Boryana Varbanov, was born, and Song took a leave of absence from school.

At the time, navy-blue Mao suits and Lenin suits were standard attire, but Song followed the trend among some CAFA students and faculty and made her own clothing, fashioning printed, fuchsia-coloured fabric into several traditional Chinese tunics. In 1958, Dong was commissioned by *People's Daily* to create a poster entitled *Diligence and Frugality in Housekeeping* for International Women's Day. Song volunteered to be the model, playing the role of a peasant

Jean Lurçat
Comme par miracle, 1945
Wool
217.2 × 322.6 cm
Collection of the
Metropolitan Museum
of Art. Gift of Seward
W. Eric, 1951.

This photo shows Song Huai-Kuei in Dayabao hutong with her family and their neighbour Huang Yongyu, 1958. On the right is Song, Maryn Varbanov, and their daughter, Boryana. On the left is Huang Yongyu with his wife, Zhang Meixi, and their children, Huang Heini and Huang Heiman. In 1952, Huang Yongyu had returned to Beijing from Hong Kong with his family and started teaching at the Central Academy of Fine Arts.

woman sewing clothing. Dong's graphic was simplified into an easily reproduced template for propaganda posters, and Song's image was consequently distributed throughout the country.

What Song did not know was that, while Dong was creating this poster, he was encountering fierce criticism. In 1957, the CPC launched the Rectification Campaign, with the initial objective of encouraging intellectuals within the party and non-communist parties to freely offer suggestions and criticisms of the government. In the event, however, many of the opinions expressed were very scathing and thus not to the CPC's liking. To party leaders, the exercise demonstrated that there were still remnants of the bourgeoisie among intellectuals. As a consequence, the campaign's objective shifted, and the public was directed to carry out an 'Anti-Rightist Campaign' by attacking the party's critics. Dong became a target of the Anti-Rightist Campaign owing to his criticism of the Ministry of Culture's educational regulations. Even his encouragement of Song's painting was denounced as evidence that he mentored only 'expert but not red' students;[9] in other words, he was accused of caring only about a student's artistic achievements while neglecting their moral and political development. Ultimately, he was forced to express his contrition by publishing 'My Self-Criticism' in the journal *Art Research*. In addition to Dong, nearly all the artists at A2 Dayabao hutong were affected by the movement. The Anti-Rightist Campaign vitiated the country's democratic system and struck heavy blows against the non-communist

In September 1957, in response to Mao Zedong's call for 'diligence and frugality in housekeeping', the All-China Women's Federation put forward a guiding policy for women's daily work, which informed Dong Xiwen's propaganda painting *Diligence and Frugality in Housekeeping* (1958). In early 1958, the Communist Party of China launched the Great Leap Forward. Mass production of propaganda art became a major political task for artists.

parties, academia, and intellectuals, promulgating numerous false accusations. The Anti-Rightist Campaign was a turning point in the history of the PRC, foreshadowing the turmoil and uncertainty of the Cultural Revolution that would arrive nine years later.

On leave from CAFA, Song was able to emerge from the political crisis relatively unscathed. Varbanov, who had transferred to the newly founded Central Academy of Arts & Design (now the Academy of Arts & Design, Tsinghua University) in 1955, went on to graduate in 1958. At that point, the family left A2 Dayabao hutong and departed for Bulgaria, marking the start of a foreign sojourn for Song that would last more than two decades.

My Mother,
Song Huai-Kuei

Boryana Varbanov

My memories are related to a time in the early 1960s when my mom and dad travelled together with me from Beijing to Sofia, a long journey that involved taking the trans-Siberian railroad to Moscow. In Bulgaria, we lived in the attic rooms of the Sofia Academy of Art until my brother was born in 1962. The first images stamped in my memory are from these times. The attic apartment had a small window looking at the golden dome of Alexander Nevsky Cathedral. The dome reflected the sunlight onto the bed, where it would shine in my eyes.

My mother was very young and innocent then, only twenty-one years old. When she left her home in China, she was not conscious of what life would be like in Bulgaria. Yet she was ready to discover the world with her 'one', whom she called the Prince of Oryahovo, my dad, Maryn Varbanov.

I remember a time when my mom came home once and sat on the steps of the stairs leading up to the attic room. She was waiting there with a lost and devastated look when my father found her. He asked her what had happened and expected the worst.

My dad had just held his first exhibition of the ink paintings he brought from China. The National Academy of Art and some national museums purchased the whole exhibition. He had given the entire envelope containing the gains to my mom, telling her to buy presents for herself and the family. She went to the only big market in Sofia at the time, the famous CUM (Central Universal Market). While browsing some garments, she did not pay attention to her bag, and the envelope with the money was gone when she wanted to pay. Devastated and crying, she was afraid to tell my dad about this.

His response was unexpected. He told her, 'You made me scared, darling. I thought something worse happened. It's only money! We are still young and we will earn it back.' My mom always said that my dad did not work for money. He needed only to have her by his side, his coffee, his cigarettes, and the means to make his art.

My mom treasured togetherness. She always told my brother and me that we were together in our past life, are together in the present, and we will be together in the future. At the same time, she was separated from her family in China during this time of the Iron Curtain. I imagined that she missed her parents deeply. We had no news at all from China in Bulgaria, yet she always believed that one day we would be able to return to Beijing.

In 1974 Premier Zhou Enlai invited all the *huaqiao*, or overseas Chinese citizens, to come back and visit their families. My mom, my brother, and I received a single passport to share for this long-awaited trip. (My dad had to remain in Bulgaria.) We packed a suitcase full of gifts, and before we left Bulgaria my mom wrote a letter to her parents to tell them that we would likely be able to reunite very soon.

My mom was prepared to accept different cultures without forgetting her own, as Zhou exhorted her in his letter granting her permission to marry a foreigner. She always knew that she would one day be able to do something for her country. She truly became the first cultural ambassador between China and the West. I could write more and more about our life, but it is not so easy to formulate a whole life of a wonderful mother, great artist, devoted wife, and outstanding public icon. She will always be remembered, and her spirit will be bright and gracious like those apsaras flying on the Dunhuang frescoes.

We are very thankful to M+, Dr Pi Li, and everyone involved in this eminent project related to Madame Song Huai-Kuei. Thank you all for your support and love.

Sofia, 3 July 2022

1958–1974:
A New World
in Sofia

ong Huai-Kuei was not yet twenty-one when she departed Beijing for Sofia with Maryn Varbanov in November 1958. Their daughter, Boryana, had just turned sixteen months old. With no direct trains, their route took them through Ulan Bator, Mongolia, and then across Siberia. After reaching Moscow, they travelled south to Sofia. The journey took more than ten days. Transferring from train line to train line in temperatures of minus 20 degrees Celsius with their daughter bundled in their arms, the young couple must have experienced tremendous hardships. They had brought hardly any personal items with them—their luggage was chock-full of artwork. The young Song, who had left everything familiar behind, was more anxious about the uncertain future than she was about the long journey fraught with challenges. She knew next to nothing about Bulgaria, this nation on the Balkan Peninsula, nor did she know Varbanov's family.

No sooner had they reached Sofia than Song hastily penned a letter to her former teacher Dong Xiwen. She was eager to learn how her friends at home were doing and to receive any words of comfort:

> It's already been a month since I left you all, and I expect that life has been rather tense for you over the past month, as so much has happened. This is even truer for me. I've come to an utterly unfamiliar place, and while everything feels very fresh and appealing, I can't help but feel lonely at times. I miss China, and everyone there.
>
> I'm sure that you are all keen to know how we are getting on, in life, in study, and in our work. My academic problems have been completely resolved, and I've begun classes. I have fourteen classmates, all very warm and welcoming. They treat me with great kindness and have been helping me out in every possible way. Our teacher is the most famous oil painter in Bulgaria, Ilya Petrov. I really like his paintings. Even so, I miss you a lot, Mr Dong. I'm extremely envious of Dong Fuzhang, Li Huaji, and my other classmates who have been continuing their studies with you, while I no longer get to do that. [...]
>
> Mr Dong, I'm very anxious to know what things are like at the Academy these days, how my classmates are doing, and how things are in the art world in general. If you're able to write back, I can assure you that the two of us would be overjoyed. If you're busy right now, it's all right if you write just a few simple sentences.
>
> Dear Mrs Dong, if you aren't too busy after work, I very much hope that you can write to me. Letters from Beijing are my greatest joy right now.[1]

In her letter, Song also mentions that her husband was preparing his first solo show, planned for late 1959. For Varbanov, who had taken up a position at the National Academy of Art in Sofia, this exhibition was of great significance. He presented several ink paintings he had produced in Beijing, along with textile works he designed in Sofia.

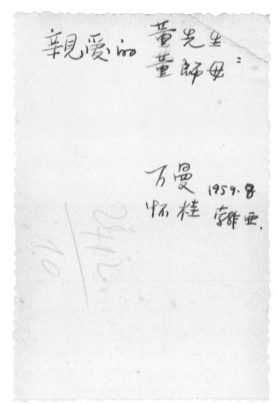

親愛的 董先生
董師母:

万曼
怀桂   1959.8
李雄亚

Above

This photo shows Song Huai-Kuei and Maryn Varbanov in Sofia. In August 1959, the couple sent the photo (inscribed with greetings on the back) from Bulgaria to Dong Xiwen and his wife, Zhang Linying, in China.

Right

Maryn Varbanov and Song Huai-Kuei visiting a carpet factory in Kotel, Bulgaria, 1959.

The opening of Maryn Varbanov's first solo exhibition, Sofia, late 1959. Song Huai-Kuei, who is wearing a *qipao*, and artists Vladimir Dimitrov and Stoyan Venev are present, as well as Bulgarian and Chinese diplomats and cultural officials.

Song wore a Chinese *qipao* to the opening. The dress accentuated her willowy figure and made her look half a head taller than her husband. She was the very picture of Asian femininity. The *qipao* was a refined adaptation of Qing Dynasty Manchu-style dress. While it had enjoyed great popularity in the early twentieth century, becoming essentially the Chinese national dress, it had fallen from favour under the communist regime. In fact, regarded as emblematic of bourgeois taste, the *qipao* had become so unfashionable that, by the 1950s, hardly anyone in China wore the garment. It had been supplanted by socialist-style clothing: female industrial workers wore white shirts and grey or blue work clothes, while well-educated women wore the double-breasted, wide-lapelled jackets known as Lenin suits. The *qipao* Song wore that night was quite possibly something she had found among her mother's old clothes. It was a tangible reminder of home and a subtle affirmation of her identity as an Asian woman.

On arrival in Sofia, the young family did not have a home of their own and had to stay with relatives. Only later were they able to move into an attic owned by the academy. Because their room was small and Song was eager to restart her study of oil painting, she and her husband sent their daughter to live temporarily with her grandparents in Oryahovo, on the banks of the Danube.

Varbanov had been adopted by a family of ironsmiths, and in 1951 he had been admitted to the sculpture department of the National Academy of Art.

After completing his foundation courses in 1953, he was sent to China for further study, and it was there that he switched his focus to textile design. Varbanov's academic trajectory mirrored post-war developments in the socialist countries of Eastern Europe. At the time of its founding, the People's Republic of Bulgaria was primarily an agrarian society. But under the regime of Valko Chervenkov, who led the nation's communist party from 1949 to 1954, Bulgaria followed the Soviet model, swiftly collectivising and industrialising while cutting off all contact with the West. Bulgaria soon came to depend on the Soviet Union for 90 per cent of its foreign trade. As the government prioritised investment in industry, many artists and art students were assigned to work or study in the field of applied arts. Indeed, Varbanov had been sent to China to study textile design because it was considered more practical than sculpture, and the emerging wool and cotton industries were crucial to Bulgaria's new economy. Meanwhile, China was following a similar path. The Central Academy of Arts & Design, where Varbanov pursued graduate studies, was a newly independent offshoot of the former Department of Applied Arts at the Central Academy of Fine Arts (CAFA). The new institution comprised departments of textile arts, ceramic arts, and decorative arts.

After his return to Bulgaria, Varbanov took the position of chief designer at the Malchika Textile Factory. He was also enthusiastic about teaching and making his own work, however, which led to his concurrent job at the National Academy of Art. He participated in the founding of a new discipline at the academy, 'Textiles', which incorporated dyeing, weaving, and fashion design.[2]

In support of this work, Varbanov was given the opportunity to return to China in 1960 for advanced research. Although the homesick Song wanted to accompany him, the couple could not afford the expense of a round-trip to China for a family of three. In the end, Song's teacher at the National Academy of Art, Ilya Petrov (1903–1975), paid for the trip out of his own pocket, enabling Song and Boryana to depart with Varbanov. Fortunately, China had recently opened a direct train line between Beijing and Moscow, reducing the travel time to fewer than ten days and making the journey less arduous.

This much-anticipated homecoming happened at a time of great adversity, however. Although they had been away for less than two years, the couple found that the atmosphere in Beijing had changed drastically. The Communist Party of China (CPC) was rushing to industrialise, spending wildly on infrastructure. This policy resulted in a dramatic downturn in grain production. In the wake of the Anti-Rightist Campaign of 1957, no one either inside or outside of the party risked voicing opposition. Between 1959 and 1961, the entire nation experienced what became known as the Great Chinese Famine. According to official statistics, the famine caused an extraordinary number of deaths; in 1960 alone, the population of China fell by ten million.[3] Although conditions were better in Beijing than they were in the countryside, city-dwellers of all ages nonetheless suffered food shortages.

Varbanov had been sent to China to study textile design because it was considered more practical than sculpture.

Above, right, and below

Song Huai-Kuei, late
1960s to early 1970s.

Right and below
Song Huai-Kuei, late
1960s to early 1970s.

Before Song could savour the joy of returning home, she was beset by new problems. Not long after the family's arrival in Beijing, Varbanov was summoned back to Bulgaria. Someone had reported him for failing to perform his mandatory military service. Then, shortly after Varbanov's departure, the couple's two-year-old daughter came down with polio. Left by herself, Song had to make the daily trip to the hospital with her child. She also taught herself how to treat Boryana's illness with the traditional Chinese therapies of acupuncture and moxibustion.

Song did find time to pay her respects to Dong Xiwen, her teacher and Dayabao hutong neighbour, but she found him in poor health. Although the internal CPC disciplinary action against him had been resolved, he still did not dare show his face at CAFA. His long-standing advocacy of an arts education combining traditional Chinese art and Western oil painting ran counter to orthodox instruction in Soviet-style Socialist Realism, and he was often criticised for having bourgeois tendencies. Song was unable even to see Yuan Yunsheng, her classmate from Dong's studio. Because Yuan had been sceptical of the Soviet-style arts-education system and had praised Impressionism, he had been sent to the countryside for reform through labour during the Anti-Rightist Campaign. In fact, Yuan had been sent to the same rural labour camp as Jiang Feng, the interim director of CAFA who had presided over Song and Varbanov's wedding. Song was distressed to see her friends in such dire straits, and she may well have sensed that it would be a very long time before she would be able to return to China. Before leaving Beijing for Sofia, she had several family portraits taken for her parents and gathered up her antiquarian books and artworks, including woodcuts by Huang Yongyu.

‡

Shortly after his return to Sofia, having fulfilled his military service obligations, Varbanov resigned from the Malchika Textile Factory and began teaching full-time on the textiles programme at the National Academy of Art. This allowed the family to apply to the municipal government for housing. Still, it was not until 1962, after Song had graduated from the oil painting department at the academy, that the government finally allotted them a three-room apartment on Oborishte Street. Their son, Phénix Varbanov, had just been born, and the family of four was able to live comfortably together at last. Boryana and Phénix shared one room, another served as a combined living room and master bedroom, and the third acted as the couple's shared studio space. The studio housed several looms and was where Varbanov and Song produced all their smaller works during the 1960s. It was also in this room that the creative output of this young couple became increasingly modernist.

If we want to understand Varbanov and Song's modernist practice, we need to briefly review the artistic environment in which they worked. Before the advent of twentieth-century modernism, two innovative intellectual trends had dominated Europe: socialism and the avant-garde. Socialists strove to overcome capitalist exploitation and establish an ideal society based on economic equality, while the avant-garde sought to overthrow ossified artistic languages and thereby pave the way for free self-expression. Every avant-garde artist—whether Impressionist, Futurist, or follower of the Arts and Crafts movement—was to some extent influenced by socialism, since they all shared the belief that social reform and artistic experimentation aimed at shattering traditional constraints were complementary.[4] When the October Revolution broke out in 1917, avant-garde artists such as Wassily Kandinsky (1866–1944) and Kazimir Malevich (1879–1935) were so inspired that they returned to Russia and threw themselves into the socialist revolution, marking the prologue to the influential, albeit short-lived Soviet avant-garde.

The newly established regime in Russia understood art's primary purpose to be spreading political consciousness and promoting a revolutionary spirit. Literary and artistic activities were subsumed in proletarian movements under the banner of Socialist Realism. Lenin believed that the 'freedom' of bourgeois artists was a false freedom, because the artist 'lives in society and yet can only be free if they leave society, and this is not possible'.[5] Therefore, avant-garde art, or anything created under the auspices of 'art for art's sake', could not be considered real art. As Lenin insisted: 'Art belongs to the people. It must be deeply rooted in the broad labouring masses. It must be understood by and pleasing to the masses. It must unite the feelings, thoughts, and will of the masses, and elevate them.'[6] Kandinsky, who was focused on exploring pure art theory, was deeply disappointed by this policy and soon returned to Germany. Those who stayed behind, such as Malevich, Alexander Rodchenko (1891–1956), and Vladimir Tatlin (1885–1953), were subsequently criticised for developing artistic styles at odds with what the Communist Party deemed to be society's needs.

In the 1950s, this Soviet aesthetic model was transplanted wholesale to China, Bulgaria, and every other nation that belonged to the socialist camp. Nonetheless, the avant-garde spirit of modernism was not completely eradicated behind the Iron Curtain. In the 1920s, both Rodchenko and Tatlin worked in bookbinding, poster design, and fashion and set design, incorporating avant-garde techniques into their work while striving for utility, visual appeal, and mass accessibility. Along with the strands of modernism that arrived in China from Latin America with the international communist movement, these traces of avant-garde aesthetics evolved into a unique form in socialist countries: Socialist Modernism.

Following the death of Stalin in 1953, the socialist nations of Eastern Europe began a process of 'de-Stalinisation'. The art world was no exception. Many Bulgarian artists took advantage of the relatively relaxed environment and renewed their engagement with traditional Balkan arts and crafts. The timely creation in 1960 of the textiles discipline at the National Academy of Art in Sofia exemplifies this trend.[7] In a departure from the previous emphasis on design for the purpose of industrial production, this new speciality aimed to integrate design and weaving techniques. Kotel, Samokov, and other mountainous areas of Bulgaria already had wool-producing districts and textile crafts that helped spur this revival.[8]

Varbanov, who had seen the exhibition of Jean Lurçat's tapestries at CAFA, immediately perceived the new possibilities. Conventional tapestry artists translated painted images into woven wall hangings. Lurçat employed Cubist techniques to create weavings independent from other mediums. This gave new

life to the traditional craft of tapestry, which had long been modelled on the practice of the French region of Aubusson. Joan Miró (1893–1983), Le Corbusier (1887–1965), and others were inspired to create their own non-representational tapestries that accentuated the medium's specific qualities.

The seeds planted by Lurçat in Beijing had travelled, and ultimately blossomed and bore fruit in Bulgaria. With the help of Lurçat's friendship, and under the banner of textile techniques and research into the decorative arts, Varbanov and Song brought Western European modernist practices to Bulgaria. Beginning in the 1960s, the couple managed to set up textile arts as a discipline of its own, distinct from pattern design, and went on to establish tapestry as a creative practice separate from the textile industry.

Throughout this period, Song continued to paint and exhibit her work in Sofia. She even had opportunities to show her paintings in Prague, Tokyo, San Francisco, and elsewhere through diplomatic exchange programmes. While art academies in China embraced Socialist Realism and rejected Impressionism, Bulgarian art institutions had historically taken inspiration from French and Italian painting schools. The National Academy of Art in Sofia remained fertile ground for modernist experimentation despite a relatively short period dominated by Soviet aesthetics. This environment allowed Song to make a clean break with the Socialist Realism that had been foundational to her education in China and incorporate Expressionist and Cubist styles into her work. The emphasis on structure and shape evident in her student pieces yielded to flatter depictions of human figures and a greater focus on the expression of complex emotions.

In 1964, two years after graduating from the oil painting department at the National Academy of Art, Song went to work at the Centre for New Goods and Fashion (CNGF), which was tasked with implementing national textile-production policies.[9] Song, who had enjoyed making clothing from scratch back in China, was in her element. She gradually became more involved in design work before receiving an official promotion to full-time fashion designer in 1970. Song's experience at the CNGF would prove beneficial when she became Varbanov's working partner and the couple began applying to exhibit at the Lausanne International Tapestry Biennial as collaborators.

All the neighbours knew the Chinese lady who walked lightly, as if she were floating on water.

‡

Varbanov and Song cultivated a working relationship similar to that of Christo and Jeanne-Claude, the Bulgarian–Moroccan artist duo. They quickly became the most popular couple at the academy, if not in the whole of Sofia's artistic community. Varbanov was known as genial by nature, highly empathetic, passionate about art-making, and unstintingly generous with his students, focusing on their individual aptitudes. The door to their home on Oborishte Street was always open, and students and friends could drop by anytime to chat and look at art books. Song would prepare simple Chinese desserts for them. Sofia was not a large city, and all the neighbours knew the Chinese lady who walked lightly, as if she were floating on water (for a time, the neighbours believed all Chinese women had this particular way of walking). Song came to embody Asian style, and not just within her social network. On occasion, she even made guest appearances on Bulgarian television. In an episode of the adventure programme *Every Kilometre*, for example, she played the part of a Japanese woman.

Less than two hundred metres from Song and Varbanov's apartment was the French Embassy. In the late 1960s, Dolores Ling (1932–1999), the Chinese-Austrian wife of French cultural attaché Jean Beaulieu, arrived in Sofia and immediately got to know Song. The two women were close in age and became good friends. Raised by her Austrian mother in Vienna, Ling had received an excellent education, studying music and dance at the Vienna State Opera, and was active on both stage and screen. Perhaps because of her Asian heritage on her father's side, she was obsessed with East Asian philosophy and art. She had studied Chinese language and art history at the University of Vienna, as well as the history of East Asian art at the University of Hamburg.

The two women's shared love of art cemented their friendship. Song gave Ling the nickname 'Miss Lin', a nod to the character Lin Daiyu in the eighteenth-century novel *Dream of the Red Chamber*. After retiring from the stage to become a diplomat's wife, Ling began to practise ink painting, something that made Song feel even closer to her. Traditional Chinese art forms had been consistent touchstones for Song. Her most respected teacher, Dong Xiwen, promoted the idea that Chinese artists should use tradition to innovate and transform oil painting (the scion of a family of collectors and connoisseurs, Dong ultimately donated his entire collection of calligraphy and

These photos (above and top right) show Song Huai-Kuei dressed in costumes of her own design, her hair loose or tied in a round bun atop her head as she performs an Eastern, Buddha-like gesture. Song was working at the Centre for New Goods and Fashion (CNGF) in Bulgaria (right) at the time and gained considerable experience in design and modelling. Through its internal bulletin, CNGF circulated translated information about the latest fashion trends from Western Europe, especially Paris, including sketches and photos of works by such famous brands and designers as Chanel, Dior, Yves Saint Laurent, and Pierre Cardin.

Film still showing Song Huai-Kuei acting in the Bulgarian television series *Every Kilometre* (На всеки километър, 1969–1971), ca.1970.

A photo of Song Huai-Kuei with two of her fellow actors during the filming of an episode of the Bulgarian television series *The Demon of the Empire* (Демонът на империята, 1971), ca.1970.

A photo of Song Huai-Kuei acting in *The Sun and the Shadow* (Слънцето и сянката, 1962).

DOLORES LING

MARTIN BERLINER

Foto By

A spread from the programme for *Das kleine Teehaus* (The Teahouse of the August Moon), a comedy produced in Berlin in the 1950s. The photo at top right shows Dolores Ling as Lotus Blossom, a Japanese geisha.

paintings to the National Museum of China); Song's other teacher, Shen Congwen, immersed himself in research on ancient Chinese costume and decoration. Even her husband had been deeply influenced by traditional Chinese culture and had also taken up ink painting. Meanwhile, Ling brought a refreshing change to Song's cultural milieu by introducing her to the artist and ink painting teacher T'ang Haywen.

Born in Xiamen, Fujian province, to parents who marketed silk cloth and rice in what are now Vietnam and Thailand, T'ang studied calligraphy and painting with his grandfather, who had held an imperial *xiucai* degree during the Qing Dynasty. To escape the warfare then engulfing China, T'ang went to Saigon as an adolescent, where he received a French colonial education. In 1948, he travelled to Paris to study art at the Académie de la Grande Chaumière. Starting in the 1960s, T'ang read widely in Laozi, Zhuangzi, and other Daoist philosophy. This contributed to the development of his own style, which melded the expressive aspects of traditional Chinese ink painting with Western abstraction. Rather than depicting the physical world, he sought to 'see the Dao with a lucid mind', emphasising the experience of the infinite through landscape painting. Even as he delved into traditional aesthetic philosophy, T'ang was hardly shackled to the conventions of ink painting. He made the bold move of painting diptychs on cardboard, using rapid and abbreviated brushstrokes to create kaleidoscopic explosions of colour. At the same time, the diptych form itself conveyed his Daoist understanding of the universe, as expressed in the saying: 'The Dao engenders the one, the one engenders two, two engenders three, and three engenders ten thousand things.' For Song, T'ang embodied a radically different set of beliefs about East Asian thought and life compared to those she had been exposed to in her formal education.

T'ang Haywen
Untitled, ca.1970
Ink on Kyro card, diptych
70 x 100 cm
Private collection

Although her teachers Dong and Shen admired traditional culture, they were burdened with the Confucian sense of social responsibility, forever yearning to change the world. But T'ang was like an itinerant bard or poet, borne on the currents of the world by a Daoist attitude, meeting life's ups and downs with equanimity. As a gay man, he was not responsible for pleasing his parents by carrying on the family line, and instead saw art-making as his destiny. For the rest of his life, he kept a studio in Paris that was so small and basic it lacked its own bathroom. He spent most of his time travelling from place to place, staying in the homes of various friends, and toting his favourite portfolio. This man who appeared to have no possessions in fact possessed the entire world. Sometime around 1970, T'ang drove his decrepit Peugeot to Sofia, its trunk crammed full of art paper. Song and Varbanov showed him around, exploring every corner of the city. After this visit, T'ang and the couple became lifelong friends. Perhaps owing to the influence of T'ang, nearly all of Song's works from this period feature Daoist-inspired images of butterflies.

While establishing professional reputations and a community around themselves in Sofia, Song and Varbanov began to see new opportunities in Western Europe. In 1971, they were invited to participate in the Lausanne International Tapestry Biennial and show their collaboratively produced *Composition 2001* (1969).

Song Huai-Kuei, Maryn Varbanov, and
Phénix having a picnic together with
Dolores Ling (second from left),
ca. early 1970s.

T'ang Haywen had lived and worked in his
small Parisian apartment-studio on rue
Liancourt since 1959. This photo, which
captures him there in a state of calm, was
taken by Hong Kong–based film director
Yonfan in the spring of 1991 and is among
the last-known photos of the artist.

When T'ang Haywen visited Bulgaria,
Song Huai-Kuei showed him around
Sofia and took him sight-seeing at old
monasteries with friends. The photo on
the left shows the group wearing flared
jeans, which were in vogue at the time.
At bottom right are Boryana and June,
the Song family's dog.

This three-metre-long work, an apparent homage to Constructivism, offered a futuristic vision in woven textiles. In 1973, their enormous work *Aporia* (1972) was selected for that year's biennial, where it captivated viewers with its imposing material presence. These two works helped spark a revolution in tapestry art by transforming the traditionally two-dimensional medium into three-dimensional constructions and showing how tapestries could be freed from purely decorative functions.[10] In 1974, at the recommendation of Dolores Ling and her husband, Song and Varbanov were offered a residency at the Cité Internationale des Arts in Paris by the French Ministry of Culture. With the special approval of the vice-president of the Committee for Arts and Culture in Bulgaria, Lyudmila Todorova Zhivkova (1942–1981), they were given permission to live abroad for research purposes.

Zhivkova was the couple's veritable patron and protector throughout the 1970s. The daughter of Todor Hristov Zhivkov (1911–1998), general secretary of the Bulgarian Party from 1954 to 1989, Zhivkova was only thirty when, in 1972, she took the post of assistant president of the Committee for Arts and Culture. Because her mother had died young, Zhivkova had long played the role of surrogate first lady, and it was widely rumoured that she would be her father's successor. Zhivkova had studied history at Sofia University and art history at Moscow State University before pursuing research on the Balkan Peninsula at the University of Oxford.

Japan's Crown Princess Michiko speaking with Lyudmila Todorova Zhivkova, at that time the president of the Committee for Arts and Culture in Bulgaria, on 10 October 1979 in Sofia.

With her exceptionally fine educational background, she sought to preserve and promote Bulgarian art during her tenure. She was open-minded about the cultural policies of Western nations and introduced popular music and art from the West. She even promoted the educational model of Maria Montessori as a replacement for rigid Soviet educational systems.

Zhivkova sought opportunities to highlight the historical ties between Bulgaria and Greece, at the same time de-emphasising Bulgaria's relationship with the Soviet Union. In connection with her work organising events in honour of the 1,300-year anniversary of the founding of Bulgaria, she had 'palaces of the arts' built all over the country and commissioned artists to create artworks on related historical themes. Varbanov's avid research into the textile handicrafts of the Balkan Peninsula coincided with Zhivkova's thinking. In 1974, with Zhivkova's support, Varbanov held his first retrospective at the Union of Bulgarian Artists. The Bulgarian Embassy in France mounted the exhibition later that year. As part of Zhivkova's programme, Varbanov was invited to make a large-scale work for the National Palace of Culture, entitled *1300 Years of Bulgaria* (1979).

‡

While the family was in the process of relocating to Paris, Song received an invitation from the Chinese embassy to return to Beijing to participate in ceremonies marking the twenty-fifth anniversary of the founding of the People's Republic of China. She had not set foot in China since her departure from Beijing in 1960. While China had been in the throes of the Cultural Revolution, anyone with international associations had been vulnerable to scrutiny and criticism. Consequently, Song and her parents had even refrained from exchanging letters. Now, with the Cultural Revolution entering its final days, and with US President Richard Nixon (1913–1994) having visited China in 1972, Chinese politics were beginning to loosen up. In 1974, to restore China's international prestige, the government took advantage of the twenty-fifth-anniversary celebrations to invite a large contingent of overseas Chinese to return. Song accepted the invitation without a second thought and flew to Moscow with Boryana and Phénix. In Moscow, they boarded a plane bound for Beijing in the company of a large group of overseas Chinese and diplomats.

When Song unexpectedly showed up at the family home in Beijing with her children in tow, her parents could hardly believe their eyes. By nightfall, however, the local police were at the door. According to the regulations, overseas Chinese and foreigners were not permitted to stay overnight in the homes of Chinese people. Song was forced to take the children and check into a nearby hotel. On the day of the major celebration, Premier Zhou Enlai, who was then in the late stages of cancer, and Deng Xiaoping (1904–1997), who had recently returned from internal exile, greeted Song and her cohort at Tiananmen, and encouraged them to return to China to spend time with their families.

Song was delighted to see Zhou again, but the spectacle of the National Day festivities could not conceal those who were still suffering. Shen Congwen had long since been banished from his job at the National Museum of Chinese Revolution and History (now the National Museum of China) and exiled to Hubei province.

Left
Installation view of
Maryn Varbanov's first
retrospective, held in 1974
at the Union of Bulgarian
Artists, Sofia. The work in
the centre of the photo is
Composition 2001 (1969),
made in collaboration
with Song Huai-Kuei.

Above
Card inviting Pierre
Cardin to the opening of
Maryn Varbanov's 1981
exhibition, *1300 Years
of Bulgaria*.

Left
Cover of the catalogue
for Maryn Varbanov's first
retrospective, held in 1974
at the Union of Bulgarian
Artists, Sofia.

Maryn Varbanov's *1300 Years of Bulgaria* (1979) is one of the government-commissioned artworks permanently displayed at the National Palace of Culture in Sofia, which opened in 1981. With the work's modular structure, Varbanov departed from the practice of creating a flat surface in traditional tapestry art. He also incorporated elements from Bulgaria's classical heritage. The two figures on either side of the sun deity, for example, reference portraits of a prince and his wife found on the wall of a Thracian tomb in Bulgaria.

Dong Xiwen's *The Founding of the Nation* was still on display at the museum, but the joyous tableau depicting the first National Day had been altered numerous times for political reasons.[11] Dong himself had died of cancer the year before Song's visit. On the day of the main twenty-fifth-anniversary celebration, Song had intended to visit Dong's wife, Zhang Linying (1912–2014), the beloved 'Mrs Dong' to whom Song had referred in her correspondence from Sofia. Zhang, however, was still in the rural village to which she had been exiled.

During this 1974 visit, Song saw few of her former classmates or neighbours from Dayabao hutong. Most of them had been sent to the countryside during the Cultural Revolution. If she were to call on her friends, it could cause them unnecessary trouble owing to her status as an overseas Chinese. She did, however, get to know one of her fellow visitors, the painter Zao Wou-Ki. Zao and Dong had been classmates at the National College of Art, and during the Second Sino-Japanese War, both had studied at the Shanghai College of Fine Arts (now the Shanghai Academy of Fine Arts). While Dong had stayed in Beijing to teach, Zao had moved to Paris to continue his studies and ended up settling there. He made his name in post-war French art circles with abstract paintings that incorporated ancient Chinese brush techniques. Beginning in 1972, Zao returned to China several times to visit family members whom he had not seen in more than twenty years.

Although Song realised that the China she was witnessing in 1974 was not the same as the China of her youth, she nonetheless regarded this visit as the best opportunity for her children to gain an understanding of her home country. She took them to see famous sites, such as the Great Wall, the Ming Tombs, the Forbidden City, and the Temple of Heaven, as well as the Working People's Cultural Palace, where she had studied painting as a young girl. Upon her return to Sofia, Song continued her preparations to move the family to Paris.

Beijing
to Paris and
Back Again

Liu Heung Shing

When the door opened onto a 40-square-metre, one-room studio space in the Cité Internationale des Arts, close by the River Seine in Paris, I was greeted by Song Huai-Kuei, beaming with her signature broad smile that would become so familiar over the next several decades as our paths crossed again and again. It was 1974, and she had recently arrived in Paris from Beijing with her artist husband, Maryn Varbanov. Having ushered me inside, Huai-Kuei proceeded immediately to prepare a bowl of northern Chinese noodles for me, a student visiting from New York. We sat and talked as easily as if we had known each other our whole lives, even though we had met just an hour ago.

Varbanov sat quietly beside us as we all squeezed around a square table of the kind used to play mah-jong. I learned that their union was the first between a Chinese person and a foreigner to be personally approved by then Premier Zhou Enlai, who had also been to Paris in his youth with fellow communist Deng Xiaoping. Huai-Kuei, a student at the Central Academy of Fine Arts in Beijing, and Maryn, an art student from socialist Bulgaria, was a love affair so rare in China that it had to be approved by Premier Zhou himself.

The following day, Huai-Kuei took me to meet the Vietnamese-Chinese artist T'ang Haywen, who in turn took us to a tiny Wenzhou restaurant for those distinctive rice noodles known to Vietnamese and people in southern China. The restaurant was very dark and had only one table. Perhaps its aura of curious intimacy worked its magic on us, but we soon found ourselves becoming firm friends. This friendship would endure over the ensuing decades, during which the work of Huai-Kuei, Maryn, and Haywen became known to artistic circles in both Europe and China.

I returned to the United States to graduate from New York University, and then plunged into my personal journey back to China, reporting on the country with my camera through the early 1980s and 1990s. I was already there when Huai-Kuei returned to Beijing from Paris in 1981. She made sure that I attended all the fashion shows and events associated with Pierre Cardin that were contributing to the new cultural energy of the Chinese capital and beyond. In 1983, I was present at the opening of the Cardin-owned Maxim's restaurant, located in the Chongwenmen district of Beijing. Cardin had invited numerous European aristocrats and fashion models to attend the opening, during which the champagne flowed, and abundant caviar was served by local Chinese waiters wearing tuxedos. That was the moment when China was opening to new experiences and new ideas from the West.

In contrast, around the same time, one could hear stories of how the former Chinese vice-premier Gu Mu had told a delegation of twenty Chinese ministers who were about to visit Europe to familiarise themselves with European etiquette, advising them to watch out for large plate-glass windows and doors to avoid crashing into them. Upon their return, it was said that one minister had asked a foreign waiter if he could 'warm up the ice cream'.

In the 1980s, China would attract visitors such as Roy Halston Frowick, Nancy Reagan's go-to fashion designer. Elton John came and played ping-pong with local students. American actor Kirk Douglas visited Beijing Film Studio. The American television series *Love Boat* brought its crew to film on location at the Great Wall. Coca-Cola returned to China with a new plant in Beijing, and American senators and congressmen could be seen jogging through Tiananmen Square. Throughout these pivotal years of China's opening to the outside world, Song Huai-Kuei often hosted social parties, bringing together Chinese artists and movie stars to meet and greet their foreign counterparts. Huai-Kuei would remain a gracious dinner host. In time, she would open a new branch of Maxim's restaurant on the ground floor of the China World complex, a space currently occupied by Louis Vuitton. It immediately became the place to be seen, where you could listen to such Chinese stars as Liu Xiaoqing [b. 1955], Jiang Wen [b. 1963], and Ge You [b. 1957] sing impromptu to the accompaniment of a Steinway piano. I took famed photographer Douglas Kirkland, whose iconic depictions of Marilyn Monroe, Diana Ross, and many other celebrities were well known in America, to photograph Chinese actress Gong Li [b. 1965]. Given Huai-Kuei's stature within this milieu, it did not surprise me that she landed a cameo role in the Italian director Bernardo Bertolucci's film *The Last Emperor*, largely filmed inside the Forbidden City.

To her last days, Huai-Kuei would continue to be a truly gracious bon vivant, through those changing years when China stepped out of the long shadow of Chairman Mao and embraced the modern world with such speed and intensity that we are still digesting its impact today.

Hong Kong, 26 May 2022

1975–1981: Adrift in Paris, Rooted in Beijing

Chapter Three

n April 1975, Maryn Varbanov and Song Huai-Kuei received permission from Lyudmila Todorova Zhivkova, president of the Committee for Arts and Culture in Bulgaria, to accept a residency at the Cité Internationale des Arts in Paris. Zhivkova held Varbanov in high esteem, and had even higher hopes that sending an artist abroad would give her a deeper understanding of French cultural policies and the general atmosphere in the country's art scene. The couple brought their thirteen-year-old son, Phénix, with them while Boryana remained in Bulgaria to study mural painting at the National Academy of Art. It was not until the following year that she was able to join the rest of her family in Paris and transfer to the École Nationale Supérieure des Beaux-Arts as a painting student.

The main building of the Cité Internationale des Arts sits on the Right Bank of the Seine. Four storeys tall, the structure has striking white exterior walls; inside is an enormous fireplace and a spiral staircase. The facility was fully equipped, providing artists with both studio and living spaces. When Song and her family arrived in 1975, the tapestry studio was overseen by an artist from the former Yugoslavia, Jagoda Buić (b. 1930). Buić had met Varbanov in Lausanne many years before, and they had formed a deep friendship. However, as an acclaimed artist, Buić travelled often, so the position of studio director was passed down to Varbanov in the second year of his residency. Although their work for the Lausanne International Tapestry Biennials brought Varbanov and Song much fame, they struggled to make ends meet in Paris, where the cost of living was much higher than in Sofia. Varbanov continued to teach part-time in Sofia, and Zhivkova also helped to arrange government commissions. Still, it was difficult to support a family of four in the French capital, what with rent, art supplies, and the children's educational expenses. In Bulgaria, they could afford to hire assistants, but in Paris they had to see to everything themselves. To work more efficiently, Varbanov created a simple loom by attaching a net to the floor and ceiling of the studio. When they ran short of sisal and goat hair, which had to be imported from Bulgaria, Varbanov and Song would sometimes pick apart their own wool cardigans and repurpose the yarn for their tapestries. When they wanted to create large-scale works, however, they had no choice but to return to their studio in Sofia.

In the 1960s and 1970s, a number of Eastern European artists, among them Magdalena Abakanowicz (1930–2017) and Jolanta Owidzka (1927–2020), gained international prominence for their tapestries. The medium allowed these artists to engage with their own cultural traditions. At the same time, they could take advantage of the labour and resources made available through the socialist system to make large-scale works without the spatial limitations imposed by a cramped studio. Varbanov and Song were part of this trend. During their time in Paris, they wholeheartedly explored three-dimensional qualities in their tapestries while bringing a majestic Balkan vitality to the Parisian art world. In the words of Varbanov specialist Assadour Markarov (b. 1961): 'French tapestry artists wove patterns on a flat surface using fine wool threads, because colour and form were crucial for them.' By contrast, 'Varbanov believed that form and structure were the most important things.'[1] Varbanov employed the Bulgarian double-sided weaving technique to make tapestries that did not have a front or back, thereby

Transforming tapestry from a two-dimensional surface into a three-dimensional structure that interacts with architectural space was a major artistic pursuit of Song Huai-Kuei and Maryn Varbanov in the 1970s. They created several gigantic tapestry works collaboratively. To achieve the ideal effect, they often experimented with different forms and mediums in their studio at Cité Internationale des Arts in Paris, as captured in the photo on the right. The photo below shows Varbanov and Song in front of their monumental work *Contrast* (early 1970s).

Above

Maryn Varbanov's work *Les orgues de Matignon* in the collection of Georges Heckly.

Varbanov

Tapisseries

Préface de Dora Vallier

Galerie Odermatt

Above

Cover of the catalogue for Maryn
Varbanov's solo exhibition *Varbanov
Tapisseries*, held at Galerie Hervé
Odermatt in 1978.

Above top

Song Huai-Kuei, Maryn Varbanov,
and their long-term patron Georges
Heckly at Heckly's gallery Art-Dialogue
in Paris, 1968.

Above

In October 1978, Maryn Varbanov's solo
exhibition *Varbanov Tapisseries* opened at
Galerie Hervé Odermatt in Paris. Standing
in front of his tapestry work, Varbanov is
with a Bulgarian diplomat (first from left)
and French-Bulgarian art historian and
critic Dora Vallier (third from left), who
introduced him to the gallery and wrote
a preface for the exhibition's catalogue.
Song Huai-Kuei was a socialite even in
the Parisian art scene. Here, she can be
seen speaking with Michel Lee's partner.

allowing the viewer to appreciate the piece from different sides. He
also followed an ancient water-treatment method used in Bulgarian
villages that involved submerging finished weavings in a swirling
water bath. By controlling the density of the weave, the duration of
the treatment, and the centrifugal force of the water, Varbanov could
produce exceptionally rich textures in the wool.[2]

In her spare time, Song worked as an illustrator for publications
about fashion design so Varbanov could fully devote himself to
art-making. The couple set their eyes on commercial galleries for
additional income. However, the market for tapestry art was small.
In part because the works are onerous to maintain and store, very few
collectors were dedicated to the field. In Sofia, Varbanov and Song had
been able to sell works through Hemus, a Bulgarian import–export
company that also handled international exhibitions for Bulgarian
artists. Although their earnings from such sales were meagre,
it was through Hemus that the couple got to know the prominent
contemporary tapestry collector Georges Heckly, who became their

Above
Song Huai-Kuei and her
family celebrating Lunar
New Year at Zao Wou-Ki's
studio in Paris, 1976.

Right
Maryn Varbanov (left)
with Zao Wou-Ki (right)
and Zao's wife, the curator
Françoise Marquet,
late 1970s.

Song Huai-Kuei (left)
with Dolores Ling (front,
centre) and Jean Beaulieu
(back, centre), late 1970s.

Below
Maryn Varbanov (first
from left) and Song
Huai-Kuei (second from
left) with T'ang Haywen
(centre) and others,
late 1970s.

Michel Lee (bottom left) was a friend of Song Huai-Kuei and T'ang Haywen. He was in the fashion business and worked for Emanuel Ungaro and Itochu Corporation. In Paris, he introduced Song to various social circles and events. Lee often invited his friends to his home, and Song and Varbanov were regulars at these gatherings. The photo on the left shows the couple attending in traditional Chinese attire, while the photo below shows Lee (front row, second from left) with Song and Varbanov and other guests. Taken in the late 1970s, both photos illustrate Lee's interest in art, notably his collection of exquisite Buddhist sculptures and Chinese calligraphy and drawings. Although the photos are of two separate occasions, Song is wearing the same outfit, one that emphasises her cultural identity.

Song Huai-Kuei (right) in traditional Chinese attire with Dolores Ling (left), late 1970s. Behind them is one of Song Huai-Kuei's tapestry works from the *Dream of Zhuangzi* (or *Butterfly*) series.

long-term patron starting in 1968. In 1974, they began working with Galerie La Demeure, which had exhibited many of Le Corbusier's tapestries. The Bulgarian art historian and critic Dora Vallier (1921–1997) also introduced Varbanov to Galerie Hervé Odermatt and organised the solo exhibition *Varbanov Tapisseries* (1978).

These exhibitions introduced Varbanov and Song to Parisian cultural circles. Several Chinese artists in Paris were especially close to the family. T'ang Haywen, who had lived in France for many years and had a wide network, introduced Song and her husband to many collectors and friends. In turn, Song introduced T'ang to Michel Lee, who was originally from Taiwan and was active in fashion and culture. Lee had come to France to escape the constraints of the traditional Chinese family, and at one point he asked Song to dress up in traditional clothing and pose for a 'family portrait' with him to alleviate his family's concerns that he was gay and unmarried. It was through Lee, at the opening reception of one of T'ang's exhibitions, that Song finally reconnected with Zao Wou-Ki.

Zao had moved to Paris in 1948, treading a path similar to that of T'ang. In some respects, he had also followed the lead of such artists as Chang Shuhong and Lin Fengmian (1900–1991), who had fused modernism with traditional Chinese culture. But Zao was less bound to tradition than his predecessors, even as he explored his cultural roots to enable artistic breakthroughs. In the 1950s, he began incorporating Chinese iconography, such as oracle bone scripts, into his paintings, marking the beginning of a move towards the complete abstraction of his 'wild cursive' period. Starting in the 1970s, almost simultaneously with T'ang,

Around 1982, Song Huai-Kuei was introduced to Peking opera singer Shi Peipu (1938–2009, pictured behind Song in the photo to the right), who was performing in Paris at the time. The two organised an impromptu photoshoot in the flat of Yoshi Takata (1916–2009), a photographer and close friend of Pierre Cardin, with Song and her family putting on opera costumes and make-up that Shi had brought along. Captured in the two photos above are Song's children dressed in some of the costumes. A year later, Shi and his French diplomat partner, Bernard Boursicot, were arrested for spying for China. Actor John Lone, Song's close friend, played a character based on Shi in the 1993 film *M. Butterfly*, whose storyline draws on Shi's love affair.

Above
Invitation for the opening of Maryn Varbanov's solo exhibition at Espace Pierre Cardin in New York, 1980.

Opposite
On 12 December 1980, Maryn Varbanov's solo tapestry art exhibition opened at Espace Pierre Cardin in New York. This was Varbanov's first exhibition in the United States and featured works from his artistic experiments of the 1970s, including those from Pierre Cardin's collection. During this period, Varbanov focused more on the independent forms of tapestries and their interactions with modern architectural space. He also adopted abstract geometric structures, textures, and colours to free tapestry art from its original narrative function.

Zao consciously used the medium of oil painting to express the abstract qualities of Chinese ink art.

After their initial meeting in Beijing, Song had attempted to contact Zao several times since her arrival in Paris. When Lee learned that Zao would be attending T'ang's opening reception, he not only invited Song to come along, but also brought her some couture from his company to wear. After all, if she was to meet with this famous artist from the elite social circles of Paris, Song needed an appropriate outfit. Lee told Song that, since coming to Paris, Zao had rarely had the opportunity to socialise with other people of Chinese descent. At the opening, Zao recognised the lady whom he had met once before in Beijing and recalled that she was a student of his old classmate from the National College of Art. He soon invited Song and her family to join him at his studio to celebrate Lunar New Year, insisting that they pick out one of his oil paintings as a gift.

In 1978, Dolores Ling returned to Paris from Chicago with her diplomat husband, and was soon reunited with her good friend Song. Life was simple but very happy, and the pair occasionally organised fancy-dress parties at which the men donned long robes and the women *qipaos*. Sometimes, guests would put on Peking opera costumes, offering a taste of Chinese traditions. For members of this elite diasporic community, such events must have been tinged with melancholy. The version of Chinese culture they longed for did not really exist in Paris, and it was also gradually fading away in the distant Asian country they had once called home. Song and Ling were like drifting duckweed, thrown together again in Paris. At any moment, however, the east wind might start blowing again, scattering the two friends in opposite directions. Nonetheless, this artistic capital was an important stop on their way towards appreciating the importance of their own cultural roots. As Zao once commented in an interview:

> Without question, Paris had a deep and long-lasting influence on my artistic development, and yet I was also gradually becoming reacquainted with China, in addition to becoming conscious of my own innate personality and characteristics ... Paradoxically, it may have been Paris that allowed me to return to the wellsprings that lay deep in my own heart.[3]

‡

In October 1980, the annual Foire Internationale d'Art Contemporain (FIAC) opened at the Grand Palais in Paris. On the final afternoon of the exhibition, the designer Pierre Cardin, who had recently won his second Golden Thimble

Award, saw the work that Varbanov was showing with Galerie Hervé Odermatt and was immediately captivated. For Cardin, who would soon be the subject of a thirty-year retrospective at the Metropolitan Museum of Art in New York, Varbanov's rough-hewn Balkan style must have presented a distinctive contrast to the refined geometric patterns and lines typical of French textile design. Cardin purchased six of Varbanov's works and decided to display them in his new arts venue in New York, Espace Pierre Cardin. This was Varbanov's first solo show in America, and Song and the children were invited to attend the opening. While the family were in New York, they were also introduced to the architect Ieoh Ming Pei (1917–2019).

I. M. Pei was the scion of an illustrious family from Suzhou; his father had co-founded the Bank of China. Pei grew up in Hong Kong, and at the age of eighteen travelled to the United States to study. In 1955, he opened his own design office. By the late 1970s, Pei had been awarded a gold medal by the American Institute of Architects (AIA), as well as the Gold Medal in Architecture from the American Academy of Arts and Letters, making him practically the only internationally recognised modernist architect of Chinese descent. At the time of his meeting with Song, Pei had spent nearly fifty years living outside China. However, he was given an opportunity to return thanks to a rather challenging project: the Fragrant Hill Hotel.

The origin of the hotel can be traced back to a series of visits Pei made to China in the 1970s. After the end of the Cultural Revolution, Deng Xiaoping gradually consolidated power. Years of political strife had brought the nation's economy to the brink of collapse, and Deng advanced the idea that economic progress was the party's foremost responsibility and legal obligation. He promoted the modernisation of China's industrial, agricultural, scientific, and defence sectors, setting a target of a USD 1,000 per capita GDP by the end of the twentieth century. In line with Deng's famous remark that 'it doesn't matter if a cat is black or white, as long as it can catch a mouse', China changed course, departing from the Mao-era quest for a pure socialist form of government in favour of a policy that put pragmatism first. As a result, the government strongly encouraged enterprises to leverage the low cost of labour to develop export businesses and work actively to attract foreign investment. Many overseas Chinese and foreign businesspeople were invited to visit China, Pei and Cardin among them.

Following his 1974 visit to China with a delegation from the AIA, Pei received an invitation to return in 1978. China's policymakers were intensely focused on the acquisition of foreign currency. Deng commented at the time: 'When doing business with foreigners, keep an eye on the bottom line. If each tourist spends USD 1,000, and if we host ten million tourists per year, then we can make USD 10 billion. Even if we only hosted half that number, we would still earn USD 5 billion. We must work as hard as we can to meet the goal of accumulating foreign exchange by the end of the century.'[4] But if that goal were to be realised, China's cities needed a makeover. China would have to create the visual symbols of modernisation if it wanted to attract more international visitors.

Every potential tourist city prioritised the construction of large international hotels.[5] The authorities hoped that Pei would design a group of hotel towers and

Song Huai-Kuei and I. M. Pei first met in New York in 1980 at Varbanov's solo exhibition at Espace Pierre Cardin. Pei's Fragrant Hill Hotel project in Beijing may have encouraged Song to return to China for work. Because Song appears in Western dress, this photo was likely taken in 1981, after she had gone back to Beijing. When she started working for Cardin, Song switched her Chinese-style wardrobe for Western outfits, especially Cardin's designs.

a flagship building in the centre of Beijing to help them achieve their goal of opening one hundred thousand guest rooms. Officials imagined that Pei's structure would be the tallest building on Chang'an Avenue, a towering monument to modern China on the capital's main thoroughfare. Pei, however, politely declined the offer of a site adjacent to the Forbidden City, concerned that a skyscraper would destroy the grandeur of the historic palace complex. He was also opposed to the Soviet-influenced 'rootless' architecture that had dominated China for three decades:[6] steel-and-concrete edifices, sometimes topped with structures resembling traditional Chinese roofs as a superficial acknowledgement of the setting.[7] Living in the United States during the 1970s, Pei reflected at length on modernist architecture, and had his own vision for the future of China's built environment. Rather than adhering to the cold homogeneity of Western modernism, he explored China's vernacular architectural vocabularies and studied garden compounds and other classic Jiangnan dwellings:

> China must find a way to create an architecture with its own unique qualities ... and see how architecture can reflect history, life, and culture ... My goal is not to build a hotel, but rather to find a path forward ... Chinese gardens are unique, with the interiors and exteriors integrated, as if the entire universe had been placed in a courtyard.[8]

Ultimately, Pei agreed to build a 300-room low-rise hotel in suburban Fragrant Hill Park. The project consisted of a scattered arrangement of buildings with whitewashed walls and dark-grey brick and tiles, all built around a Chinese-style

When I. M. Pei's Fragrant Hill Hotel opened, it was not well received by the Chinese, who were unimpressed by its elegant but modest decor. Nevertheless, Song Huai-Kuei brought Chinese models to the hotel for fashion photoshoots. In this photo, the models are in the hotel atrium wearing Pierre Cardin dresses in several colours, creating a fascinating contrast with the hotel's ornamental rock, moon gate, and geometric wall—all elements from traditional Chinese gardens.

garden. Surrounded by rockeries, the garden had cobblestone pathways winding through it, and the reflections of the buildings on the surface of the water swirled with the reflections of the trees, organically blending into the environment. The hotel's passageways and courtyards incorporated many traditional elements, including arched doorways and latticed windows.

Song learned from Pei that the hotel had been built on the former site of the Fragrant Hill Kindergarten, where his mother had once taught. Pei also invited Song's friend Zao to paint a pair of ink paintings for the hotel. In conversations with Song, Pei revealed some of the difficulties he had encountered during the hotel's construction owing to the builders' poor management. Working with his wife and assistants, Pei had had to remove spots of paint from the floors. They had even had to clean up the bathrooms themselves.

Song had sophisticated taste in Asian aesthetics, informed in part by her years abroad. She eagerly awaited the opening of the hotel in the autumn of 1982, when scarlet leaves covered Fragrant Hill. But neither she nor Pei was prepared for the mixed reception the complex received. The architect had enjoyed official

Far left
Pierre Cardin in front of
Mao Zedong's portrait,
taken shortly after his
arrival at Beijing Capital
International Airport
on 30 November 1978.
It was Cardin's first visit
to China.

Left
Pierre Cardin on the Great
Wall in Beijing, late 1970s.

Below
Pierre Cardin in the
streets of Beijing during
his first visit to China,
1978.

Left
Pierre Cardin toasting with
Chinese officials in China,
late 1970s.

Above

In 1979, Pierre Cardin visited China
for the second time. He brought with
him models from France and Japan to
showcase his designs at a fashion show
at the Cultural Palace of Nationalities in
Beijing. In this photo, one model wears
a dress and the other a suit; most of the
audience members, by contrast, are in
thick cotton jackets. The Chinese foreign
trade authorities restricted the show to
'internal viewing', so only designers and
practitioners within the fashion business
could attend.

Right

Pierre Cardin backstage at his fashion
show at the Cultural Palace of Nationalities
in Beijing, 19 March 1979. It was the first
fashion show to be held in China.

support from start to finish, and the authorities had not interfered with his designs. But the final building appeared to be at odds with the style they had expected. Other architects praised the elegance and intelligence of Pei's design. Far more people, however, found fault with the structure's remote location and disparaged the hotel's understated elegance, which struck them as inadequate for hosting tourists. Critics also felt that Pei had spent far too much money on artisans in his quest for fine craftsmanship, pointing to his seemingly excessive devotion to traditional brick polishing and setting. They also thought shipping Taihu rocks and cobblestones from South China had been an unnecessary extravagance.[9] Some people even poked fun at the architect, saying that the cobblestones he used were even more expensive than chicken eggs. But for Pei, who had shed blood, sweat, and tears for the project, the harshest blow of all was seeing the collapse of his dream that the Fragrant Hill Hotel could spur the growth of modern architecture rooted in China.

This hope disappeared like 'moonlight in a ditch', as the Chinese saying goes. Indeed, the project was ridiculed precisely for its ostentatious ambition to define a distinctly Chinese style for the era. 'Being profligate is incompatible with the country's current condition,' one critic wrote. 'Even if it became successful, it won't be of any universal significance.'[10] Another quipped about the low-rise structure: 'to explore "the path for modern Chinese architecture", all you have to do is wander through the spaces between high-rises ... Something is only valuable if it works.'[11] Many architects in China also viewed international hotels as a vehicle for bringing Western techniques, models, and sometimes investment into the country. They imagined they could modernise by churning out quick copies of foreign buildings, thereby accelerating China's lagging development. Pei offered an alternative course. He thought of architecture in terms of how it reflects people's lives and culture. It has taken people in China four decades to understand Pei's work at Fragrant Hill. In the end, this missed connection exemplified the enormous gap between the modernisation that China was rushing into headlong and the hybrid modernism that Pei had conceived in the West.

‡

Compared with Pei, Pierre Cardin had a much easier time in China. When he first visited the country, in 1978, Cardin brought along his staff as well as a reporter from *Paris Match*. They visited Beijing, Tianjin, Shanghai, and Hangzhou, observing what a Western reporter had dubbed 'blue ants': the people of China dressed from head to toe in indigo cotton.[12] The officials hosting him thought that Cardin was merely a French tailor, and so took him to see clothing factories and textile mills. Before the tour was over, Cardin put on an impromptu fashion show of his own designs for officials in Shanghai, with his assistants and other staff members serving as models.

After Cardin returned to France, all the leading media outlets in North America and Europe reported on his travels. While an article in the *New York Times* said inaccurately that Cardin had been appointed as a fashion consultant to the communist nation, it correctly conveyed the hope that Cardin would 'advise

Song Huai-Kuei and Maryn Varbanov at Yoshi Takata's flat in Paris, mid-1981 to 1982. They are pictured with Dida Javacheff, sister-in-law of Christo Javacheff of the artist duo Christo and Jeanne-Claude. Song had started working for Pierre Cardin in China and returned to Paris from time to time to be with her family. Song's work *Butterfly* hangs on the wall between two containers holding her family's Chinese ink brushes, most often used by Varbanov to paint, highlighting her transition at the time from a life of art-making to a career in fashion.

the Chinese on how to style their textile products to make them more marketable in the West'.[13] Cardin also saw China's immense economic potential, telling officials he wanted to bring a delegation of a dozen or so models to the country to present his designs. He even floated the prospect of opening a factory.

In 1979, Cardin received an official invitation to return and flew to Beijing with more than two hundred pieces of clothing to stage a fashion show at the Cultural Palace of Nationalities. Only people from the Ministry of Foreign Trade and the clothing industry had access to this 'internal viewing' event, but it marked the first up-close encounter between a Chinese audience and the work of a top international fashion designer. It was also on this trip that Cardin's model Maryse Gaspard (b. 1947) posed for a famous image. Dressed in a rainbow-striped outfit designed by Cardin, Gaspard dances on the Great Wall against a backdrop of craggy mountains while so-called blue ants look on with astonished faces.

At the start of his career, Cardin had served as an apprentice in the atelier of Christian Dior, who worked exclusively in haute couture. In the late

This is the most famous photograph of Pierre Cardin's 1979 trip to China. Cardin asked his favourite model, Maryse Gaspard, to dance on the Great Wall for a photoshoot. Her rainbow dress stands out against the dark, muted clothing of the Chinese people watching her. The photo captures the state of Chinese fashion at the time, as the country began to reform and open up under Deng Xiaoping.

1950s, Cardin came up with an imaginative idea to democratise fashion. With mass-produced ready-to-wear items, Cardin shook up the old-guard leadership of the Fédération de la Haute Couture et de la Mode. Although he was expelled from the group for his irreverent approach, he would later win the organisation's prestigious Golden Thimble three times. With the advent of youth culture in the 1960s, haute couture needed to evolve. A new generation derided the extravagance of traditional fashion houses, which appeared stuck in the past. Cardin seized on this cultural shift just as the new ready-to-wear market was taking off. With equal foresight, Cardin saw the potential of the Chinese market: 'If I could make one button for each person in China, then that would be nine hundred

Yuan Yunsheng

Memories of Water Towns, 1962
Oil on canvas
243 × 245 cm
Collection of Art Museum of Central
Academy of Fine Arts

Memories of Water Towns is Yuan Yunsheng's first mural drawing and Dong Xiwen's favourite work by a 1962 graduate of the Central Academy of Fine Arts. Rather than a realist approach that highlights key figures, the mural adopts a multi-point perspective commonly found in traditional Chinese painting, presenting a bird's-eye view of Jiangnan's bustling water towns. Mexican muralist influence is evident from the work's composition and in the characterisation of the figures. Yuan was subsequently criticised for deviating from Socialist Realism.

million buttons!'[14] For China, an under-developed country longing for modernisation, the picture of Western life painted by Cardin was simple, straightforward, and accessible—at least compared to Pei's highbrow reflection on international modernism.

Cardin's trademark licensing production model was especially suitable for China, where his first step was to establish the Pierre Cardin brand. To accomplish this, Cardin needed a representative who understood the country. His visit to New York had left him quite impressed with Song, whose qualifications included experience in Europe, artistic training, a good disposition, excellent taste, and a solid network within China's art world. For her part, Song seems to have greatly admired Cardin's practical outlook. The two hit it off immediately. With the signing of a handwritten contract, Song became Pierre Cardin's chief representative in China.

At the age of forty, Song switched from art to commerce without hesitation. Although we can never know for sure what motivated her, the dangerously unpredictable political situation in Bulgaria might have been a factor in Song's decision. Several months before the celebrations for the 1,300-year anniversary of the founding of Bulgaria, Song and Varbanov's long-time supporter Lyudmila Todorova Zhivkova died suddenly under mysterious circumstances. Rumour had it that her interest in mysticism exceeded what government officials were prepared to tolerate. Within a year, all her closest aides in the Ministry of Culture had been purged, and with them Varbanov lost his main source of protection in Sofia. At the same time, Boryana was about to graduate from art school, and Phénix had also decided to study art. For a family that was barely scraping by to begin with, the prospect of supporting four artists seemed like a luxury beyond their means. Thus, in 1981, Song boarded a plane bound for Beijing and embarked on her new life. From that point on, she rarely mentioned that she herself was a highly accomplished artist, and people knew her only as the businesswoman and fashion connoisseur Madame Song.

‡

When Song landed at Beijing Capital International Airport in March 1981, she entered a newly completed terminal adorned with a mural that was the subject of heated debate. The painter of this mural was none other than Yuan Yunsheng, one of Song's younger classmates in Dong Xiwen's studio. Like Song, Yuan had been thrilled and inspired by the slideshow of Mexican murals presented by David Alfaro Siqueiros at the Central Academy of Fine Arts in 1956; however, as we saw earlier, he had been denounced as a rightist for his dissenting views and sent to the countryside for reform through labour. He was not considered rehabilitated until two years later, at which point he was permitted to return to his studies in Beijing. For his graduation project, Yuan produced a set of studies for a mural entitled *Memories of Water Towns* (1962), which combined modernist and Chinese folk art styles. Although Dong effusively praised the work, other faculty members who upheld the Socialist Realist line expressed their dissatisfaction. But Dong did not

Above

This photo shows Yuan Yunsheng's mural *Water-Splashing Festival: Ode to Life* (1979) at Beijing Capital International Airport before it was completed. On the right are the bathing female nudes that caused controversy among both Chinese officials and members of the public. The nudes were covered in 1981 and subsequently boarded up around the time of the Anti-Spiritual Pollution Campaign in 1983.

Right

Yuan Yunsheng and his assistants, Fei Zheng (back) and Lian Weiyun (front), painting the mural *Water-Splashing Festival: Ode to Life* at Beijing Capital International Airport in the summer of 1979.

Water-Splashing Festival: Ode to Life presents young Dai women as symbols of vitality and idealism in southern China.

back down, and ultimately the piece received high marks. However, when it was presented in an exhibition the following year, critics attacked the work for its supposedly cartoonish renderings of labourers. Although Yuan was widely acknowledged to be the most talented of all the students in his cohort, he was nonetheless assigned to do propaganda work in the cold northeast, where he would spend fifteen years.

It was not until the late 1970s that Yuan received a telegram from Beijing offering him a new creative platform. In response to Deng Xiaoping's calls to develop the tourism industry, a mural was commissioned for the new terminal at Beijing's main airport. Invited to participate, Yuan designed a scene depicting a traditional festival of the Dai ethnic group of southern China. Entitled *Water-Splashing Festival: Ode to Life*, the sprawling work presents young Dai women as symbols of vitality and idealism. While echoes of Mexican murals are evident, the painting also reveals the influence of Dong's ideas about oil painting with Chinese vernacular characteristics. Yuan's proposal was very well received. However, after its completion, two of the figures—nude Dai women—soon became the focus of public controversy.

Yuan had been quite conscious of the limitations imposed by the censors. When the project was still at the drafting stage, he had drawn lines over the chests of the young women so that the censors would assume that he planned eventually to add garments. But when the painting was unveiled, there were no dresses to be seen. If Yuan had not taken steps to obscure his intentions, accusations of pornographic content would have halted the project before it had got off the ground. At the time, the depiction of nudes in Chinese painting and sculpture was experiencing a renaissance of sorts, and arts magazines had been steadily publishing reproductions of such works. But these depictions, too, were subject to fierce attacks by members of the public.

Yuan's mural became a principal target in an ongoing debate. When *Meishu* magazine published photographs of the mural, it received the following letter to the editor: 'I know that when customs officials are looking for contraband, one of the things they look for is nude photos ... Doesn't your publication agree that there are differences between socialist culture and capitalist culture? Is the enjoyment of buttocks and breasts your publication's idea of "modernisation"? What a joke.'[15] Alarmed officials suggested that the mural be revised to clothe the naked women. But when Deng visited the airport, he quipped: 'What's all the fuss about? Artistic expression is a perfectly normal thing, and I think it's fine. I think we should print copies of it and sell them to foreigners.'[16] Unfortunately, the matter continued to simmer until it entered the arena of national politics. A compromise was found, and by the time Song landed, the nudes had been hidden behind a huge curtain.

The debate in China about the representation of the human form, and the nude in particular, was not limited to the art world. For Song, who had travelled to Beijing to assist Cardin in opening a boutique and putting on fashion shows with

Song Huai-Kuei with
colleagues at Pierre
Cardin's Beijing office
in the now-demolished
Baoluo Building, 1995.
From left: Song's
subordinate Zhang Wei;
her assistant, Fang Fang;
Song herself; and Song's
French interpreter,
Zhao Huamin.

Right

The Pierre Cardin Beijing showroom was
established in the Palace of Abstinence
at the Temple of Heaven in Beijing on 21
November 1981. Here, Cardin is addressing
the press on opening day with Song
standing next to him.

Below

Pierre Cardin adjusting the collar of a
model at the opening of his showroom
in the Palace of Abstinence on
21 November 1981.

Song Huai-Kuei's main job in the 1980s was to identify local manufacturers and distributors for Pierre Cardin in China, thereby greatly reducing production costs. On the left is Hugues-Alexandre Tartaut, who also worked for Cardin alongside Song. On the right, judging by their attire at least, are two Hong Kong businessmen.

Chinese models, the central concern was how modern people might use fashion for the purpose of self-expression. Leveraging Cardin's reputation, as well as her own network of contacts among fellow alumni of Bridgman Girls' College and CAFA, she quickly secured a suite at the Beijing Hotel, which served as both her residence and her office. She coordinated with the Beijing Foreign Trade Company to open a Pierre Cardin showroom in the Palace of Abstinence at the Temple of Heaven, the first Western clothing boutique to be located near one of China's historic sites. To celebrate the opening, she planned to hold a fashion show at the Beijing Hotel the very same day. With the venue chosen and written permission in hand, she lacked only models to show off the clothes.

In China in 1981, the job of 'fashion model' barely existed. During the revolutionary era, Mao Zedong had exhorted women to 'reject make-up and put on military uniforms'. Such directives promoted an asexual image; women did not wear skirts or dresses, and they bobbed their hair. This convention was clearly at odds with the need for a fashion model to be confident in showing off her femininity. And there was another problem: the outfits Pierre Cardin had brought with him had been made to fit the measurements of Europeans. They were too large to fit the petite frames of many Chinese women. Influenced by the fashion show Cardin had staged several years previously, a number of clothing factories in Shanghai

Pierre Cardin and Chinese models dressed in his designs outside the Palace of Abstinence, 1981.

NOT EXACTLY ABOUT
皮爾卡丹在北京
鄧小宇

27

had recruited female workers to display the factories' products; however, asking workers to parade around in Western designs was a different matter.

Offering to help, the Beijing Foreign Trade Company put Song in touch with a military song-and-dance ensemble. The members of the ensemble were tall and slender with well-toned bodies. But when Song asked them to put on Cardin's designs, it quickly became apparent that their stern military comportment was completely at odds with the clothing. The People's Liberation Army dancers were also hesitant to participate in an activity that had a suspiciously bourgeois hue. Then Song had a flash of inspiration. She went to the Beijing Shichahai Sports School to scout for models among the basketball and volleyball teams. From time to time, she would also approach a tall and slender young person who stood out from the crowd. After a period assessing these prospects, she eventually selected more than twenty charismatic but wholly inexperienced 'models'. Among them were college students, actors, and athletes. All were curious to try something new, but none dared tell their families about their new occupation.

Several months before the show, Song rented a space in the Working People's Cultural Palace near the Drum Tower. Relying on the instruction she had received at the Centre for New Goods and Fashion in Sofia, she proceeded to train her new recruits, none of whom had any previous runway experience. Song

contacted Michel Lee and other friends in France and asked them to send glossy magazines and fashion photos. She also used audio-visual materials during her training sessions, having brought from France a VCR and cassette tapes—rare items in China at the time. A few days before the opening, Song invited the Hong Kong–based film director Yonfan (b. 1947), whom she had met in Paris, to join her in Beijing to help with training. Travelling with him was Peter Dunn Siu-Yue, co-founder of the Hong Kong publication *City Magazine*.

Dunn wrote a humorous, behind-the-scenes account of the show's trials and tribulations. From the very beginning, the performance into which Song had poured her heart and soul was underappreciated. As far as Cardin was concerned, the event was simply an opportunity to promote himself. As long as the international media showed up and wrote about the spectacle, he was not concerned about the quality of the fashion show itself. Dunn reported on the infighting and backbiting within the Cardin company, noting that some staff 'thought the show was a joke, and when they saw Yonfan and Song Huai-Kuei ... painstakingly trying to teach those kids how to walk down the runway, they stood to the side and secretly snickered'.[17] Song carried on, impervious to criticism, doing her best to look after her 'kids'.

In contrast to Song's cool, calm, and collected attitude, the Chinese officials observing the show were very anxious about the models and urged them

to comport themselves with 'self-respect, propriety, and poise'. The officials also inspected each item of clothing. If a garment proved to be overly revealing, either the model would have to cover potentially scandalous areas with their hands or Song would have to grab a random piece of clothing for them to wear over the offending garment. The final show was fifteen minutes shorter than originally planned, in part because many outfits had been disallowed. The Chinese models were also unaccustomed to the rapid changes of clothing typical of a fast-paced runway show. As a result, the American model whom Cardin had brought along appeared essentially non-stop. The task of modelling all the low-cut—and even the relatively low-cut—evening gowns also fell to her.

After all the fluster, the display came to an end. As Dunn concluded in his article, the important thing was not that Pierre Cardin had held another fashion show, but rather that the Chinese models had gained an invaluable experience: 'If this succeeded in making these young people so happy that they would remember it for the rest of their lives, then it couldn't have been all that bad.'[18] Indeed, this was the first group of 'professional models' to receive relatively formal training, and some of them embarked on careers as models with Song's encouragement. For all its clumsiness and confusion, this fashion show appears in retrospect as a watershed moment for professional modelling in China.

Above
Through Song Huai-Kuei's active involvement, the first public show of Western fashion in China was held at the Beijing Hotel in 1981. Pierre Cardin employed only one male and one female model from outside of China. Here, the foreign female model is changing her outfit in an open area backstage. To her right, a Chinese official lowers his gaze; he and the Chinese models would have been shocked by such a practice, which was common in international fashion shows. Since Chinese models were forbidden from wearing outfits that were considered too revealing, the foreign model was tasked with presenting all the designs featuring lower necklines.

Opposite
The only foreign female model at Pierre Cardin's fashion show held in the ballroom of the Beijing Hotel in 1981.

Like a Butterfly: Revisiting Madame Song the Artist

Wu Mo

Most people in China remember Madame Song as the restaurateur of Maxim's in Beijing, or as the country's earliest fashion guru. By comparison, her life as an artist is relatively unknown. Beginning in her adolescence, art was consistently among Song Huai-Kuei's core interests, nurturing her creative aspirations and fostering several pivotal transformations in her career. Trained initially as a painter, Song's independent works in the 1970s demonstrate a mastery of textiles as a medium and a profound understanding of the female body that resonated with the era's global feminist movements.

In 1954, Song was admitted to the Central Academy of Fine Arts, Beijing, to study oil painting under the famous artist Dong Xiwen. Dong encouraged his students to express their unique characters rather than rigidly follow the academy's teachings of Socialist Realism. Painted as a class assignment in 1956, Song's *Portrait of an Old Man* offers a glimpse into how her teacher influenced her. She depicted her subject shirtless and vividly presented his thin physique and sagging muscles. The work's greatest appeal comes from the face: the old man is staring into the void with a trace of sadness that points to a heavy heart. Song treated her model not as a passive target of scrutiny, but as an individual charged with emotions.

In 1958, Song and her husband, Maryn Varbanov, left China to settle in his native Bulgaria, where she enrolled at the National Academy of Art in Sofia. Song found herself in a milieu that included artists and intellectuals. Her portrait of Bulgarian actress Nevena Kokanova (1938–2000), known as the 'first lady of Bulgarian cinema', shows how her painting style changed while abroad. Compared to *Portrait of an Old Man*, this painting features lighter and more relaxed strokes that leave the under-drawing

visible in places. Song no longer created texture by piling on pigments; she also eschewed realistic depictions of anatomical details. Instead, she ever-so-slightly lengthened the actress's proportions, especially the neck, to make her appear calmer and more poised.

Among Song's few extant paintings is a group portrait of her own family from the late 1960s. All four family members have elongated necks, a feature that had become Song's motif. For the background of her portrait of Kokanova, Song created a misty shroud in a colour that matches the actress's skin tone. In the family portrait, Song depicted herself and Varbanov in cyan, creating a striking contrast with the background and the skin tone of the two children in the foreground. This visual effect creates the illusion that the parents are a screen behind their children, while also affirming the bond between Song and her spouse.

Even while demonstrating promise as a painter, Song began to focus on another aspect of her artistic career: the tapestry art she

Song Huai-Kuei

Portrait of an Old Man

1956

Oil on canvas

63 × 48 cm

Private collection

made in collaboration with Varbanov. The 4th
International Lausanne Tapestry Biennial in
1969 marked the liberation of tapestry art from
a two-dimensional form—its shift from 'wall'
to 'space'—which brought it closer conceptually
to such modern art forms as 'soft sculpture'
or 'spatial installation'. Varbanov and Song's
Composition 2001 (1969) and *Aporia* (1972), which
were shown at the 1971 and 1973 biennials
respectively, embody their responses to this
new direction of tapestry art. The two works,
both very large, possess majestic structures that
render them self-contained within their spaces.
Composition 2001, woven with white wool, forms
a perpetually spiralling 'fortress', at once closed
and open. One can imagine it hanging in space,

Left
Song Huai-Kuei in front of *Composition 2001*
(1969) at the 5th Lausanne International
Tapestry Biennial, 1971.

Below
Song Huai-Kuei and Maryn Varbanov
Composition 2001, 1969
Wool
320 × 160 × 160 cm
Collection unknown

free warp threads gently dancing. *Aporia* features
even more sophisticated weaving artistry. The
work consists of two semi-cylinders with a
crevice between them that seems to be both
inviting as an opening and prohibitive, evoking
the classical Greek philosophy underlying the
work's title.

   As a female tapestry artist, Song employed
a style that was vastly different from Varbanov's,
despite their close collaboration. Her experience
tailoring and making clothes since adolescence,
as well as her growing understanding of the
feminist movements that were taking Europe
and the United States by storm in the 1970s,
likely informed her approach. Song sought to
express feminine experience in an introspective
way, and independently conceptualised the
series *Dream of Zhuangzi*, or *Butterfly*.

   The tapestries in this series have a wide
range of palettes, but they all share a form
that resembles a butterfly with spread wings.
Song conceived the series as an allusion to the
classical Daoist parable *Zhuang Zhou Dreams
that He Is a Butterfly*, which explores the state
of 'union of self and object'.[1] One can regard
these butterfly tapestries as incarnations of Song
herself, especially when these 'butterflies' are
quite obviously shaped like vulvas. Compared to
the vaginal forms of Judy Chicago's controversial

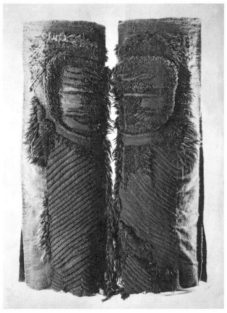

**Song Huai-Kuei
and Maryn Varbanov**
Aporia, 1972
Wool
340 × 225 × 40 cm
Collection unknown

Song Huai-Kuei with *Aporia*
(1972), ca.1972.

table settings in *The Dinner Party*, created around the same time, Song's 'butterflies' appear more playful than provocative.[2] This has to do with their soft material and decorative details, such as the dangling, pine cone–shaped components. These 'butterflies' also have an unexpected use. In a photo taken by her daughter, Boryana Varbanov, in 1979, Song has draped a 'butterfly' over a mannequin, like a cape. Shortly after the photo was taken, Song switched professional identities, becoming the representative of a designer label in China and a pioneer in the modelling industry.

Madame Song's oeuvre offers a pleasure-infused feminine experience that was uncommon in the artistic landscape of the 1970s, reflecting her own assessment of her personal life. In addition, as a cosmopolitan female artist who traversed opposing ideologies during the Cold War, Song's artistic creations reflect her openness to different art forms and ethnic cultures, from which she was particularly adept at extracting ideas and combining them with Chinese cultural heritage in order to develop her own artistic language. Even though Song slowed down her artistic practice after the 1980s, this eclectic attitude remained embedded in her life and continued to nourish her subsequent career. As a close friend commented: '[S]he was someone who was true to her ideals as an artist.'[3] Retracing the long-neglected context of her artistic creations and her identity as an artist offers an indispensable dimension to understanding Madame Song as a person.

Dr Wu Mo is De Ying Associate Curator of Visual Art at M+

Right

Mannequin displaying Song Huai-Kuei's tapestry work *Butterfly* at Espace Pierre Cardin during the 1979 Salon d'Automne, Paris.

Below left

Song Huai-Kuei
Dream of Zhuangzi, 1970s
Sisal and wool
130 × 99 × 12 cm
M+, Hong Kong

Below right

Song Huai-Kuei
Composition Rouge, 1974
Vegetable fibres and horsehair
210 × 157 × 32 cm
Collection of Centre National des Arts Plastiques

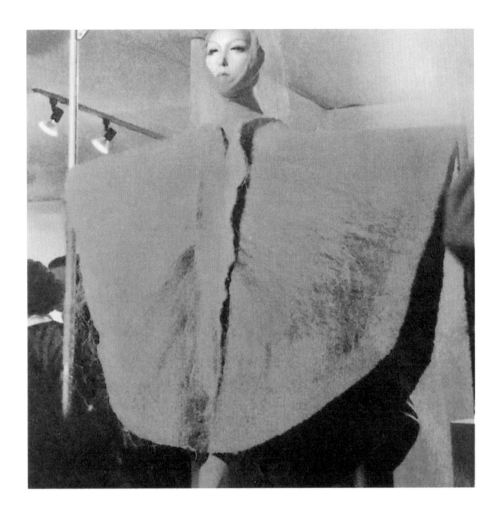

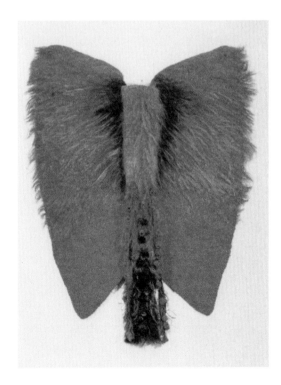

Dressing the Modern Woman: Madame Song's Wardrobe

Tanja Cunz with Isobel Harcourt
and Natalie Harding

As Pierre Cardin's ambassador to China, Song Huai-Kuei had to dress well. Her archive at M+ includes some hundred and twenty-five garments, most designed by Cardin. This collection is a testament to her multiple identities and complex professional activities. From days signing contracts with clothing manufacturers and training China's first supermodels to evenings hosting cultural luminaries at Maxim's in Beijing, Song crafted the perfect look for every occasion. The following section presents thirty-four of these garments, a selection of photographs depicting Song and her contemporaries in the course of her days and nights in Beijing, as well as more recent images that reflect her legacy.

M+ curators have worked closely with conservators to catalogue these garments. Each caption begins with a list of materials and production techniques, followed by a description of the garment and a short text about the context in which it was worn. This systematic approach to analysing and contextualising fashion is a prelude to the full cataloguing of all textiles in Madame Song's archive held by M+. The project aims to stimulate further research and prompt discussion about fashion as an important part of the disciplines of design and visual culture.

**Evening dress from Haute Couture
Spring/Summer 1984 collection**

Designed in 1983

Silk chiffon printed with a paisley design in pink,
beige, and black | fawn silk georgette | cord
(probably nylon) | braided elastic | metal press
studs | interfacing (probably synthetic)

Machine and hand sewn

Large symmetrical chiffon rosettes with corded
edges obscure the wearer's silhouette in this
strapless paisley print dress. The neckline is
decorated with a chiffon bow at the centre.
In 1985, Song Huai-Kuei was photographed
wearing the dress at Maxim's. She paired it with
a statement bib necklace and a dress ring with
blue stone, the latter being one of her favourite
and most-worn accessories.

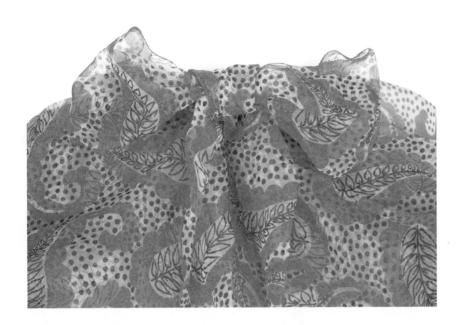

**Evening dress from Haute Couture
Autumn/Winter 1987/88 collection**

Designed in 1987

Black silk chiffon with a tartan pattern of
machine-stitched plastic sequins in black, brown,
and bronze | silk georgette | black satin ribbon
(probably silk) | synthetic zip fastener | foam
shoulder padding (probably polyurethane)

Machine and hand sewn

Glamorous full-length sequined evening
gown with a jewel neckline, long sleeves, padded
shoulders, and a form-fitting bodice. The flared
skirt gathers at the left hip to form a flounced
slit with a bow at the opening. Song Huai-Kuei
often showcased Pierre Cardin's collections by
wearing his garments herself or having her models
present them, as the two archival photos show.
In particular, the model (opposite, top) is seen
featuring the dress—accessorised with oversized
statement earrings and a fur collar—at a fashion
show held at Maxim's in January 1988.

Evening dress

Designed between 1984 and 1987

Black satin (probably silk) | black silk velvet | black silk habutai | synthetic zip fastener | foam shoulder padding (probably polyurethane) | metal weight

Machine and hand sewn

Black full-length evening gown with a deep V-neck satin bodice, dolman sleeves, and padded shoulders above a straight-cut velvet skirt with a centre back slit. In both photos, taken at an event at Maxim's, Song Huai-Kuei dazzles with her sophisticated look by combining this dress with a long lariat necklace and matching chandelier earrings, as well as two dress rings with coloured stones.

**Evening dress from Haute Couture
Autumn/Winter 1985/86 collection**

Designed in 1985

Red silk crêpe de Chine printed with a black
ivy-leaf pattern | black gaberdine (probably silk) |
black enamelled metal press studs | interfacing
(probably synthetic) | foam shoulder padding
(probably polyurethane)

Machine and hand sewn

Red-and-black silk crêpe de Chine dress with
an ivy-leaf print, long sleeves, padded shoulders,
and a bias-cut tapering skirt gathered at the
front to form panniers at the sides. The waist is
emphasised by a black belt. In this photo of Song
Huai-Kuei and a group of models at Maxim's, the
dress is being worn by the model second from
the right. The royal-blue wedge dress worn by the
model second from the left was also designed by
Pierre Cardin (see page 114). Song is at the centre
in a black evening gown (see page 111); as she is
wearing the same jewellery as seen in the archive
photos on page 111, this photo might have been
taken on the same occasion.

**Evening dress from Haute Couture
Spring/Summer 1986 collection**

Designed in 1985

Royal-blue silk satin | blue silk habutai |
metal press studs | foam shoulder padding
(probably polyurethane)

Machine sewn

Drop-waist silk satin wedge-cut dress with
a choker collar, padded shoulders, and long
dolman sleeves. The hip is encircled by a deep
flounce, dipped in the back and open at the
front with a centre front slit. Like many of Pierre
Cardin's designs, this royal-blue dress, also
seen in the archive photos on pages 112 and 143,
captivates with a distinctive silhouette and an
intriguing combination of contrasting stylistic
details. Dating many of the dresses in Song Huai-
Kuei's archive has proved difficult owing to the
lack of specific clues. However, in the case of this
dress, the observation that Cardin frequently
used high-gloss satin between 1984 and 1987
provided an initial time frame that helped identify
the exact collection.

Evening dress from Haute Couture Spring/Summer 1984 collection

Designed in 1983

Black gaberdine (probably synthetic) | black silk organza | black silk habutai | silver lamé ribbon | silver plastic sequins | multicolour paint | synthetic horsehair ribbon | synthetic zip fasteners | foam shoulder padding (probably polyurethane)

Machine sewn

This three-quarter-length black shift dress with dolman sleeves and boat neck features latticed sequins on wavy organza panels, which culminate in a playful, oversized bow on the left shoulder. The archive photo shows three of Song Huai-Kuei's models at an event at Maxim's. The dress is worn by the model on the left, while the model on the right is in a black evening gown, also part of Song's archive, with a distinctive stand-up cape made of reinforced organza ruffles.

Evening dress

Designed between 1980 and 1988

Black wool crêpe | white plain weave (probably linen or cotton) layered with fusible interfacing | black silk habutai | synthetic zip fastener

Machine and hand sewn

Black one-shoulder shift dress with a contrasting white asymmetrical flyaway collar forming a crest above the left shoulder. The photos show Song Huai-Kuei in the dress on two occasions: once during a promotional event for Peugeot in March 1988, and another at an event with Humbert des Lyons de Feuchin (right), manager of Maxim's Beijing, and Hong Kong actor Tony Leung Ka-fai (left). Interestingly, in both archive images, Song is seen wearing the dress backwards. While barely visible in the group photo, a black silk rose is fixed on Song's shoulder between the wings of the collar.

Evening dress from Haute Couture Autumn/Winter 1985/86 collection

Designed in 1985

Dark-green silk velvet | permanent-pleated sea-green silk taffeta | synthetic horsehair ribbon | metal hooks and eyes | braided elastic | interfacing (probably synthetic)

Machine and hand sewn

Strapless dark-green velvet evening gown with deep-pleated taffeta ruffles that make a peplum skirt before travelling down the back to form a train. Two taffeta cord bows secure the bodice at the back. Brought from Pierre Cardin's Paris studio to Beijing, this dress was featured in a fashion show at Maxim's in January 1988 alongside Cardin's extravagant evening wear from the 1980s, examples of which are included in this section. The dress was also used at a promotional event for Peugeot two months later, worn by a different model but accessorised with the same striking choker. The choker, also designed by Cardin, has mixed synthetic tubing with gemstone and rhinestone crystals.

Evening dress

Designed between 1980 and 1987

Burgundy silk velvet | black silk taffeta | black satin ribbon (probably silk) | burgundy silk dupion | braided elastic | synthetic zip fastener

Machine and hand sewn

Made of burgundy silk velvet, this shift dress showcases billowing black taffeta ruffles that frame the dipping backline and extend, winglike, above the shoulders. Three black ribbon bows are attached to the ruffles, embellishing the shoulder blades and lower back. This elegant fit is characterised by the contrast between the high-neck front and the sensual back, as well as the combination of soft fabrics with stiff sculptural details. One of Song Huai-Kuei's models wore the dress at a fashion show in 1988 (opposite), the same event at which the green evening gown on page 121 was featured. The other photograph (above) was taken during the shooting of the 2010 short film *Beijing Love*, directed by John-Paul Pietrus and starring Ling Tan. A homage to Song, the film features several garments from her archive, including dresses on pages 108, 113, and 128.

**Evening dress from Haute Couture
Autumn/Winter 1986/87 collection**

Designed in 1986

Black silk velvet | black silk taffeta | black
satin ribbon (probably silk) | white metal and
rhinestone ornament | black silk habutai | synthetic
horsehair ribbon | synthetic fusible interfacing |
synthetic zip fastener

Machine and hand sewn

Black evening gown with short kimono sleeves and
an asymmetrical ruffle skirt that rises above the
knees in the front. The ribbon belt at the dropped
waist is ornamented with a bow and a rhinestone
brooch. Presented during a fashion show at
Maxim's in January 1988 (see page 120), this velvet
and taffeta dress plays with lengths and volumes
as well as the contrast between the opulent skirt
and the slightly oversized, almost T-shirt-like
top. The accessories were also carefully chosen:
the model in the archive photo wears a single
statement earring on the opposite side of the
decorative clasp at the waist, giving the outfit
a whimsical twist.

**Evening dress from Haute Couture
Autumn/Winter 1989/90 collection**

Designed in 1989

Black textured synthetic tube-knitted textile |
black synthetic permanent-pleated mousseline |
cording (probably nylon) | black synthetic ribbon
with adhered rhinestones | black plain-weave silk
and wire flower | steel hoop | black enamelled
metal press studs

Machine and hand sewn

Textured synthetic black halter-neck tube dress
with a low back and an asymmetrical hooped
peplum, trimmed with pleated organza and
rhinestones. A silk rose lies beneath the peplum
on the back of the right hip. This dress is another
example of Pierre Cardin's playful treatment
of soft fabrics and sculptural elements, one of
the key features of many of his designs. In the
archive photo, the Forbidden City functions as an
atmospheric backdrop for Song Huai-Kuei and
four models she had trained. They are all wearing
striking black-and-red outfits designed by
Cardin, with Song in the foreground in an intense
red dress, a pleated cape, and sunglasses.

Evening dress

Designed between 1980 and 1989

Black gaberdine (probably synthetic) | black plain-weave silk | multicolour plastic sequins | multicolour glass beads | stiffening (probably buckram) | braided elastic | synthetic zip fastener | foam shoulder padding (probably polyurethane)

Dress body: machine and hand sewn; beading and sequins: machine and hand sewn

This full-length shift dress has a flyaway collar that goes above the left shoulder and is embellished with multicolour sequins and glass beads, resembling a butterfly with folded wings. In the photo, Song Huai-Kuei is wearing this dress at Maxim's in the 1980s. As in the case of the vine-like design of the green evening gown on page 121, this dress exemplifies the influence of nature on Pierre Cardin's evening wear in the 1980s.

Cocktail dress

Designed between 1980 and 1989

Black gaberdine (probably silk) | white metal and diamanté ornament | black silk habutai | foam shoulder padding (probably polyurethane) | synthetic zip fasteners

Machine and hand sewn

Black three-quarter-length shift dress with padded shoulders and long dolman sleeves with cuff zip closures. Secured by a square-shaped statement brooch with tassels on the left shoulder, the floating panel drapes across the body towards the waist in the opposite direction of the asymmetrical neckline. This dress is a good example of the incorporation of asymmetry into Pierre Cardin's style from the 1970s, in this case emphasising the wearer's shoulders. Song Huai-Kuei wore the dress for an actor friend's visit to Maxim's.

Cocktail dress

Designed between 1980 and 1989

Silk chiffon with satin and gold lamé stripes, overprinted with a multicolour tartan pattern | black satin ribbon (probably silk) | black silk georgette | synthetic zip fastener

Machine and hand sewn

This colourful, flowy silk chiffon dress with tartan print features an asymmetrical neckline and a statement cape collar with a slanting, off-shoulder design, underlining Song Huai-Kuei's cosmopolitan femininity and her pioneering role in creating a new perception of Chinese women. As in the case of the black, one-shoulder dress on page 118, Song wore this dress back to front—an interesting fact that was only discovered during the conservational work on her archive.

**Suit from Haute Couture
Autumn/Winter 1985/86 collection**

Designed in 1985

Plain-weave red-and-black wool tweed | black silk
habutai | stiffening (probably buckram) | jacket:
black plastic buttons and black buckle (probably
cellulose acetate) | skirt: metal hook, metal press
stud, and synthetic zip fastener

Machine and hand sewn

A dark-red-and-black wool tweed jacket with a
stand-up collar, overlapping lapels, waist pocket
flaps, belt-and-buckle closure, and large cuff
and pocket buttons. The jacket comes with
a matching mid-length peg skirt with side slits.
To make fashion accessible to a wider audience,
Pierre Cardin designed his first ready-to-
wear collection for women as early as 1959,
a pioneering move that led to his temporary
expulsion from the Chambre Syndicale de la
Haute Couture. Cardin used haute couture as
a field for experimentation while operating ready-
to-wear lines for menswear and womenswear.
Many of his designs were created with the modern
woman in mind—women who were active
and working, like Song Huai-Kuei. In this photo,
Song is with Humbert des Lyons de Feuchin
at Maxim's, the suit emphasising her identity
as a businesswoman.

Jacket

Designed in the early 1990s

Yellow twill-weave wool or wool blend layered with fusible interfacing | black synthetic patent leather | black enamelled metal press studs | foam shoulder padding (probably polyurethane)

Machine sewn

Collarless high-chroma-yellow jacket with padded shoulders and black synthetic-leather press studs resembling frog fasteners. In the archive photo, probably taken in the 1990s, Song Huai-Kuei is shown wearing the jacket while posing with three women and the actress and businesswoman Liu Xiaoqing (centre). Part of the main cast of *The Little Flower* (1979), the first Chinese film to be made after the Cultural Revolution, Liu became one of the very first stars of contemporary Chinese cinema and, later, China's first female millionaire. The sleeves of the jacket are reminiscent of Pierre Cardin's iconic 'car wash' dress from the 1960s with fringed hems, while the box cut and other design features are characteristic of early 1990s fashion.

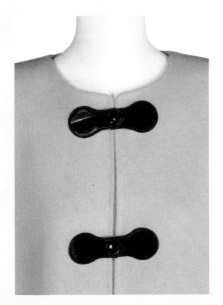

Day dress

Designed between 1980 and 1984

Yellow wool crêpe | yellow silk habutai | black buckle (probably cellulose acetate) | foam shoulder padding (probably polyurethane) | black enamelled metal press studs

Machine sewn

This short yellow shift dress with padded shoulders has a deep U-neckline and a peplum skirt, which opens at the front and dips in the back. The waist is accentuated by a belt made from the same fabric, as well as a large bow and an oval buckle at the front. The archival photo, taken in January 1985, shows Song Huai-Kuei at an exhibition opening with, among others, artists Jin Shangyi (front row, first from left), at that time also vice-president of the Central Academy of Fine Arts (CAFA), and Zhan Jian-Jun, who was also a professor in the academy's oil painting department. Bright and jovial, Song's outfit makes her stand out from the crowd while still being dressed for the occasion.

Day dress

Designed in the mid-1980s

Camel-coloured wool crêpe | camel-coloured silk habutai | brown enamelled metal press studs | interfacing (probably synthetic) | foam shoulder padding (probably polyurethane)

Machine sewn

Camel-coloured tapered midi dress with wide kimono sleeves that open at the lower seams and a deep bib panel at the front decorated with enamelled studs. The horseshoe neckline is accentuated with a flat collar that is open at the back. As a tribute to Song Huai-Kuei, London-based photographer and creative director John-Paul Pietrus created the *Madame Song Hommage* series (*Hommage*), which features clothes from Song's archive presented by a new generation of Chinese models. *Hommage* was shot in Beijing in 2008 and 2010. This photo, from the latter shoot, shows this particular dress worn by model Lina Zhang.

Cocktail dress from Haute Couture Autumn/Winter 1987/88 collection

Designed in 1987

Black silk velvet | teal silk satin | black satin ribbon (probably silk) | black silk habutai | synthetic zip fastener | synthetic horsehair ribbon | foam shoulder padding (probably polyurethane)

Machine and hand sewn

This short, long-sleeved velvet shift dress with padded shoulders captivates with four teal silk godets across the hipline decorated with black ribbon bows. Playful and flamboyant, the dress features Pierre Cardin's signature geometric touch. It was worn by Song Huai-Kuei in June 1988 for the visit of Spanish opera singer Montserrat Caballé (1933–2018), who had become popular among the general public the previous year thanks to a song she had recorded with Freddie Mercury (1946–1991) for the 1992 Olympic Games. In the archive photo, Song wears a pair of fancy drop earrings accentuating the glossy material of the dress.

Evening dress

Designed between 1980 and 1989

Organza (probably silk) printed with a large, abstracted floral pattern in multiple colours | cord (probably nylon) | braided elastic | interfacing (probably synthetic) | synthetic zip fastener

Machine and hand sewn

This full-length floral cape dress features an off-shoulder design, with six large petal-shaped organza panels with corded edges attached to the shoulders, bodice, and waistline. Inspired by the natural world, Pierre Cardin made use of flower prints and sculptural elements reminiscent of organic shapes in several of his collections, as demonstrated by some of the garments shown in the accompanying photo (see also page 120). Except for the blue dress worn by the model second from the right, which seems to be a version of this floral cape dress, all other garments are part of the Song archive. Many of these dresses, including this one, feature an internal reference number from Cardin's atelier instead of an official label, suggesting they are samples produced for his couture runway shows.

Cocktail dress

Designed between 1980 and 1989

Silk organza printed with an abstract floral
pattern in shades of pink on an off-white
background | metal press stud | synthetic
horsehair ribbon | synthetic interfacing

Machine and hand sewn

Floral print halter-neck dress with a choker collar
and three layers of stand-out skirt frills. Playful
and vibrant, this short cocktail dress was worn by
model Becky Zau at an event at Maxim's in May
1989. It originally came with a matching scarf or
stole, but, as the archive photo shows, Zau used
it as a sash to accentuate the waist and make
the frills more prominent. The red blouse with
an ivy-leaf pattern (see page 160) worn by Song
Huai-Kuei is also part of her archive, as is the
blue silk dress worn by the model on the left
(see page 114). The latter also comes in pink and
is worn by the adjacent model (second from left),
but it was not among the garments when M+ took
over the archive in 2013.

Cocktail dress

Designed between the late 1980s and early 1990s

Pink silk chiffon | pink silk habutai | dyed pink nagoire feathers (probably goose) | braided elastic

Machine and hand sewn

Midi shift-cut silk chiffon dress with three-quarter sleeves, an elasticated off-shoulder scoop neckline, and a feathered hem. In John-Paul Pietrus's *Hommage*, the dress is presented in two variations, with different feathers and shades of pink, by models Zhu Lin and Fei Fei Sun. Taken in Beijing in 2008, the photo evokes the nonchalant *joie de vivre* commonly associated with the fashion world, resonating with the lifestyle Song Huai-Kuei established and celebrated at Maxim's.

Day dress

Designed between 1985 and 1988

Silk jacquard printed with an abstract floral pattern in black, grey, and white | white plain weave (probably cotton) layered with fusible interfacing | dress body: black enamelled metal press studs | collar: white enamelled metal press studs | synthetic horsehair ribbon

Machine sewn

Short, sleeveless dress with a dropped-waist design, a white, detachable choir-boy collar, and a two-tier pleated skirt. The archive image shows Song Huai-Kuei wearing the dress during the first edition of the Dalian Fashion Festival held in late August 1988. The festival was established to connect fashion professionals all over the world, promote the latest industry trends and developments, and foster intercultural exchange. It was renamed the Dalian International Fashion Festival in 1991 and still takes place annually in mid-September.

Day ensemble

Designed between 1980 and 1986

Gaberdine (probably synthetic) printed with a large floral design in cream and black | black satin ribbon (probably silk) | synthetic horsehair ribbon | synthetic zip fasteners | black enamelled metal press stud

Machine and hand sewn

Three-quarter-length tunic top with a black-and-cream floral print and a matching peg skirt. The tunic has wide, short kimono sleeves and a flared hem, both stiffened with synthetic horsehair ribbon for an exaggerated silhouette. In what appears to be a later remodelling, the loose fabric of the tunic is gathered into pleats at the back and decorated by a black ribbon bow, which may have been made from an original belt. The archive image shows Song Huai-Kuei wearing this outfit in the presence of Pierre Cardin, Deng Lin (front, centre)—an artist from CAFA and the daughter of Deng Xiaoping and Deng's third wife, Zhuo Lin—and the French singer Mireille Mathieu (front, right). As numerous other archive images demonstrate, Deng Lin was one of Cardin's most prominent clients in China and a close acquaintance of Song. Mathieu was one of Cardin's muses; she met Song when she was invited by the Chinese Ministry of Culture to visit and perform in Beijing and Shanghai in 1986.

Cocktail dress

Designed between 1985 and 1989

Black plain-weave silk | grey synthetic permanent-pleated mousseline | red satin ribbon (probably silk) | cord (probably nylon) | synthetic horsehair ribbon | synthetic zip fastener | interfacing (probably synthetic) | braided elastic

Machine and hand sewn

This short, strapless dress with a large, stiffened oval panel at the front showcases Pierre Cardin's experimentation with completely new ways of playing with body silhouettes. The front is decorated with concentric organza frills and a red satin ribbon bow at the centre. The back is also lined with red satin ribbon at the edges. Following his internationally acclaimed bubble dress of 1954, launched in the same year as Eve, his first womenswear boutique, Cardin made round geometric shapes a key feature of his designs. Inspired by the Space Age, Cardin took the bubble shape one step further from the 1960s onwards with completely round garments, like the one pictured here in a photo from *Hommage* with models Liu Wen and Zhu Lin. The black shift dress embellished with red silk flowers on discs at the hem also belongs to Song Huai-Kuei's archive.

Day dress from Maxim's de Paris line

Designed between 1981 and 1989

Cream silk jacquard printed with black polka dots | cream silk habutai | interfacing (probably synthetic) | foam shoulder padding (probably polyurethane) | synthetic zip fastener

Machine and hand sewn

Cream-coloured silk jacquard dress with black polka-dot print, cap sleeves, a pleated tunic bodice, and a box skirt gathered at the front and back to form panniers. This dress belongs to Pierre Cardin's Maxim's line and is worn by model Zhu Lin in a photo from *Hommage*; in the same photo, model Fei Fei Sun wears the dress featured on page 147. Cardin founded the line after he took over Maxim's restaurant in Paris in 1981 and seems to have used it to explore different kinds of fabric, such as the flowing silk used to make this particular dress. Apart from clothing, the line also included other lifestyle products that became part of Cardin's successful licensing business.

Cocktail dress

Designed between 1988 and 1993

Pink synthetic stretch fabric with stamped paisley pattern | black satin ribbon (probably silk) | braided elastic | corset boning (probably steel)

Machine and hand sewn

Pink off-shoulder paisley shift dress with three-quarter sleeves and three asymmetrical hooped frill fans. A black ribbon bow with hanging tails is attached on the right hip where the hoops converge. From the 1970s onwards, Pierre Cardin incorporated moving elements, such as pompoms and fringes, to enrich geometric elements in his designs. From the 1980s onwards and more often in the 1990s, he further experimented with rigid hoops, a defining feature of this dress. The photo, which shows the dress worn in another way by the model, was taken at the first edition of the Chinese International Clothing and Accessories Fair in 1993. Cardin was invited to participate in the fair by the Chinese government alongside Italian designers Gianfranco Ferré and Valentino.

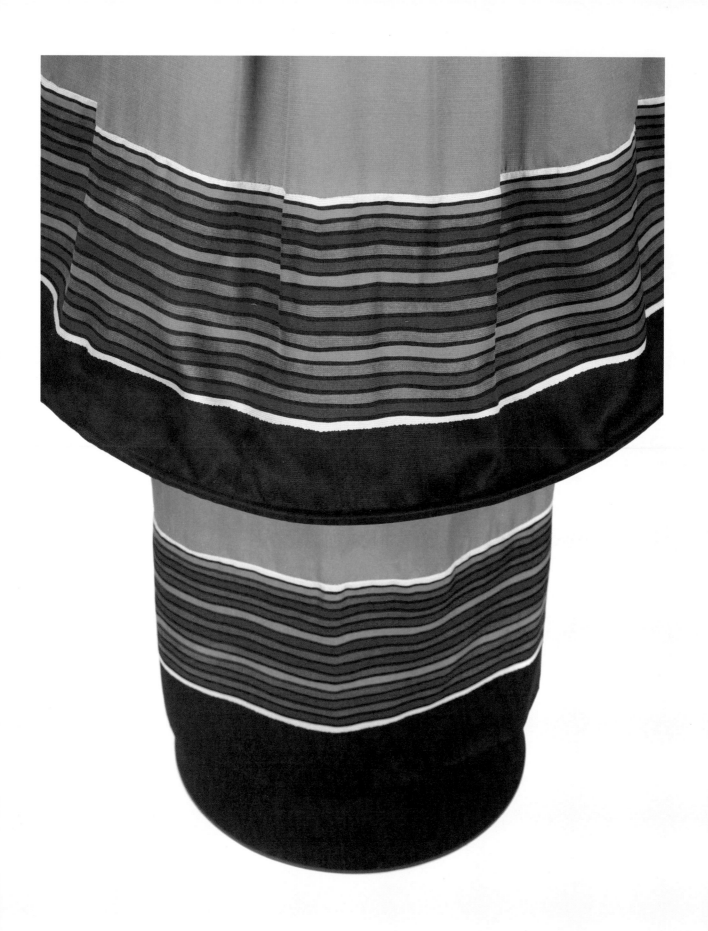

**Evening dress from Haute Couture
Spring/Summer 1987 collection**

Designed in 1986

Synthetic or synthetic cotton blend textile with
textured weave, printed with irregular emerald-
green, black, cream, purple, orange, and pink
stripes | synthetic horsehair ribbon | interfacing
(probably synthetic) | braided elastic | corset
boning (probably steel) | synthetic zip fastener

Machine and hand sewn

Striped tube dress with a loosely fitted bodice,
gathered waist, straight skirt, and deep hooped
peplum overskirt. Pierre Cardin was fascinated
with sculptural–architectural constructions
animated by the natural quality of different
fabrics. In the 1980s, summer dresses made up
of several tube-shaped pieces and tube dresses
with rigid hoops were among his recurring motifs,
as shown in this photo from *Hommage* featuring
model Zhu Lin. Cardin was also interested
in the relationship between people and their
surroundings and emphasised the importance
of movement in his designs. Like a sculptor
working with their materials, Cardin executed
many of his creations directly on models.

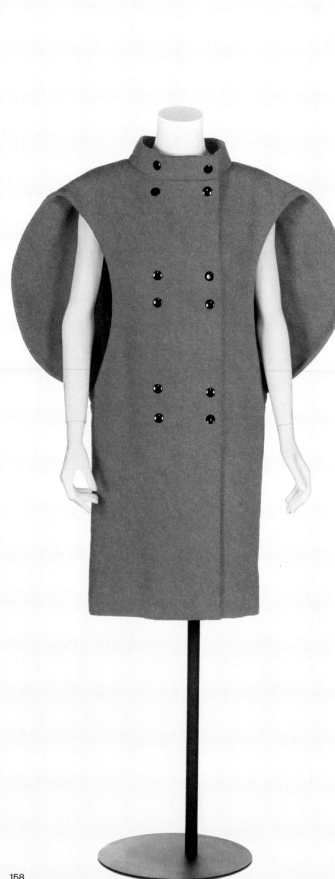

Coat

Designed between 1985 and the early 1990s

Twill-weave magenta wool layered with fusible interfacing | plain-weave magenta silk | synthetic interfacing | black enamelled metal press studs | foam shoulder padding (probably polyurethane)

Machine sewn

This mid-length double-breasted magenta wool coat features a moat collar and exaggerated wings at the back between the padded shoulders and the waist. Press-stud closures are arranged in groups of four at the front. Showcased by model Du Juan in a photo from *Hommage*, the coat brings together several of Pierre Cardin's signature design traits: bright and bold colours, a defining element of his outerwear since the 1960s and 1970s; a preference for precise cuts; and a keen interest in geometric shapes and sculptural silhouettes, all coupled with a futuristic aesthetic. From the 1980s onwards, Cardin employed sharper, edgier cuts, and after his first visit to China in 1978, he came up with even more creative designs for armholes.

**Blouse from Maxim's de Paris 1987
Spring/Summer collection**

Designed in 1986

Black silk jacquard printed with an abstract red leaf motif | black enamelled metal press studs | synthetic interfacing | synthetic horsehair ribbon | foam shoulder padding (probably polyurethane)

Machine sewn

Red-and-black silk jacquard blouse with bishop sleeves, tie collar, dolman shoulder padding, and deep ruffles at the dropped waistline. This was one of Song Huai-Kuei's favourite outfits, which she wore for numerous events (see also the archive image on page 143). The blouse originally came with a matching pleated skirt with the same distinctive red leaf print, but images from her archive show that Song preferred to pair the blouse with a black pencil skirt and a matching belt that accentuated her waist, as the photo above demonstrates. Taken in October 1988, the photo shows Song standing in front of her artwork *Composition in Rose* (1983–1985), which was part of the exhibition *New Direction in Contemporary Chinese Tapestry* at Hong Kong Arts Centre the same year.

Cocktail dress from Maxim's de Paris 1987 Spring/Summer collection

Designed in 1986

Black silk jacquard printed with an abstract green leaf motif | synthetic zip fastener | synthetic interfacing | synthetic horsehair ribbon | foam shoulder padding (probably polyurethane)

This green-and-black silk jacquard shift dress has the same leaf print as the red-and-black outfit on page 160, implying they are from the same collection. It has long dolman sleeves with shoulder padding, a scoop neckline, and three-tiered skirt ruffles. Several archive photos of the dress displayed in Maxim's shop window suggest

that both the dress and the blouse might have been made under the Maxim's de Paris label instead of the Pierre Cardin brand. The dress, which appears to have been a favourite of Song Huai-Kuei's, was later featured by model Lina Zhang in *Hommage* (opposite) and by another model at an event in Paris, with Song attending in her favourite red-and-black blouse (see page 161). On one occasion, the dress was also borrowed by prominent Chinese media proprietor and journalist Yang Lan (above left). Yang, who started her career in 1990 as a co-host of China Central Television's famous *Zheng Da Variety Show*, is now the co-founder and chairperson of the Sun Media Group.

Day dress from Haute Couture Autumn/Winter 1985/86 collection

Designed in 1985

Teal wool crêpe | teal silk habutai | black enamelled metal studs | synthetic zip fastener | self-adhesive interfacing (probably cotton)

Machine sewn

Teal wool crêpe tapering shift-cut dress with loose leg-of-mutton sleeves. The upper sleeves are accentuated with a circular pleating and disc design with a central stud. Many of Pierre Cardin's creations feature distinctive cuts for the shoulders highlighted by unique details. As photos from her archive demonstrate (see page 195), Song Huai-Kuei wore this dress on various occasions and usually paired it with a black belt accentuating her waist and a choker with a large disc pendant. The occasion depicted here is the visit of French politician Édith Cresson (b. 1934) to Maxim's in April 1985. A member of the French Socialist Party, Cresson was at that time minister of industrial restructuring and external trade; later, in 1991, she would become France's first female prime minister.

Day dress

Designed between 1981 and 1989

Black, red, purple, and teal wool crêpe | black silk habutai | interfacing (probably cotton) | foam shoulder padding (probably polyurethane)

Machine sewn

This knee-length wool crêpe dress features a boat neck, wide, open kimono sleeves, and layers of asymmetrically placed panels in contrasting colours of red, purple, and teal over a black dress shell. While the dress evokes a certain 1980s flair, it looks especially fresh and fashionable among outfits with the same palette, as this *Hommage* photo featuring Liu Wen, Fei Fei Sun, and Zhu Lin shows.

Jacket

Designed in the early 1990s

Cream wool crêpe | cream plain weave (probably rayon) | black calf or kid patent leather | black buttons (probably cellulose acetate) | foam shoulder padding (probably polyurethane)

Machine sewn

This collarless cream wool crêpe jacket with padded shoulders is characterised by an overlapping scalloped front with three oversized black buttons surrounded by patent leather. Scalloped edges and large buttons were part of Pierre Cardin's style early in his career, and, like many of his signature elements, recur and are reinterpreted in later collections. In addition to this jacket, seen here in a photo of Song Huai-Kuei with American television and radio host Larry King at Maxim's, three other designs with similar features exist in Song's archive. One appears to be a replica of this particular jacket and was probably made by a Chinese tailor.

1982–1989: Striving in Hangzhou and Beijing

Chapter Four

n 1981, shortly before travelling to Beijing to attend his second fashion show in China, Pierre Cardin purchased the restaurant Maxim's de Paris at an exceptionally high price. First opened in 1893, Maxim's de Paris underwent an Art Nouveau makeover in 1899 under its second owner, Eugène Cornuché (1867–1926). The revamped venue exemplified the most popular style of the era and seized the international spotlight during the 1900 World Expo in Paris. Registered today in France as a historical monument, the restaurant has maintained its decor ever since. It is said that Ho Chi Minh (1890–1969), father of the August Revolution in Vietnam, worked there while in exile. Cardin, a frequent customer, designed various products for the expanding Maxim's brand starting in the 1970s, including men's evening suits. Only a year after his acquisition, he opened the restaurant's first branch outside of Paris, in Brussels. It was Cardin's vision to replicate this quintessential Parisian symbol around the world.

Impressed by Song Huai-Kuei's successful staging of his 1981 Beijing fashion show, Cardin made a wild gamble: to expand Maxim's to the other side of the world. After 1949, Western restaurants, deemed indicative of a capitalist lifestyle, almost completely disappeared from China. For decades in Beijing, there was only a handful of fine-dining establishments. Most served borscht, fish au gratin, and other Russian specialities to the Soviet experts there to assist the country. Before Deng Xiaoping's economic reforms, these restaurants accepted payment only in the form of Foreign Exchange Certificates (FECs). Since the average citizen did not have the privilege to convert Chinese banknotes into FECs, Western cuisine remained alien to the vast majority of the population. Following the launch of reform and opening-up policies, foreign tourists and merchants flocked to China, some even settling down. Western restaurants were soon felt

The newly opened Maxim's attracts the attention of Beijing citizens, 1983.

Above

Pierre Cardin and a Chinese official signing the contract for opening a branch of Maxim's in China. Song Huai-Kuei is standing behind Cardin. The photo was taken in Paris on 13 December 1982.

Left

This photo shows foreigners shopping at a branch of the Friendship Store, a state-run business established in 1958. The Friendship Store sold Euro-American products, which were hard to come by in China, as well as Chinese handicrafts. Located in Beijing, Tianjin, Guangzhou, and other large cities, the stores were not open to the local population, admitting only foreign visitors and workers or overseas Chinese. The stores also did not accept renminbi (RMB), only foreign currency, making them the designated place for shopping for privileged groups. It was only in the 1990s that the Friendship Store opened its doors to locals.

Above
Song Huai-Kuei and Pierre Cardin inspecting the construction of Maxim's, ca. early 1983.

Right
The interior of Maxim's, 1983.

to be in short supply. With Deng's direction to increase foreign-exchange income by boosting tourism, many large-scale, high-end hotels opened with restaurants serving Western cuisine, including I. M. Pei's Fragrant Hill Hotel, the Jianguo Hotel, and the Great Wall Hotel.

Song Huai-Kuei, Hugues-Alexandre Tartaut, and restaurant staff outside Maxim's at its opening in 1983.

Song came up with the idea of collaborating with existing hotels to host Maxim's. In the winter of 1982, after extensive negotiation, Cardin signed an agreement with the Beijing Bureau of Tourism to open a branch of Maxim's on the second floor of the Chongwenmen Hotel. Song's first experience of the restaurant had occurred much earlier, in the 1970s. Song had been helping Yonfan, at the time an aspiring artist, organise a photography exhibition. When Yonfan's sister visited France from the United States, Song and Varbanov decided to take their guests to Maxim's de Paris. They were rejected at the door because Yonfan and Varbanov were both wearing jeans. Now, however, Maxim's was not only opening in Song's hometown, but doing so with Song—a customer who had once been turned away—as its vice-chair, a role she would hold for a decade. (Song could not take the top job because, at the time, government policy concerning the operation of foreign joint ventures specified that the chairman had to be a member of the Chinese partner, in this case the Beijing Bureau of Tourism.)

With extensive experience in art production, the perseverance to navigate difficult conditions, and a profound knowledge of China, Song successfully

Song Huai-Kuei with Chinese models
and staff at the bar at Maxim's, mid-
to late 1980s.

A Chinese official trying a cigar at the
opening banquet at Maxim's, October
1983. Although there was a major tobacco
market in China, smoking cigars was
considered decadent and bourgeois.
However, the country gradually accepted
aspects of the Western lifestyle in the
1980s. Song Huai-Kuei can be seen
on the right of the photograph.

Above

Soon after the opening of Maxim's, it became one of the few unofficial places where Chinese officials and businessmen could gather with their foreign counterparts. As the Chinese government was eagerly attracting foreign investment in the 1980s, many businessmen travelled to the country from the West. Chinese officials had yet to adopt Western-style suits at the time, so most of them at these gatherings wore grey Mao suits adapted from Sun Yat-sen suits. Despite the jovial atmosphere, Chinese officials were not particularly fond of Maxim's, as they were not used to fine French food served in portions they did not consider hearty enough. Song Huai-Kuei later improved the menu by making the dishes more filling.

Left top

A party at Maxim's, mid- to late 1980s.

Left

Song Huai-Kuei with friends at Maxim's, mid- to late 1980s.

assembled a team capable of replicating the magnificent decor of Maxim's main restaurant in Paris. From the signature bar to chromatic glass paintings, every detail was reproduced exactly to scale, and all within a year. Porcelain and silverware were devised in the style of the French originals, but produced in China. The construction crew managed to create furnishings they had never attempted before using only photographs for reference.

Considering the trials and tribulations that Pei had faced at the Fragrant Hill Hotel, Song seemingly accomplished the impossible. The young, handsome waiters at the restaurant were all hand-picked by Song from hospitality and tourism courses, which meant they came equipped with both customer-service and English-language skills. Management staff and chefs were sent to Paris for training. Song also specifically requested that Cardin send Humbert des Lyons de Feuchin to Beijing. Born into a noble French family, Humbert had worked in the protocol division of the French Ministry of Foreign Affairs for many years prior to joining Maxim's. In Beijing, he became responsible for diplomatic relations and business banquets. Material scarcity in Beijing made it necessary for most restaurant offerings—champagne, caviar, foie gras, as well as most meats and vegetables—to be imported from Hong Kong. The prices at Maxim's soared even higher than those at Gaddi's at the Peninsula, Hong Kong's oldest French restaurant.[1]

In September 1983, Maxim's had its grand opening. Every day since, as the sun has started to set and the streets grow empty, the night at Maxim's has begun. Aerodynamic wall lamps in classic Art Nouveau style and glass murals reflect soft light, while the flickering shadows of candles dance across cosy red sofas. Waiters in tuxedos and bow ties move elegantly between tables as guests whisper and toast. Music plays in the background, accompanied by the crisp sounds

A banquet at Maxim's, 1980s.

David Tang Wing-cheung's
wedding reception at
Maxim's, November 1983.

Left

Song Huai-Kuei (front,
fourth from left) and Jiang
Zemin (1926–2022), the
then minister of industry
and electronics in China
(front, third from right),
having their photo taken
with a government official
and restaurant staff to
celebrate Maxim's first
anniversary in Beijing,
October 1984.

Song once told Peter Dunn Siu-Yue that China simply needed to modernise, and that Beijing, as the capital of the country, must be at the forefront of this modernisation.

of silverware on porcelain. Here, everything remains mysterious and exciting, a completely different sensory experience from what awaits outside its doors: the bicycle kingdom, 'blue ants', sandstorms, brassy radio broadcasts, and enormous propaganda banners.

The first major event that Song hosted after the restaurant's opening was a wedding banquet for Hong Kong business tycoon David Tang Wing-cheung (1954–2017). Born to a prominent family in Hong Kong, Tang received his education in the United Kingdom before returning to his home city. Having earned a PhD in philosophy from the University of Cambridge, he was well on his way to becoming a lawyer. In 1983, as China and the UK continued their negotiations on Hong Kong, Tang switched career paths to teach Western philosophy and English literature at Peking University. He earned a monthly salary of a few hundred RMB—a substantial sum for the average citizen in China but amounting to volunteer work for Tang—teaching a class composed of a dozen doctoral students, the first group of Chinese students to have studied in the UK at public expense after the Cultural Revolution. Known for charting his own course in life, Tang married the Hong Kong television actress Susanna Cheung in Beijing. After the ceremony held at a small church, the party moved to Maxim's for dinner. A fixture of high society, Tang was close to many prominent figures, even Charles, Prince of Wales (now King Charles). His wedding dinner at Maxim's brought together a panoply of dignitaries, including Lady Pamela Youde, the wife of the then governor of Hong Kong.

A year later, in 1984, Tang became the chief representative in Hong Kong of the UK-headquartered Cluff Oil, overseeing exploration of petroleum reserves in the South China Sea. In 1991, driven by his passion for Chinese culture, Tang opened the China Club, a luxurious private establishment inside the Bank of China building in Central, Hong Kong; soon afterwards, he opened another branch at the Sichuan Hotel in Beijing, not far from Maxim's. Tang loved cigars and art. He was one of the earliest prominent collectors of contemporary Chinese art, and most of his collection still hangs inside the Hong Kong China Club. Particularly enamoured by the modernist glamour of 1930s Shanghai, he later founded the modern Chinese clothing brand Shanghai Tang, one of the few high-end fashion brands in the world to celebrate Chinese-style garments.

Song's taste in art differed in many ways from Tang's penchant for the exquisite, but the two shared similar career trajectories. Equally driven by their rebellious nature, they both believed a modernising Chinese society would greatly benefit from increased cultural exchange between East and West. Song regarded this as her lifelong pursuit, far more than just a job. She once told Peter Dunn Siu-Yue that China simply needed to modernise, and that Beijing, as the capital of the country, must be at the forefront of this modernisation. As she said in one of her interviews with Dunn, one could not let foreigners eat Chinese imperial cuisine, Peking duck, and mutton hotpot forever.[2] Deep in

Song's heart, Maxim's came to be an indispensable part of China's development. Even so, in early 1980s China, the lifestyle embodied by the restaurant was not without political risk.

‡

Throughout the 1980s, China was in a constant state of political turmoil. Deng Xiaoping had pinpointed economic liberalisation as the country's priority as soon as he had come to power. Western culture, art, lifestyles, and even political ideas began to enter China along with foreign investment. As the economy became more dynamic, however, political reform stagnated. The government was divided between reformists supporting a market economy and conservatives insisting on a planned economy. Despite this rift, officials maintained a unified front in a hard-line culture war. The government launched waves of campaigns against what they deemed to be the latest problems caused by bourgeois ideology.

After the Cultural Revolution, many unemployed young people returned to the cities from the countryside. With limited education and few marketable skills, they began to cause increasingly serious security concerns. In response, Deng announced in 1983 a three-year nationwide 'Strike Hard against Crime' campaign, introducing a series of sweeping measures intended to deter crime. But sloppy judicial processes—including a loose definition of 'hooliganism'—led to controversy. The anti-crime campaign followed a crackdown on private dance parties, which had become popular following an earlier ban on social balls in public settings. The Ministry of Public Security and the Ministry of Culture issued a document entitled 'On the Spirit of Banning

Song Huai-Kuei with singer Teresa Teng. Born in Taiwan, Teng was a pioneer of global Chinese pop music. Her music reached mainland China in around 1979 and she established a wide fanbase. However, in the 1980s, Teng's records were criticised as decadent, vulgar, and obscene. Despite the condemnation, her music remained extremely popular.

Fashion show at Maxim's
organised by Pierre
Cardin and the Beijing
Costume, Cosmetics,
and Beauty Research
Association, November
1987.

Commercial Dancing and Discouraging Social Dancing' to further discourage
dance parties in private homes. Meanwhile, recordings by Taiwanese pop singer
Teresa Teng (1953–1995) were deemed 'yellow music' and banned for promoting sexual indecency.[3] During the three-year crackdown, many were punished
under the anti-hooliganism law for listening to Teng, for hosting dance parties
at home, or for engaging in premarital sex. A notable case was Chi Zhi Qiang,
a famous actor who was sent to jail for nothing more than hosting private parties
and engaging in consensual sex with women. Today, these behaviours would
be considered matters of personal choice; in the 1980s, however, officials of the
Communist Party of China (CPC) were disturbed by the prospect of young people
adopting liberal social ideals and embracing 'bourgeois lifestyles and culture'.

In response to fierce criticism from liberal intellectuals who demanded
political reform, Deng delivered a defiant speech at the Second Plenary Session
of the 12th Central Committee of the CPC, in which he denounced Western
lifestyles and humanistic thought as 'spiritual pollution':

> In essence, spiritual pollution involves the spread of all kinds of
> corrupt and decadent ideas from the bourgeoisie and other exploiting
> classes, and the spread of distrust in the socialism, communism, and
> leadership of the Communist Party ... The bourgeoisie often boast
> of their humanity and attack socialism as inhumane. I am amazed to
> find that some of our Party comrades are now preaching humanism,
> the value of the human being, and so forth, in abstract terms.[4]

Less than a month after the Beijing outlet of Maxim's had opened, *People's Daily*, the
government's de facto mouthpiece, published a front-page article entitled 'Protect

Pierre Cardin fashion
show at Maxim's,
October 1984.

Inherent Qualities of the Working Class against Spiritual Pollution'. Almost as soon as the paper had hit the news-stands, Yuan Yunsheng's controversial mural at the airport, the one featuring three naked women, was covered with boards.

In this suffocating social environment, and despite considerable political resistance, Song remained determined to develop the modelling industry in China. She soon hit upon a solution: regular fashion shows at Maxim's. These events would not only help to promote Cardin's designs, but also allow the models under her mentorship to gain experience on the runway. As a veritable extra-legal space catering to foreigners, Maxim's provided much-needed protection.

At a cocktail party at Maxim's in 1984, Cardin and Song made a proposal to Yang Bo (1920–2016), minister of light industry in China. To promote the burgeoning Chinese fashion industry and project a modern image of the country, why not let Chinese models take part in an haute couture show in Paris? Naturally, they would be wearing the latest Pierre Cardin outfits. Yang agreed, and secured approval from the government, contingent on Cardin covering all expenses. A few months later, Song flew to Paris with eight Chinese models during Paris Haute Couture Week, marking the debut of Chinese models in the French capital. Strutting down the runway of the Pierre Cardin Haute Couture show, the young women from China captured the attention of the media and audiences alike—including Claude Pompidou (1912–2007), France's first lady from 1969 to 1974. Amid a tight schedule, the women made time to go to the Place de la Concorde for a photo shoot. Sitting in an open-top Cadillac, they drove past the Arc de Triomphe on the Champs-Élysées

Above

The first group of Chinese models
to appear during Paris Haute Couture
Week, something that would not have
been possible without Song Huai-Kuei's
involvement. Taken on 22 July 1985,
the photo shows the models riding in
a 1956 Cadillac along the Champs-
Élysées, carrying the flag of the
People's Republic of China.

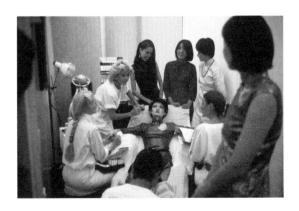

Left

Becky Zau, one of the
eight Chinese models who
travelled to Paris, at a hair
and make-up session at
Carita with fellow models,
22 July 1985.

Above

In this photo, taken on
22 July 1985, the Chinese
models are seen crossing
the Pont des Arts in Pierre
Cardin's apparel.

with their red national flag flying behind them. This moment was captured in one of the most iconic images in the history of Chinese fashion, marking China's first step into the world of international modelling. However, while Cardin paid standard industrial rates for manufacturing, the models received less than a hundred RMB each—about the same as the monthly wage of an ordinary Chinese worker. Prior to returning to China, Song asked Cardin to gift each model a tailored garment from the latest season, and quietly left some francs in the garments' pockets.

‡

The opening of Maxim's accelerated the pace of Song's life. During the day, she was busy with the clothing business; at night, she focused on the restaurant. It soon became clear she could no longer maintain a lifestyle that involved flying between Beijing and Paris. Boryana had accompanied her since the beginning of the Maxim's project, working as her interpreter and contributing to the brand's graphic design. Phénix was now old enough to take care of himself. Other than teaching and making art, Varbanov had nothing else to do in Europe, and so Song asked him to move to China. It was, of course, not as simple as moving house. To produce his large-scale tapestries, Varbanov needed a sizeable studio and assistants. In 1984, through a former classmate teaching at what was then known as the Central Academy of Arts & Design, Varbanov received an appointment as a substitute teacher. He was also allowed to make art in the Beijing Carpet Factory near the Great Wall Hotel.

Varbanov moved into the Beijing Hotel, a ten-minute drive from the Central Academy of Fine Arts (CAFA), and went to Maxim's for a drink every night. One evening, he passed a group of art students who had sneaked into the hotel for coffee and heard them discussing avant-garde art. Varbanov approached them and introduced himself as a CAFA alumnus. His impeccable Chinese surprised the students, among them the curator Hou Hanru (b. 1963), still a graduate

Left
This photo shows Song Huai-Kuei with Air China flight attendants in the signature blue uniform that was in use until 2001. The uniform was designed by Pierre Cardin and features a blazer with a matching skirt, trousers, and a white-collared striped shirt. Air China was established in 1988 as an offshoot of the Civil Aviation Administration of China, previously the only civilian airline in the country, and was given chief responsibility for intercontinental flights. Song prompted Air China to invite Cardin to design its aircrew uniform, and he remains the only foreign designer Air China has ever hired.

student at the time. This encounter sowed the seeds of a short but profound friendship. At the time, Varbanov was likely the only artist both based in China and active in the Paris art scene. His work, which had developed into site-specific installations, hinged on the relationship between people and public spaces in a way that inspired Hou, who was obsessed with the concept of social sculpture proposed by Joseph Beuys (1921–1986). Hou adopted Varbanov as a sort of spiritual father, with avant-garde art as a bond between them. When they were together, which before long was almost every day, Varbanov discussed his ideas for new tapestries and plans to set up an institute. He introduced Hou to his students Han Meilun (b. 1957), Zhao Bowei (b. 1957), and Mu Guang (b. 1945).

Maryn Varbanov (back, fourth from left), Hou Hanru (back, sixth from left), and workers from the Beijing Artistic Tapestry Center during the installation of *Exhibition by Beijing Artistic Tapestry Center* at the National Art Museum of China in Beijing, 1985.

Hou, meanwhile, worked to translate such concepts as 'installation' and 'soft sculpture' into Chinese. He also helped to organise the *Exhibition by Beijing Artistic Tapestry Center* in the West Hall of the National Art Museum of China (NAMOC). As Hou aptly observed in the exhibition's brochure, 'the work can no longer be contained by a flat wall, but instead assumes a three-dimensional form in space.' To distinguish the fine-art tapestries on show from commercial applied art and design, Hou coined the term 'woven sculpture'.[5] (At the group's second exhibition, in 1986, their work was simply identified as 'soft sculpture'.) Being held at the same time in the other hall at NAMOC was an international touring exhibition of the work of American artist Robert Rauschenberg (1925–2008), who left a comment in the group's guest book calling their show one of the best exhibitions he had seen in China.[6]

The currents of new art swirling around Varbanov and Hou at the time would later be identified as the '85 New Wave, the most significant movement in contemporary Chinese art. Most of the New Wave artists were among the first group of students to have graduated from art academies following the resumption of enrolment after the Cultural Revolution. Through magazines and foreign art books, they could access information about Western art and theories. Given their recent experience of the Cultural Revolution, these young artists were all preoccupied with a particular set of questions: how to employ liberal and humanist ideas to avoid the recurrence of historical tragedy, how to develop their country, how to evaluate traditional culture. While reflecting on these concerns, they faced serious obstacles. In particular, their avant-garde, abstract, or non-realistic works were rejected from the *Sixth National Fine Art Exhibition*, dismissed by jurors as 'spiritual pollution'. In response, the artists decided to form their own collectives, publish new manifestos, and organise their own exhibitions, all of which gave rise to the New Wave.

Varbanov's style was perhaps too avant-garde for his contemporaries in Beijing, and his visiting professorship at the Central Academy of Arts & Design

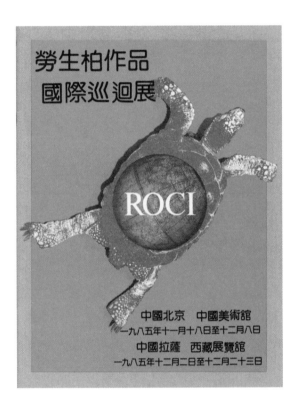

Above top
Maryn Varbanov (second from left), Hou Hanru (second from right), Han Meilun, Zhao Bowei, and Mu Guang at the National Art Museum of China in Beijing, 1985.

Above
Maryn Varbanov and Chinese artists at the Beijing Artistic Tapestry Center, ca.1984–1985.

Above
In November 1985, Maryn Varbanov's *Exhibition by Beijing Artistic Tapestry Center* opened at the National Art Museum of China at the same time as Robert Rauschenberg's *Rauschenberg Overseas Culture Interchange* (*ROCI*) show, which was part of a cultural exchange between China and the United States aimed at improving relations between the two. Rauschenberg's exhibition brought Pop Art to China as well as such mediums as performance, photography, and installation, exposing Chinese artists to influences from outside the country.

was not extended. Song then contacted two classmates from her years in Dong Xiwen's oil painting class, Cai Liang (1932–1995) and Song Ren (b. 1932), both of whom were teaching at the Zhejiang Academy of Fine Arts (ZAFA), with its main campus located close to West Lake in Hangzhou. Along with CAFA, ZAFA was known as one of the two best art academies in China. The predecessor of ZAFA had been the National College of Art, the birthplace of modernism in China, where both Dong Xiwen and Zao Wou-Ki had studied.

In May 1985, at the age of sixty-four, Zao Wou-Ki was invited to return to his alma mater, the Zhejiang Academy of Fine Arts, to hold a month-long painting workshop. The Ministry of Culture selected twenty-seven 'progressive teachers and students' from nine art schools in China to attend. This was the first time that abstract painting had been taught systematically in a Chinese art school.

Owing to its distance from the capital, ZAFA was able to maintain a relatively independent and open educational system and traditions, in contrast to CAFA's dogmatism. In 1985, Zao had returned to his alma mater to teach an oil painting class, introducing to his students a new path utterly different from Socialist Realism. The following year, Varbanov was invited to set up a tapestry institute at ZAFA, which later became the Institute of Art Tapestry Varbanov (IATV). As soon as he arrived in Hangzhou, Varbanov launched a series of experiments with new materials, such as bamboo, rice paper, elastic bands, and even laser lights,[7] thereby enhancing the experimental and conceptual novelty of his works and elevating his artistic career to a new level.

Varbanov put everything into the IATV—at the time, the only institute in China systematically teaching the spatial and material language of modern

Above

Gu Wenda

*United Nations—China Monument:
Temple of Heaven*, 1998
Human hair, white glue, and burlap
Dimensions variable
Collection of the Hong Kong Museum
of Art Installation view at MoMA PS1,
New York, 1998

Left

Maryn Varbanov and his students at
the Institute of Art Tapestry Varbanov,
mid- to late 1980s.

On 7 May 1987, the *Contemporary China Tapestry Exhibition*, organised by the Institute of Art Tapestry Varbanov, opened at the Shanghai Exhibition Centre. Jiang Zemin, at that time mayor of Shanghai, attended the opening accompanied by Song Huai-Kuei and Maryn Varbanov. The monumental tapestry in the background is Varbanov's *Silk Road* (1987), in which he incorporated many elements of Dunhuang art. Pictured in front of the tapestry are (from left) Shi Hui, Song Zhongyuan, Song Huai-Kuei, Jiang Zemin, Maryn Varbanov, Xiao Feng, and Song Ren.

In both applied and fine arts, Varbanov provided his students with a comprehensive set of resources and a system for the study of space, materials, and concepts.

art—and his creative methods left a lasting impact on a generation of artists. Gu Wenda, having originally trained in ink painting, was confused during his first tapestry class. Noticing Gu's long hair, Varbanov told him that he could use any material to make tapestries, even hair. Many years later, Gu would indeed use hair to create his seminal work *United Nations* (1998). In 1987, Varbanov led Gu and three of his other students, Shi Hui, Liang Shaoji, and Zhu Wei (b. 1966), as they mounted the *Contemporary China Tapestry Exhibition* in Shanghai; that same year, he brought Gu's *Wisdom Comes from Tranquility* (1986), Shi Hui and Zhu Wei's *Longevity* (1986), and Liang Shaoji's *The Art of War* (1986) to the Lausanne International Tapestry Biennial, marking the first time emerging Chinese artists had participated in the event.

A thorough study of the diverse practices that comprise the '85 New Wave would reveal a degree of thematic unity with strong undertones of cultural criticism. Varbanov took a different approach with the IATV. He was dedicated to forging a concrete artistic language and could be indifferent to theoretical research into grand historical narratives.[8] In both applied and fine arts, he provided his students with a comprehensive set of resources and a system for the study of space, materials, and concepts. He and Rauschenberg might well be credited with the sudden rise of installation art as a significant medium in contemporary Chinese art at the end of the 1980s, a phenomenon exemplified by the works that both Gu and Liang submitted to the 1989 *China/Avant-Garde* exhibition.

Every few months, Varbanov returned to Beijing. Song, meanwhile, was a frequent visitor to Hangzhou and Shanghai, and attended nearly all the exhibitions organised by the IATV. With her exceptional talent for business, Song was able to persuade the gallery of the Shangri-La Hotel in Hangzhou to exhibit and sell works by members of the institute—a remarkable achievement at a time when there was not yet an art market in China. Once Varbanov was settled, Song was able to focus on her own responsibilities and interests. In 1986, she also found the time to make a cameo appearance in Bernardo Bertolucci's *The Last Emperor*.

‡

Bertolucci was a politically active figure. An avowed Marxist, much of his early work took an explicitly critical stance against fascism and supported youth revolt. During the protests of May 1968, left-wing literary and art circles in Europe, and especially in France, developed a fanatical reverence for Mao Zedong and the Cultural Revolution. Although Bertolucci was not as enthusiastic about developments in China as one of his close friends, French New Wave auteur Jean-Luc Godard (1930–2022), the Italian director made no secret of his general sympathy for the country and its politics.[9] The Italian Communist Party (PCI)

In June 1987, these tapestry works, all produced at the Institute of Art Tapestry Varbanov, were selected for the 13th Lausanne International Tapestry Biennial. Clockwise from left: *Wisdom Comes from Tranquility* by Gu Wenda (no longer extant), a mixed media installation featuring elements from ink painting; *The Art of War* by Liang Shaoji, a tapestry of bamboo scrolls inscribed with *Thirty-Six Stratagems*, a classic Chinese military text, secured by hemp ropes; and *Longevity* by Shi Hui and Zhu Wei, which references oracle bone inscriptions. This was the first time Chinese artists had been selected to participate in the biennial.

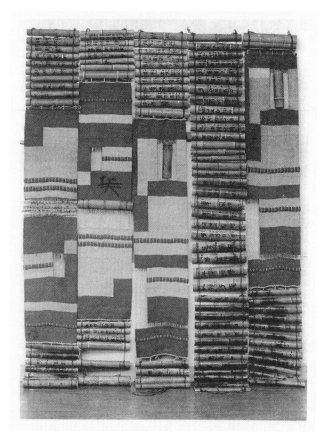

remained on good terms with the Chinese government throughout the 1970s and 1980s. Rumour has it that the then general secretary of the CPC, Hu Yaobang (1915–1989), received a note from his counterpart at the PCI requesting permission for Bertolucci to shoot a film in China. The country had always remained open to those directors and artists who publicly supported Marxism and internationalism, regardless of their creative aspirations. Bertolucci's PCI membership earned him a reference letter from the China Film Co-Production Corporation and an invitation to fly to Beijing.[10]

The film Bertolucci made, *The Last Emperor*, became the most celebrated foreign film to have been shot in China during this period, but it was not the first production in the country by an Italian leftist director. Michelangelo Antonioni (1912–2007) had undertaken a Marco Polo–style adventure in China ten years earlier. Following Nixon's 1972 visit to China, Italian public broadcaster

Above

Song Huai-Kuei and Maryn Varbanov attending the celebration marking the first anniversary of the Institute of Art Tapestry Varbanov, 1987.

Right

Shi Hui's *Implications* (1987) on display at the Tapestry Gallery run by the Institute of Art Tapestry Varbanov at the Shangri-La Hotel, Hangzhou, 1987.

Rai (Radiotelevisione italiana) received approval from the Chinese government to produce a documentary about the country. Antonioni was invited to shoot what became *Chung Kuo, Cina* (1972). The director, known for his depictions of life in post-war Italy, had assumed it would be acceptable to go about the project in accordance with his usual humanistic values and style. With a wandering camera attuned to quotidian subtleties, he attempted to capture the truth of everyday life. Yet his portrait was slammed by *People's Daily* as a deliberate attempt to 'slander and vilify China, borrowing methods from reactionary art'.[11] When the film was shown at the Venice Film Festival, Chinese diplomats even attempted to halt the screening. The film was banned in China for many years—a huge blow to Antonioni, who had great respect and admiration for the country.

How do you tell a story about China? This was not only a question the Chinese government had to face while establishing its international image in the 1980s, but also the core of Bertolucci's challenge. In 1984, the director arrived in Beijing with two proposals: either he could adapt *Man's Fate* (1933), the Prix Goncourt–winning novel by left-wing French writer Georges André Malraux (1901–1976), or he could tell the life story of Aisin-Gioro Puyi (1906–1967), the last emperor of the Qing Dynasty. Set in 1927 against the backdrop of the April 12 Incident in Shanghai, *Man's Fate* focuses on the existential travails of its characters amid the armed workers' uprising. Puyi's story is one of transformation,

The Last Emperor was the first Western narrative feature to be shot in China since 1949, and the first production granted permission to film on location.

through many regime changes, from a lofty emperor into an ordinary, self-reliant citizen of socialist China. Since Malraux's novel touches on such sensitive topics as the arrest and execution of CPC members—and despite Bertolucci's attempt to lobby for *Man's Fate*, maintaining that, 'All the workers in the West fall in love with Chinese communism because of this book, because it's such a romantic story of revolution'[12]—the Chinese government chose the Puyi biography.

While editing the script for *The Last Emperor* in Beijing, Bertolucci frequented Maxim's, where he got to know Song. Ever the consummate hostess, Song provided considerable assistance to the project. In 1986, *The Last Emperor* began filming in the Forbidden City. This was the first Western narrative feature to be shot in China since 1949, and the first production granted permission to film on location at historical sites, including the Hall of Supreme Harmony inside the Forbidden City and the Imperial Palace of Manchukuo in Changchun (now the Museum of the Imperial Palace of Manchukuo). From producers, editors, and screenwriters to cinematographers and sound designers, the film crew was remarkably international, consisting of professionals from Italy, the United Kingdom, China, the United States, Japan, and elsewhere. The size of the cast was even more impressive: more than ten thousand extras supported a cast featuring John Lone (b. 1952), Joan Chen (b. 1961), Peter O'Toole (1932–2013), and Ryuichi Sakamoto (b. 1952). Many well-known figures made cameo appearances. Ying Ruocheng (1929–2003), the then deputy minister for culture, played the warden of the Fushun War Criminals Management Centre, while fifth-generation film director Chen Kaige (b. 1952) played the captain of the imperial guards. Bertolucci invited Song to play Puyi's adoptive mother, Empress Dowager Longyu, a tragic figure who lived the life of a widow in the harem for decades, with no emotional connection with either her husband or her adopted son.

Song was no stranger to filmmaking. Following her brief roles on Bulgarian television in the 1960s, she befriended Hong Kong filmmaker Yonfan in the 1970s and cultivated a substantial network of acquaintances in the film industry. When Li Han-hsiang (1926–1996), another Hong Kong filmmaker, was shooting in Beijing, Song visited the set and became friends with the leading actors Liu Xiaoqing and Tony Leung Ka-fai (b. 1958). The filming of *The Last Emperor*, however, was on an entirely different scale, with its majestic sets and sophisticated costumes. Upon seeing real people wearing the clothes once described by writer Shen Congwen, Song must have felt as if she were in a dream. Unsurprisingly, *The Last Emperor* swept the board at the world's major film awards: the Oscars, the Golden Globes, and the BAFTAs. Moreover, ever since its release, it has had a subtle yet far-reaching influence on the evolution of Chinese visual culture.

Qing palace drama, a narrative genre based on court life in the Forbidden City, developed in the 1920s. At first, the genre did little more than cater to foreigners' exotic fantasies, just as the Turkish harem had once done for Romantic artists.

Left
Song Huai-Kuei and
Bernardo Bertolucci at
Maxim's, ca. mid-1980s.

Below
Bernardo Bertolucci
directing a night scene for
The Last Emperor at the
Forbidden City in Beijing,
1987.

Opposite
Song Huai-Kuei and
Bernardo Bertolucci
on the set of *The Last
Emperor*, ca. mid-1980s.

Most early twentieth-century Chinese film productions were based in Shanghai, with cosmopolitan life and anti-Japanese nationalism as favoured themes. Qing palace drama received little attention. After 1949, the Chinese-language film industry relocated to Hong Kong, and it was there, among the colony's multicultural inhabitants, that such genres as *wuxia*—adventures of martial-arts heroes in ancient China—and Qing palace drama found their audience. A particularly notable work is *Sorrows of the Forbidden City* (1948), directed by Zhu Shilin (1899–1967). Set in the Forbidden City during the reign of the Guangxu Emperor, the film tells the story of the power struggle between Guangxu and the Empress Dowager Cixi, shedding light on the political conflict between reformists and conservatives in the late Qing Dynasty. However, the Chinese government denounced the work as treasonous. Critics accused the filmmakers of legitimising foreign invasion and slandering the anti-colonial Boxer Rebellion that began in 1899. Hardliners used the film as a rhetorical tool to attack potential reformers during the Cultural Revolution. As a result, stories with Qing Dynasty themes became highly restricted.

The key figure in bringing Qing palace drama back to the silver screen was Li Han-hsiang. In 1980s China, with the government newly committed to developing tourism, many landmarks were opened for filming. No longer obliged to build sets inside film studios, Li could at last travel to northern China to film on location instead. *Reign behind a Curtain* (1983) and *The Burning of Imperial Palace* (1983), both co-produced with the China Film Co-Production Corporation (now the China Film Group Corporation), continued the standard Qing palace drama narrative, with Empress Dowager Cixi as lead and the Guangxu Emperor as her rival. Consequently, the principal filming locations for both works were female living spaces such as the Chengde Mountain Resort, the Summer Palace, and the harem of the Forbidden City. *The Last Emperor*, on the other hand,

A photo of Song Huai-Kuei (centre) during the filming of Puyi's wedding to Empress Wanrong and Consort Wenxiu in *The Last Emperor*. The grandiose scene was produced with the help of hundreds of extras from the Chinese military and cultural groups. The actors were given exquisite costumes, make-up, and props, resulting in an immersive recreation of the event.

Right

A photo of Song Huai-Kuei during the filming of one of the classic scenes from *The Last Emperor*. From a lotus pond, the widowed Longyu witnesses teenage Puyi's attachment to his nursemaid and orders her to be sent out of the palace.

Song Huai-Kuei and Hong Kong actor Tony Leung Ka-fai on location during the filming of Li Han-hsiang's *Reign behind a Curtain* and *The Burning of Imperial Palace* in 1983. Li was a Hong Kong director who specialised in filming works set in the Qing court. The two films were shot in the Forbidden City. The photo below shows leading actress Liu Xiaoqing, who was playing a young Empress Dowager Cixi.

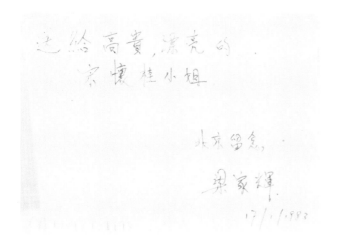

Left

The back of a photo Tony Leung Ka-fai gave to Song Huai-Kuei on 17 January 1983. The inscription reads: 'To the elegant and gorgeous Ms Song Huai-Kuei'.

set in the very different Chinese society of the tumultuous twentieth century, centred on the titular emperor, and was filmed mostly in architectural spaces in the Forbidden City symbolic of masculine power, such as the Hall of Supreme Harmony, Meridian Gate, and Tiananmen Square. The golden-yellow palace rooftops, white stone railings, and highly saturated cinematography evocative of oil paintings together conveyed the density of Chinese history and departed from the gloomy, dejected ambience of the standard imperial narrative, introducing a brand-new visual dimension to Qing palace drama. This turn allowed Chinese directors to envision new possibilities; among other things, it was now permissible to employ the Qing court as an aesthetic theme, and even to use it in propaganda for the national image. Without doubt, the international production of and worldwide acclaim for *The Last Emperor* enabled the re-establishment of the genre. The film's success also inspired Chinese artists and intellectuals, Song included, to start looking at tradition from the perspective of modern Western society.

‡

Under Song's management, Maxim's became the talk of the town. Cardin regularly invited dignitaries to China from Europe and other parts of the world to help promote the Maxim's brand. Having once led the bohemian life of an artist, Song recognised an opportunity to foster high-level cultural exchange between East and West. When foreign directors and actors came to the restaurant, she made sure to invite Chinese directors and actors to join them for dinner; when there were visiting foreign dancers, she invited Chinese dancers. Before long, Maxim's became known as a haven for avant-garde art and popular culture. Rather than being a strictly hierarchical club catering exclusively to the elite, Maxim's allowed Chinese artists to express themselves comfortably while mixing with people from different backgrounds. As she befriended directors and film stars, Song effectively became the social queen of Beijing with a front-row seat from which to observe the development of the Chinese film industry. Favourite guests of Song's included Liu Xiaoqing and Tony Leung Ka-fai; Jiang Wen and Ling Zifeng (1917–1999), the star and director, respectively, of the 1988 feature *Chun Tao: A Woman for Two*; and Zhang Yimou (b. 1950) and Gong Li, the director and star, respectively, of *Red Sorghum* (1988).

It was in this milieu that Song learned of plans by the then unknown director Mi Jiashan to shoot *The Troubleshooters* (1988), a black comedy adapted from a novel by Wang Shuo. *The Troubleshooters* tells the story of three young *flâneurs* who set up a company to help people realise their dreams. In the early 1980s, Wang was marginalised in literary circles because his contemporary themes were considered out of step with the dominant tendency to reflect on history. Mi also met with various discouragements during his career. In particular, his preference for the 'entertaining film' over weighty dramas elicited resentment and mockery. 'Entertaining film' was almost a derogatory term among 'serious' Chinese directors captivated by New Wave filmmakers from Europe and the aesthetics of Akira Kurosawa (1910–1998), which melded German Expressionism with classic Hollywood narratives.

Song Huai-Kuei and French actor Alain Delon (b. 1935) at a press conference held in conjunction with Delon's fiftieth birthday celebrations at Maxim's in Beijing, 1985.

In the course of adapting Wang's novel, Mi added a fashion show to *The Troubleshooters*, an event that does not appear in the original narrative, but which marks the film's zany high point. Over the course of a scene that lasts more than twenty minutes, ten slender, stylishly dressed young ladies walk down the runway. Suddenly, a three-year-old little emperor appears and becomes entangled in the models' long, bare legs. A parade of characters from recent Chinese history then takes to the stage: landlords, Kuomintang officials, farmers, and Red Guards gathering for a grand celebration. Song, who had trained the featured models with Jerry Zhang, founder of the Beijing Textile Bureau's fashion show unit, could not miss the filming of this scene, and even persuaded French fashion brand Dior to sponsor the make-up—likely one of the first instances of a Chinese film receiving sponsorship from a Western brand. *The Troubleshooters* received six nominations at the 1988 Golden Rooster Awards, but was slammed by Zhong Chengxiang, vice-chair of the China Federation of Literary and Art Circles, as 'the most reactionary film since the founding of the People's Republic of China'.[13] At a moment when a wave of consumerism was about to hit their country, Wang and Mi had adopted a seemingly vulgar aesthetic as a vehicle for otherwise risky ruminations on social realities. Cementing a connection between high fashion and popular culture, the film also directly anticipated the arrival of Cynical Realism and Political Pop as major trends in contemporary art.

Left and below

Maxim's in Beijing replicated the Art Nouveau style of the restaurant in Paris. Its decor conjures fantasies of a Western lifestyle and was used as a setting for many films, becoming a hallmark of popular culture in the 1990s. These stills are from the films *Someone Falls in Love with Me* (1990), directed by Ning Ying, and the kung fu film *Once Upon a Time in China III* (1992), by Hong Kong director Tsui Hark.

CLUB
MAXIM'S
PEKIN

Left

Promotional poster for Maxim's.

In 1987, Song Huai-Kuei visited the set
of *Chun Tao: A Woman for Two*, a film
directed by Ling Zifeng (top, first from
left). The leading roles were played by
Jiang Wen, then a budding young actor,
and Liu Xiaoqing. Jiang later starred
with Gong Li (bottom, first from left) in
Red Sorghum (1988), directed by Zhang
Yimou, one of the leading fifth-generation
filmmakers. The photo in the centre shows
Jiang and Song at Maxim's celebrating
the Crystal Globe award given to *Hibiscus
Town* (1986)—in which Jiang starred—
at the 1988 Karlovy Vary International
Film Festival in Czechoslovakia (now the
Czech Republic).

The disorienting rush of city life depicted in *The Troubleshooters* was a subject that artists throughout the rapidly urbanising country attempted to process. One of the most memorable examples is the classic rock song 'It's Not That I Don't Understand', which Cui Jian (b. 1961) performed at Maxim's:

> I never knew what it was to be magnanimous
> I never knew there was so much strangeness in the world
> The future I'd envisioned is nothing like the present
> Only now does it seem I'm clear about what the future is
> I can't tell if all the things I've done were good or bad
> Past times fade and I can't recall the years
> The things I thought were simple I now can't understand
> at all
> I suddenly feel the world in front of my eyes is not where
> I really am

A still from *The Troubleshooters* (1988), directed by Mi Jiashan. In this scene, the three protagonists are holding a 'fashion show' before a literary-award ceremony they have fabricated, hoping it will attract a youthful audience. The show opens with Peking opera characters, who are then followed by stylish fashion models. The runway soon becomes chaotic when historical events from China's different eras are enacted: Red Guards attack the ruling class, Chinese communist soldiers suppress Kuomintang spies, and traffic policemen clear the road for bikini-clad bodybuilders and disco-dancing youths. Like an abridged cynical parody, the scene highlights the absurdity of parts of Chinese history.

At a time when rock music was still a little-known genre in China, Song was the main conduit for arranging rock concerts at Maxim's. Shortly after the restaurant's opening, Song had met Liang Heping (b. 1954), a former member of the Central Philharmonic Orchestra, and had invited him to perform. Liang was a trailblazer in Chinese music from the 1980s to the 1990s, exploring various musical genres—pop, rock, jazz, and avant-garde—and becoming well versed in playing and composing for several instruments, as well as production. Representative of a new generation of Chinese avant-garde musicians eager to break away from the official system, Liang invited a group of 'iconoclastic' rockers to perform at Maxim's.

Among them was Liu Yuan (b. 1960), a pioneer of Chinese jazz. Trained in Chinese folk music, Liu later switched to saxophone, and was allegedly able to play any wind instrument. For his part, Cui Jian—now one of the most well-known musicians in China—had first learned to play the trumpet from his father, a military band player, before getting into rock. Bands formed by expats in Beijing also performed on occasion. Song, with her discerning eye for talent, recognised the vigour and wildness in these young musicians—a kind of determination to live their own way—and ultimately provided a stage on which the first generation of Chinese rockers could showcase their music.

Owing to the eccentricity of official Chinese policy, rock music could not be performed in ordinary venues, and was able to gain traction only under the patronage of restaurants such as Maxim's that ostensibly catered to foreigners. An oft-repeated saying from the era was, 'Rock and roll is not close to the people, rock is only close to Maxim's'. By extension, rock would never have flourished at Maxim's without Song's influence. Every Saturday night at around ten o'clock, after seeing off the dolled-up diplomats, businessmen, and government officials, the restaurant staff would move the tables and chairs away from the stage to create a small dance floor. Then, band members would begin selling tickets at the entrance, usually for RMB 50 each. The average monthly income of ordinary Chinese citizens at the time was around RMB 70 to 80, which meant that, for the most part, only foreigners could afford this door cover. But the bands often let their musician friends attend for free; they would tell them to sneak in a cup so they could get tap water from the bathroom. Song was well aware of this trick but always turned a blind eye. After all, she had once made tapestries by tearing up her own jumpers.

As Maxim's became a Xanadu of Chinese rock, an activity called 'partying'—always denoted by the English word—had begun to creep into the night lives of ordinary people. When the British pop duo Wham! performed in China in 1985, the seated audience members were forbidden from standing up: it was decreed that police would remove any unauthorised dancers from the venue. By the end

Cui Jian began collaborating with the rock band ADO in 1987. Here, Cui (second from right) is pictured with members of the band in Tiananmen Square, late 1980s. Accompanying Cui are (from left) Kassai Balázs, Zhang Yongguang, Eddie Randriamampionona, and Liu Yuan.

of the decade, far from sitting upright in their chairs, people were getting into the groove with their bodies, screaming at the top of their lungs. Rock shows at Maxim's could be full-throated affairs.

The works of Mi Jiashan, Cui Jian, and the rock musicians at Maxim's are emblematic of a tension in China between the avant-garde and pop culture that lasted throughout the second half of the 1980s. While both were at odds with official socialist ideology, they were quite different from each other. The avant-garde had been born out of an intuitive reflection on historical tragedy, whereas pop culture was a purer outgrowth of consumerism. Although pop culture had arrived on the scene a little later, its disciples soon realised that practitioners of the avant-garde were still more or less tied to the epistemology of socialist ideology and education, always trying to instil their values in others. Like the title of the 1994 album by Cui Jian, avant-garde artists, despite their formal radicalism, were all equally 'balls under the red flag', products of a socialist system, however tough their posturing. The defenders of pop culture had to break free of the rules and conventions set by their vanguardist peers. The spirit of resistance inhabiting a pop culture labelled as vulgar or kitsch could be more avant-garde than that of the avant-garde proper.

While Varbanov cultivated avant-garde artists in Hangzhou, Song provided shelter to emerging forms of pop culture in Beijing. This close-knit couple, in both life and art, maintained their dedication to cultural pursuits. Then came the bad news. In the spring of 1989, Varbanov fell off a ladder while working in Hangzhou. In the course of treating him for his injuries, his doctors discovered that he had advanced lung cancer. Song immediately arranged for Varbanov's transfer to the China–Japan Friendship Hospital in Beijing.

The protests in the aftermath of Hu Yaobang's death in April that year were heating up, and Beijing seemed on the verge of a revolution. Shortly after

After China opened its borders, many foreign artists came to visit. In 1985, British pop duo Wham! became the first Western music group to perform in the country after the Cultural Revolution. The duo held two concerts during their ten-day visit, one in Beijing and the other in Guangzhou, and were enthusiastically received by Chinese fans (left). The group also visited such famous locations as Tiananmen Square (above). In 1987, Steven Spielberg filmed *Empire of the Sun* at various landmarks in Shanghai (below), evoking the city's vicissitudes in the 1930s. As they created work about China, these artists shaped the West's conception of the country; their international practices also stimulated China's cultural life.

In the early 1980s, many state-produced Chinese films broadened the people's understanding and perception of fashion. In *Romance on Lushan Mountain* (1980), leading actress Zhang Yu, who plays a Chinese national returning from overseas, showcases forty-three different outfits in eighty-two minutes of screentime. As the garment manufacturing industry was still in its youth in the early stages of China's reform and opening-up, some women brought their tailors to the cinema so they could reproduce the actress's outfits for them. The film stills shown here are from *Romance on Lushan Mountain* (left) and *Hei Qing Ting* (1984; below).

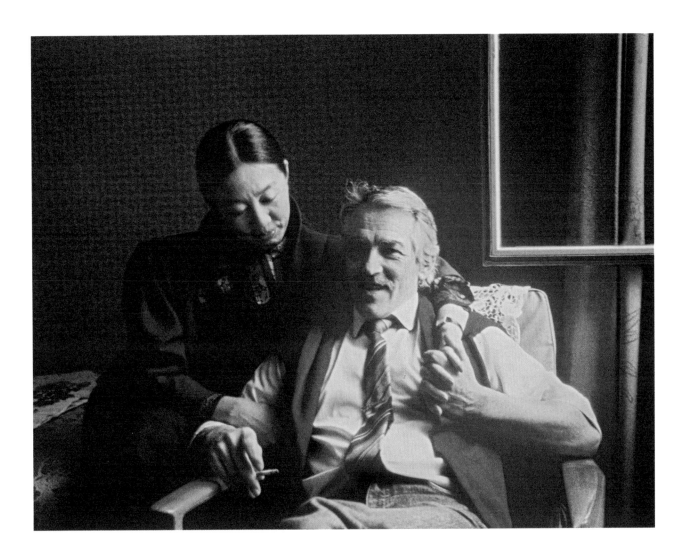

his arrival at the hospital, Varbanov's condition began to deteriorate rapidly. On 5 June, before returning to Guangzhou from Beijing, Hou Hanru paid him a visit. Varbanov dragged Hou to the balcony to sneak a forbidden cigarette. Blowing out a smoke ring, Varbanov told Hou that, when he had heard the noise coming from Tiananmen Square the night before, he had grown extremely emotional because it had reminded him of Eastern Europe during his youth. After the cigarette, Hou left to catch a plane. Later, when Song asked Hou to look for some Chinese medicine for her husband in Guangzhou, she told him he must hurry up and return to Beijing so he could see his 'Uncle Varbanov'.

In the early morning of 10 July, as soon as he had arrived in Beijing on his return visit, Hou found a pay phone and called Song Huai-Kuei's house. It was Phénix who answered. His father had died a few hours earlier.

On Stage
at Maxim's:
An Interview
with Cui Jian

Pi Li and Wu Mo

After the dinner service had ended at Maxim's, the dance floor would come alive. Under Song Huai-Kuei's management in the 1980s and 1990s, the venue hosted performances by independent musicians, among them the pioneering rocker Cui Jian. Artists, filmmakers, diplomats, and businessmen all rubbed shoulders in the audience, spawning new trends that gradually spread throughout China. In September 2022, M+ curators Pi Li and Wu Mo spoke with Cui Jian, who had first met Song in the late 1980s.

Pi Li *What was it like to survive as a gigging rock musician in the years of China's reform and opening-up?*

Cui Jian We didn't give too much thought to survival because the cost of living was low. On one hand, I had employment and a steady income. On the other, I gained quite a lot of attention after singing 'Nothing to My Name' ['Yiwu Suoyou'] at the *Let There Be Love on Earth* concert in 1986. A few record companies and actor friends began to recruit me to do small shows. But we didn't call them shows back then; we called them parties. There was no clear standard for remuneration. Sometimes it was just someone buying you drinks. Sometimes I earned a lot, sometimes a little.

Pi Li *Why were those shows called parties? How were they different from today's commercial shows in terms of format?*

Cui Jian Parties were more relaxed than shows. They were closer to a gathering for cultural exchange. There would be music at parties and alcohol was sold. Some venues charged an entrance fee, some didn't. Sometimes invitations were given out and some people even sold them for profit. All in all, parties were cultural events, a kind of entertainment.

Wu Mo *Can you briefly describe a party night at Maxim's?*

Cui Jian Parties were frequently held at Maxim's. Most of them were private gatherings and company activities. If a party was held during a festival, the atmosphere would be even more explosive. We were regulars. Most of the time, Song or her close friends would call to invite us. There were usually two or three groups performing each night. Many of the ticket-buyers were foreigners, though our friends often got in for free. The party would begin sometime between nine and a little after ten o'clock. Someone would go onstage to speak, everyone would drink, then the show would start. After the performances, people continued drinking, like in a bar. The programme was also flexible. Sometimes we had longer setlists; if it was a last-minute gig, we may finish early. We didn't rely on our gigs at Maxim's to make a living. Parties were for meeting friends and having a great time. They were a way of life.

Pi Li *So you didn't go to the parties for business or to bring food to the table, but simply for enjoyment and meeting friends. Did this last until the early 1990s?*

Cui Jian Yes. Parties gradually became a widespread phenomenon. Any sizeable gathering or event would be followed by a party. Most were held in private residences. People would bring simple musical instruments, or the host may have a piano. We would sing and enjoy ourselves like in those aristocratic, oh-so-elegant salons in European films. But we weren't trying to be like anyone. Parties were part of life.

Wu Mo *From the late 1980s to the early 1990s, what other places in Beijing held such parties besides Maxim's? Were there many venues?*

Cui Jian Public shows were subject to restrictions, but there were places for underground gigs in the compounds of government agencies and school halls like the Central Academy of Fine Arts and the Service Bureau for Diplomatic Missions. The rules were more relaxed there, and we didn't need performance permits. We were usually invited by event organisers to go and liven things up.

Pi Li *What was your impression of Maxim's?*

Cui Jian Maxim's was a window to the world through which we received news and information from overseas. I remember we would zealously discuss the Grammys every year; the vibe of the place was the same even up until 2000. Maxim's was also a place for meeting new friends. Besides the shows, Song would organise different events every weekend and promote them in venues frequented by diplomats in Beijing. Therefore, Maxim's had a following of Chinese interested in the West and foreigners interested in China, as well as artists, musicians, fashion models, filmmakers, and actors. I feel this coming-together of diplomatic and cultural circles was unique to Beijing. It was a small utopia of sorts.

Wu Mo *Maxim's started out as a restaurant and hangout for Beijing's diplomats, businessmen, and the like. Then artists started frequenting too. The crowd is different from the finely stratified society one sees today. In hindsight, what was this get-together of different social characters like? How would you describe their relationships?*

Cui Jian I feel Maxim's was an everyday hangout that embodied a certain lifestyle. Everyone was comfortable with interacting regardless of where they were from. Looking back at the 1980s, I realise I'd thought I was taking steps towards becoming more international, but I didn't finish what I started. This is why I always remind myself not to give people the wrong impression—that my dissatisfaction with the present is manifesting as a romanticised past. The 1980s were an unfinished enlightenment. It woke people up and opened a window looking towards the outside, but the door was not open.

Pi Li *In retrospect, what do you think is the legacy of Song Huai-Kuei and Maxim's?*

Cui Jian I never saw Song as an elder. She was gentle and gracious; she spoke softly and never gave anyone pressure. She was always her natural and easy-going self with people regardless of their social status. Although she was responsible for the commercial operations of Pierre Cardin and Maxim's, she came across more strongly as an artist than a businesswoman. You could tell she was someone who was true to her ideals as an artist.

As the country opened up, Maxim's was a groundbreaker for East–West cultural exchange in Beijing. That said, it wasn't as romantic and legendary as many online articles claim. [Some writers have] projected their own unnecessary imaginings about the 1980s and the bourgeois lifestyle onto the restaurant and portrayed it as this very exclusive place. Everyone who went there had the simple wish to get inspired by other individuals and congregate, not for the sake of information or material gain, but for culture. The effect this atmosphere had on us was inimitable. It made me feel the West and the East were not that far apart.

1989–2006: A Global Life and Legacy

The late spring and early summer of 1989 was a time that would be etched in Song Huai-Kuei's memory. While Maryn Varbanov had been in hospital, she had brought him food every day, shuttling back and forth from her residence in the Beijing Hotel. Passing through Tiananmen Square, she had encountered crowds of people and mounds of wreaths. Then, it was totally empty. The city had entered a period of martial law. Varbanov's death left her feeling even more acutely that the world was crashing down around her. Song's younger brother Song Huaibing (b. 1948), who had met up with the couple frequently at Beihai Park, wrote the following epitaph on a funerary wreath: 'Dear Maryn Varbanov, your last words to me will bring everlasting strength to my life.' Nobody knows what Varbanov's final words were, but he likely spent time in his last days taking stock of his accomplishments while also reflecting on his unfulfilled ambitions.

Varbanov had wanted to open a library in the courtyard house that Song had recently acquired. It would have been a place for students from the art academy to pore over the many foreign art books he had collected over the

A letter of condolence from artist and Zhejiang Academy of Fine Arts teacher Zheng Shengtian to Song Huai-Kuei following the death of Maryn Varbanov in 1989.

Above

Maryn Varbanov's
manuscripts on
frameworks for the
teaching of tapestry art.
Written between 1986
and 1988, they were
later published in *Maryn
Varbanov and the Chinese
Avant-Garde in the 1980s*
(2011).

Left

Song Huai-Kuei and Maryn
Varbanov with friends
in Hong Kong during the
exhibition *New Direction
in Contemporary Chinese
Tapestry*, October 1988.
Front row, from left:
Wong Pao-Cheng, Alice
King, Yonfan, and Zhang
Meixi. Back row, from left:
Zheng Shengtian, Huang
Heiman, Xiao Feng, Maryn
Varbanov, Huang Yongyu,
and Song Huai-Kuei.

Song Huai-Kuei and Maryn Varbanov with artist Lin Fengmian (second from left) and his student Feng Ye (first from right) at the exhibition *New Direction in Contemporary Chinese Tapestry* at Hong Kong Arts Centre, October 1988. Behind them is Wang Gongyi's tapestry *Forbidden City*.

years. In 1987, with limited cash, Varbanov had used seven of his wall hangings as a deposit towards the purchase of a studio in the Cité Internationale des Arts in Paris, which he later donated to the Zhejiang Academy of Fine Arts. This endowment established a residency programme in Paris for two faculty members every year. Varbanov also set about founding the Centre International de Recherche sur les Arts Contemporain (International Centre for Contemporary Arts Research), where audio-visual and plastic arts were treated as two distinct subcategories of contemporary art.[1] Varbanov had also long hoped to have a solo exhibition in China. Alice King (b. 1940), of Alisan Fine Arts gallery in Hong Kong, proposed mounting a show for him, but Varbanov selflessly used the budget to showcase his work alongside that of his colleagues from the Institute of Art

On 14 February 1990,
Maxim's was the venue
for one of the first fashion
shows in China since the
Tiananmen Incident and
a period of martial law.

Right
Pierre Cardin helps ink artist Deng Lin put
on one of his new designs during her visit
to France. The daughter of Deng Xiaoping,
Deng Lin was also an alumnus of the
Central Academy of Fine Arts, Beijing.

Below
Passers-by study the window display
of a boutique in Beijing, October 1984.

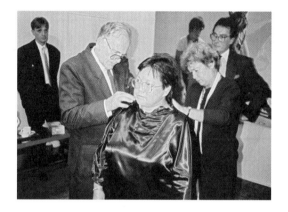

Pierre Cardin (first from left) and singer Mireille Mathieu (second from left) accompany President François Mitterrand (third from left, partially obscured) and his wife, Danielle Mitterrand (first from right), at a meeting with Hu Yaobang (third from right), the then general secretary of the Communist Party of China, 1986. It is said that Hu, who had travelled to France for a state visit at the Élysée Palace, was the first senior Chinese official to put on a Western suit and tie for official and diplomatic occasions.

Tapestry Varbanov (IATV). Together they presented the group show *Contemporary Chinese Tapestry Exhibition* at the Shanghai Exhibition Centre in 1987. With support from Alisan, some of the pieces from that exhibition went on to be shown at the Hong Kong Arts Centre the following year. When attending the celebration marking the founding of the IATV at the Shangri-La Hotel in Hangzhou, Song had been confident that her husband's artistic career in China was about to take off; she never imagined that, in just twelve months, everything would come to such an abrupt end.

While Beijing was under martial law, Maxim's closed for six months. In November 1989, Song slowly emerged from mourning and got back to work, preparing the restaurant for its re-opening. In the eyes of its well-heeled patrons, Song was the elegantly attired proprietor of Maxim's. What most of her guests did not realise is that, when she showed up each night at the restaurant, she had already spent an entire day at her desk organising fashion shows and helping to establish Pierre Cardin as the first luxury brand in China.

Cardin registered his name as a fashion trademark in 1950 and subsequently licensed it for thousands of products, including children's clothing, accessories, stationery, and furniture. Although some of his peers in the world of haute couture disparaged him for this practice—he was mocked as 'the grocer' for offering such a wide variety of consumer goods—Cardin's business model was hugely profitable, and the company maintained tight control of the brand. At its peak, Pierre Cardin had more than eight hundred licensing agreements for items produced in more than five hundred factories worldwide. In just ten years, Song secured deals with about a dozen authorised distributors in China, chief among them a contract for the manufacture and sale of Pierre Cardin menswear with the Jin Tak Garment Company Ltd of Tianjin.[2] Because the arrangement substantially lowered production costs, locally manufactured garments were more profitable in China than those imported from Japan or Europe.

Originally known for womenswear, Pierre Cardin became a dominant presence in China's menswear market, in part through the deal with Jin Tak that Song had overseen. At a time when the average monthly income in such major Chinese cities as Beijing, Shanghai, and Guangzhou was just above RMB 100, a Pierre Cardin suit retailed for RMB 1,000 or more. For China's up-and-coming nouveau riche in the 1990s, the garment was a coveted status symbol.

During the early years of the Republic of China, in the first decades of the twentieth century, intellectuals widely adopted Western-style suits. Officials, meanwhile, tended to favour the Sun Yat-sen suit, named after the influential statesman who helped design it. After 1949, the style was adapted and became better known as the Mao suit. Chinese officials wore it exclusively as formal attire. Only in the post-Mao era of reform and opening-up did national leaders begin to appear in Western suits. Zhao Ziyang, premier of the People's Republic of China (PRC) from 1980 to 1987, wore such a suit when he shook hands with the then British prime minister, Margaret Thatcher, in Berlin at the 1984 signing of the Joint Declaration on the handover of Hong Kong; Hu Yaobang wore one on an official state visit to France in 1986.

Opposite

The Pierre Cardin fashion show at the Imperial Ancestral Temple in Beijing, 1990.

Below

Pierre Cardin (centre, left), Song Huai-Kuei (centre, right), and Chinese models at Cardin's fashion show at the Imperial Ancestral Temple in Beijing, 1990, held in conjunction with the 11th Asian Games.

Cardin's menswear arrived in the Chinese market just as the re-popularised Western suit was becoming a symbol of China's new openness.

‡

In the 1990s, China developed according to an entirely different logic from that which had guided its early rise in the previous decade. Nearly all the reformers in the government had stepped down following the Tiananmen Incident. Nonetheless, conservatives widely approved of Shanghai mayor Jiang Zemin's moderate approach to handling the student movement, and he ascended to power in Beijing. Jiang lacked an established personal network in the capital, and the economy languished in the wake of the turmoil. Foreign investors had lost confidence in China, capital flowed out, production declined, and the tourism industry contracted dramatically. Ominous clouds obscured the path towards reform.

As they witnessed the radical transformation of Eastern Europe and the break-up of the Soviet Union, Jiang and his circle recognised that only a flourishing economy would allow the Communist Party of China (CPC) to stay in power. In 1990, stock exchanges opened in Shanghai and Shenzhen, part of a trial reform of the shareholding system. In response to these modest efforts at introducing market economics, the conservative faction within the CPC went on the attack. Tensions simmered until shortly after the New Year of 1992, when Deng Xiaoping,

who was no longer in office but nonetheless retained significant political influence, concluded his now-famous inspection tour of the South. In a series of remarks delivered in different cities, including Shenzhen, Zhuhai, Guangzhou, and Shanghai, he admonished officials to drop unnecessary debates about economic systems and throw their support behind development-focused policies regardless of whether they were called 'capitalist' or 'socialist'. The reformers were finally given free rein. China entered a market-economy era, and society rapidly urbanised.

For most of its history, the PRC had been subject to international sanctions. As reforms began to stimulate the economy, the CPC saw vigorous diplomacy as a means to both revitalise society and improve the country's image on the world stage. In 1990, Beijing hosted the 11th Asian Games, the first large-scale international event in the capital after the Tiananmen Incident. Despite the gloomy atmosphere in China at the beginning of the new decade, Song never stopped working. During the Asian Games, she organised a fashion show at the Imperial Ancestral Temple featuring Cardin's designs, with more than two hundred outfits flown in from France. Compared with the 1981 show that she had mounted for Cardin at the Beijing Hotel, where two dozen inexperienced models fumbled their way through wardrobe changes, the Asian Games event was a polished spectacle that went off without a hitch. It was clear that professional modelling in China had come a long way in a decade.

The Imperial Ancestral Temple, renamed the Working People's Cultural Palace by Mao, was the very place where Song had studied painting some thirty years earlier. The lively atmosphere of the palace in its heyday had since faded, and the venue came alive only when hired for events. A site rich with personal memories had been changed by the vicissitudes of history. We can picture Song,

Above left
The award ceremony of the Supermodel
Competition of the World China Division &
the 2nd Best Fashion Models Competition
of China, October 1991. Chen Juanhong
(centre), Qu Ying (left), and Liu Li (right)
came first, second, and third respectively.

Above
Song Huai-Kuei and Chen Juanhong in
Los Angeles while Chen was representing
China at the 1992 Supermodel of the
World competition.

having only recently emerged from mourning her partner, revisiting her old haunts and being overcome by bittersweet emotions. If she had not studied art at the Working People's Cultural Palace, she would not have attended the Central Academy of Fine Arts (CAFA) and would never have met Varbanov. But life is not made up of what-ifs. Song, too, had changed over time. She was no longer a young girl blessed with innocent fearlessness. She could feel the effects of age. Returning to the place where her creative ambitions had been ignited, she likely realised that it was precisely because life is short and fragile that she needed to seize the moment and bring unfulfilled dreams to fruition.

Staging a fashion show at the Imperial Ancestral Temple was no mean feat, and Song relied on the assistance of a co-organiser, Jerry Zhang. A generation younger than Song, Zhang had previously tried to hold a fashion show in Tiananmen Square, but the project had fallen apart when authorities rejected the foreign sponsors' idea of releasing brand-name balloons. When Song heard about the episode, she persuaded Pierre Cardin to hire Zhang. Cardin and Song had met Zhang previously when he worked at the Beijing Textile Bureau, and he was frequently in the audience for Cardin fashion shows. Inspired by what he had seen, Zhang recruited a 'performance team' of models composed of female textile workers.

China's textile industry was transforming itself from a processor of raw materials to an exporter of finished goods. The Beijing Textile Bureau supported Zhang's initiative to promote garments made in China, but there was a dearth of training materials for his performance team. These ad hoc models even had to construct their own runway for their first show. When Zhang asked Song for advice, she happily shared videotapes of Cardin fashion shows so that the workers previously tasked with creating garments could learn how to present them while

Chen Juanhong having her make-up applied on a beach in Los Angeles while representing China at the 1992 Supermodel of the World competition.

strutting down a runway. This also marked the beginning of a deep friendship between Zhang and Song, and they remained close collaborators in the final decade of her life. Neither was fussy about following the rules, nor were they wildly unconventional; rather, taking advantage of every available resource, they quietly transformed the business of fashion in China.

Before collaborating with Song on the Imperial Ancestral Temple show, Zhang had leveraged Beijing Textile Bureau resources to stage China's first modelling contest. In October 1989, the Best Fashion Models Competition of China had taken place in Guangzhou. The event highlighted the immense market potential of a billion Chinese people and enticed multinational business interests to invest in the country. Events like Zhang's competition helped convince Eileen Ford (1922–2014), founder of the half-century-old Ford Modeling Agency, that a modelling industry could grow at the foot of the Great Wall. Through Cardin, Ford contacted Song and Zhang and they worked together on a production. Zhang's second modelling contest, held in Beijing in 1991, had a long and elaborate name that combined his initiative with that of Ford: 'Supermodel Competition of the World China Division & the 2nd Best Fashion Models Competition of China'. Following a decade of painstaking work by Song and her peers, this event marked the beginning of a new era in which modelling was considered a serious profession—unlike in the 1980s, when models had been regarded as little more than 'fashion show performers'. Gone for good was the notion that assembly-line workers who made garments for state-run industries could also be tasked with modelling them. Song attended this competition and invited a couple of friends from Hong Kong: Loletta Chu (b. 1958), a former amateur model who had been crowned Miss Hong Kong in 1977, and Ellen Liu (1944–2019), a famous model who later became the styling director for Miss Asia. Their presence offered an additional seal of approval, since Hong Kong served as a source of inspiration for the commercial culture developing on the mainland.

Jiang Zemin, the then president of the People's Republic of China (front, centre), with Pierre Cardin (front, fourth from right), Gianfranco Ferré (front, second from left), Valentino (front, fourth from left), and Song Huai-Kuei (back, second from right) in Zhongnanhai, Beijing, 1993.

The competition had an interesting side note. Many in attendance did not understand the difference between a modelling competition and a beauty pageant. When it came time to declare the champion, the Chinese organisers wanted to put a crown on her head. Ford, the grande dame, was adamantly opposed to the idea: this was a display of professional skills, not a mere pageant. In the end, the organisers had to allow Vice-Premier Tian Jiyun (b. 1929) to place a crown on the head of the winner, undoubtedly the first and only time that a senior member of a socialist goverment has participated in such a coronation. The recipient of the award, Chen Juanhong, was an outstanding athlete, tall and lean, who carried herself very gracefully. But she had always been ashamed of her height and had found employment in a textile factory. Her life changed forever when she responded to an advertisement seeking models in Shenzhen. After her triumph in China, Chen's next step was the Supermodel of the World competition in the United States. Zhang took care of her training, and Song introduced her to Western manners, starting with the basics of using cutlery. Song looked after Chen as if she were her own child. Chen, in turn, affectionately referred to her mentor as 'Mama Song'. Chen did not disappoint: in the twelfth Supermodel of the World competition, she made it to eighth place, officially becoming the first person from China to hold the title 'World Supermodel'.

‡

As the pace of globalisation in China accelerated, the differences between Chinese and Western culture remained. Zhang and his models, all of whom were new to the international industry, had to deal with novel pressures and prejudices. 'Mama Song', with her long experience promoting Chinese culture abroad, provided crucial mediation. Song was well versed in Western culture and professional standards, but she never took a hard line with her Chinese colleagues. She solved problems through perseverance, patience, and determination. Song had a naturally even temperament and spoke softly, often projecting a disarming image rather than presenting herself as a forceful female leader. She offered needed emotional support to Zhang, Chen, and their peers as they stepped out into the world.

After tourism, fashion became China's favoured means to earn foreign
currency and burnish the country's international image. In 1993, the China Fashion
Research and Design Centre of the Ministry of Textile Industries, the China Centre
for International Trade of the Ministry of Foreign Trade and Economic Cooperation,
and other organisations devoted to promoting the garment industry convened the
first Chinese International Clothing and Accessories Fair (CHIC) in Beijing, inviting
international designers and brands. While he was in charge of Shanghai, Jiang Zemin
had attended with keen interest the *Contemporary China Tapestry Exhibition*, featuring
the work of Varbanov and his students. As president of the PRC, Jiang invited three
eminent designers—Valentino, Gianfranco Ferré, and Pierre Cardin—to visit him
at the CPC's headquarters in the Zhongnanhai complex adjacent to the Forbidden
City. The organisers of CHIC wished to establish Beijing as an international fashion
capital. A handful of fashion shows and press conferences announcing new products
was not enough, so state broadcaster CCTV was tasked with hosting 'Centuries of
Style', a gala at the Temple of Heaven showcasing China's costume culture. The
event was widely reported, contributing to the efforts to publicise China's continuing
economic improvement.

The gala took place at the same venue at which Pierre Cardin's arch-rival,
Yves Saint Laurent (1936–2008), had presented a retrospective of his designs in
1985. Separated by less than a decade, the two displays may as well have occurred
in different worlds. Saint Laurent's exhibition had been sparsely attended, a far cry
from the public interest in CHIC. In 1985, Boryana Varbanov had served as Saint
Laurent's interpreter and guide, taking him to CAFA, major historical sites, and

Above
Above
Valentino with a model
in front of Mao Zedong's
portrait in Tiananmen
Square, May 1993.

Left
The closing ceremony
of the first Chinese
International Clothing and
Accessories Fair at the
China World Trade Center,
19 May 1993.

even to visit a Peking opera troupe. But in the eyes of the aesthetically conservative and materially impoverished Chinese fashion world, Saint Laurent's designs were too foreign in their sensibility, and his love for China was unreciprocated.

As part of CHIC, Zhang directed a fashion show for Valentino and Ferré—the first runway presentation of international brands to be overseen entirely by a Chinese director. One can only imagine the pressure he was under contending with linguistic and cultural differences, not to mention the temperaments of the designers. The pioneering Chinese models Zhang enlisted were unhappy about the prohibition on wearing underwear on the runway. They suspected Cardin of being a 'dirty old man', but they believed Ferré was even worse. His insistence on inspecting the models as they tried on his clothes so that garments could be altered to better fit was more than they could take. To resolve the tension, Ferré had to come out to them as gay. With hindsight, the situation might seem amusing; at the time, however, the misunderstanding was a source of great stress backstage, where every second counted.

Zhang's involvement with CHIC taught him that it was essential to have language skills in the international fashion world. At Song's behest, Zhang stayed in America after accompanying Chen to the Supermodel of the World competition to study English. He also spent time at the Ford Modeling Agency and at Elite Modeling Management, learning their management and representation systems on the job. In 1998, he resigned from New Silk Road Model Inc. (formerly the China Fashion Show Group) and, along with Chen Juanhong, co-founded the Galaxy Model Management Company. Galaxy pioneered the joint stock ownership business model for a modelling agency and eventually broke state-run New Silk Road's domination of the market. Inspired by Zhang's example, more than fifty locally operated modelling agencies sprang up all over China, a number that grew over time to some two hundred agencies. The country's modelling industry rapidly developed a production chain that included training, selection, management, and representation.

The Wind of the Century evening fashion show at Qinian Hall in the Temple of Heaven, 19 May 1993. The show was one of the events marking the end of the first Chinese International Clothing and Accessories Fair.

Song was delighted to see her protégés Zhang and Chen on the world stage. She had returned to China in 1981 as Pierre Cardin's chief representative and had appeared at events large and small attired in Cardin's designs. It seemed that now was the time for her to don her own styles and express her true self, showing the world an image of a brilliantly talented contemporary Chinese artist who adored tradition. She went back to her studio and began work on a project she had long held in her heart: the *Five Dynasties*.

‡

The *Five Dynasties* project, which had first come to her as an idea when she was living abroad, enabled Song to affirm her own modern identity through traditional culture. In 1981, the year Song had returned to Beijing, her teacher Shen Congwen's long-awaited and painstakingly assembled treatise, *A Study of Ancient Chinese Costumes*, had finally found its way into print. This groundbreaking work incorporated archaeological evidence, archives, and paintings as source material for the study of the history of Chinese costume. (In an interesting turn of events, Guo Moruo, who had openly criticised Shen for being a counter-revolutionary, wrote the preface to the book in 1964 during his term as president of the China Federation of Literature and Art Circles.) Shen had originally intended to submit the manuscript to a publisher in time for National Day 1964, so that the book could appear in honour of the fifteenth anniversary of the founding of the PRC. Unfortunately, Shen's efforts coincided with Mao Zedong's attacks on imperial court dramas and old-fashioned love stories featuring young scholars and beautiful ladies. Historical works, such as the film *Sorrows of the Forbidden City* (1948), received harsh criticism as well. During the Cultural Revolution, all of Shen's research materials had been destroyed. Only in 1972, after returning to Beijing from his exile in the countryside, had Shen been able to retrieve and supplement the manuscript. Following some further detours, the book was published in Hong Kong by the Commercial Press. From start to finish, it had taken Shen nearly two decades to complete.

Song, meanwhile, had seen Cardin use Chinese pagoda eaves as a design element in his dramatic, broad-shouldered coats, and had also taken note of designs by Saint Laurent that treated Chinese visual culture with a predatory colonial eye. What she had learned in Shen's classes had suggested an alternative path towards rediscovering cultural history on her own terms. Moreover, everything she had seen and heard during the filming of *The Last Emperor* and during her visit to the set of *The Troubleshooters*, with its absurdist fashion show, had rekindled her youthful interest in tradition. During the rock 'n' roll era of the 1960s, many haute couturiers in the West, influenced by hippy culture, had drawn inspiration from the traditional dress and motifs of Eastern Europe and South Asia.[3] In the early 1970s, Song had also incorporated folk elements into her designs for evening wear at the Centre for New Goods and Fashion in Bulgaria in an effort to create socialist fashion free from aesthetics derived from the capitalist West.[4] Although designers in China were a generation behind these trends, some, like Wu Haiyan (b. 1958) and Ma Ke (b. 1971), found inspiration in traditional Chinese crafts and designs.[5]

Below
Song Huai-Kuei (back,
left) with Shen Congwen
(front, second from right);
Shen's wife, Zhang Zhaohe
(front, second from left);
Huang Yongyu (front, first
from right); and Hugues-
Alexandre Tartaut (back,
centre) in Beijing, ca.
early 1980s.

Right
The cover of *A Study
of Ancient Chinese
Costumes* by Shen
Congwen, published
in 1981.

Right
Song Huai-Kuei and
John Lone at the Thirteen
Tombs of the Ming Dynasty
in Beijing. Lone would
have just finished filming
M. Butterfly (1993). Song
was in the early stages
of preparing for the *Five
Dynasties* show and visited
some of China's famous
historical sites with the
actor.

Song Huai-Kuei and models at a photoshoot for the promotion of the *Five Dynasties* show, late 1990s.

Models in costumes from the Tang Dynasty collection presented at the *Five Dynasties* show, ca. late 1990s.

The *Five Dynasties*
show held in Beijing,
12 November 2000.

Right

On 9 November 2000,
models showcased
costumes from the
Tang Dynasty and Qing
Dynasty collections at
Song Huai-Kuei's *Five
Dynasties* show held
at the Shanghai Grand
Theatre. The garments
in *Five Dynasties* are not
exact copies of ancient
costumes. Instead, Song
incorporated many of her
own ideas when creating
them, making use of her
design experience from
her time in Bulgaria.

Above
Song Huai-Kuei and Jerry Zhang,
ca. late 1990s to early 2000s.

Left
One of the *Five Dynasties* shows,
ca. late 1990s to mid-2000s.

Song's priority was not to start her own fashion brand, but to cultivate in her audience a passion for Chinese culture. She decided to present ancient costume on the runway. Consulting Shen's book and other guides, in the early 1990s Song visited such historical sites as the Shaolin Temple, the Longmen Grottoes, and Dunhuang, where Dong Xiwen had worked. She began to recreate historical costumes dating from the Tang to the Qing dynasties. The project required the collaboration of numerous design studios and clothing factories. Ever the perfectionist, Song scoured suppliers for suitable fabrics. Projects of this scale were typically undertaken by museums or foundations, but Song managed to do the work on her own and in her spare time. After she had exhausted most of her savings, she sold off part of her art collection to fund the project. In addition to her work with Pierre Cardin and at Maxim's, she now had another 'baby', and she produced nearly three hundred exquisite outfits in less than five years.

With *Five Dynasties*, Song aimed to bring the history of Chinese costume to life by finding ways to make her research feel relevant to contemporary audiences. She invited John Lone to participate in the show, and enlisted actors Pu Cunxin and Xu Fan for publicity photos. She also arranged a small preview at Maxim's. Progress was incremental, with some ideas fizzling out and others taken halfway. The final project came to fruition only when Zhang returned from the United States and stepped in to assist. Handing off details of the project she had been working on for years to Zhang and his colleagues at Galaxy, Song stayed on in the capacity of funder, artistic director, designer, and producer. In celebration of the return of Macau to the PRC in 1999, *Five Dynasties* was performed at Senado Square, an iconic plaza in the former Portuguese colony. More than eighty models took part in the show, presenting about three hundred costumes. Moving back in time from the 'Dramatic History' of the Qing Dynasty, through the 'War and Fall' of the Yuan Dynasty, and arriving step-by-step at the 'Zenith' of the glorious Tang Dynasty,[6] the show featured demonstrations of Shaolin martial arts and acrobatic performances in a marriage of strength and beauty. After this triumphant premiere, the extravaganza was performed more than twenty times worldwide in locations as far afield as Bangkok, Paris, São Paulo, and Sydney.

A 2004 performance, part of a programme in honour of L'Année de la Chine en France (the Sino-French Culture Year), marked almost two decades since Chinese models had first set foot in Paris. If 1985 had been a time when models were trying out Western clothes and creating an image of Chinese women dressed in international styles, in the new millennium they projected a lively image of Chinese tradition. We will never know what Song felt, but we can see how much the cultural environment, the image of women, and the image of China had changed.

In 2002, American director Quentin Tarantino (back row, fifth from left) travelled to China to shoot key parts of his film *Kill Bill* at the Beijing Film Studio. With the popular success of Bruce Lee, Jackie Chan, and other Hong Kong martial arts stars, Hollywood was experiencing a renewed craze for kung fu films. Around the same time, Song Huai-Kuei established the China Tai Chi Kung Fu Troupe in China with the aim of promoting kung fu abroad, which contributed to kung fu becoming a key element of Chinese culture in international cultural exchange. The photo shows Tarantino and Song at Maxim's with the China Tai Chi Kung Fu Troupe. Interestingly, one of the other guests at Maxim's that night was Shaolin Temple abbot Shi Yongxin (not pictured).

From the founding of the PRC and throughout the Cultural Revolution, traditional culture was viewed as anachronistic at best, regarded as a potential source of reactionary feeling. At the beginning of the era of reform and opening-up, many in China were eager to discover Western culture. It was not until the 1990s, as the country was drawn into globalisation, that traditional Chinese culture gradually entered the consciousness of society at large. Perhaps counterintuitively, greater transnational communication made tradition an increasingly important means for people to construct and affirm their identities. At the same time, Chinese people were influenced by interpretations of their own culture emanating from the West. From Yves Saint Laurent's 1977 *Les Chinoises* collection to Bertolucci's *The Last Emperor*, Westerners adapted and remoulded the aesthetics associated with imperial China. Chinese directors who found favour at international film festivals, such as Zhang Yimou (*Raise the Red*

These film stills are from *Ju Dou* (directed by Zhang Yimou, 1990; left), *Farewell My Concubine* (Chen Kaige, 1993; below), and *Peony Pavilion* (Yonfan, 2001; below left). Song Huai-Kuei was friends with all three directors. After 1949, the visual culture of the Republican period and the aesthetics of Peking opera and Kunqu opera were denigrated as decadent and outdated. With bright colours and a visual language straddling the fantastical and the real, these films represent the era in a different light, their releases marking the acceptance and popularisation of the Republican setting from the 1990s onwards.

In 1996, Zhang Yimou was invited by Florentine Opera to direct the 70th-anniversary production of Giacomo Puccini's opera *Turandot*. It was staged in front of Xiang Hall at Beijing's Imperial Ancestral Temple from 5 to 13 September 1998, as seen here. Taking inspiration from Peking opera, Zhang's *Turandot* exuded royal splendour through lavish costumes and the temple's majestic structure, departing from the oppressive eeriness of previous productions in Europe. Zhang Yimou's *Turandot* was subsequently performed in other venues, including Beijing's National Stadium and New York's Metropolitan Opera House.

Lantern, *Ju Dou*), Chen Kaige (*Farewell My Concubine*), and Yonfan (*Peony Pavilion*), also contributed to this process.

The Imperial Ancestral Temple in the Forbidden City became a symbolic site for this complex cultural exchange. In 1996, Zhang Yimou was invited to stage Puccini's opera *Turandot* in the courtyard of Xiang Hall, bringing this story from the Orient back to the place where Puccini had found his inspiration. Constructed for the use of the imperial family and later transformed into the Working People's Cultural Palace, the Imperial Ancestral Temple was reconstructed once more, this time as an exotic stage. The imagery employed to tell the opera's story of courtly love boomeranged from China to the West and back again, converging with a massive state project to bolster the national image in the twenty-first century.

In 1998, following a failed bid three years earlier, the Chinese government launched a campaign to host the 2008 Summer Olympics in Beijing. Rupert Murdoch (b. 1931) of News Corp advised the then mayor of Beijing, Liu Qi, to engage Sir Timothy Bell's public relations firm, Bell Pottinger. With the help of another public relations firm, Weber Shandwick, they successfully persuaded the nations of the British Commonwealth to cast their ballots for China. More importantly, they spun the nationalistic propaganda strategy typically employed by the Chinese government into a cosmopolitan narrative flush with traditional imagery. Zhang Yimou had been given the job of producing a five-minute publicity film for the application. The film begins with the gates of the Forbidden City opening. Depictions of structures representing tradition and power flash by, including the Hall of Prayer for Good Harvests and the Great Wall, interspersed with quick cuts to views of skyscrapers, expressways encircling Beijing, athletes, Peking opera performers, fashion models, practitioners of tai chi, and so on. Appearing in rapid succession, these images map a cultural landscape in which history and modernity coexist, bearing the message 'China joins the world'.

Song had envisioned this version of Chinese culture early on and had devoted her professional life to making it a reality. But she did not live to see its flowering. In 2005, Song was diagnosed with cancer. She first confided this news to her beloved younger brother Song Huaibing, and only later shared the news with her son and daughter. After that, she withdrew from public life. On 21 March 2006, Song Huai-Kuei died in Beijing.

Two years after Song's death, Beijing announced the opening of the 2008 Summer Olympics. More than one hundred famous singers joined a rendition of 'Beijing Welcomes You' at the Imperial Ancestral Temple. It was a truly joyous occasion. Although Song was not there to witness it, the day might never have arrived had it not been for her. Half a century earlier, her life as an artist had begun at the place where China symbolically 'joined the world'. She had journeyed to Sofia, Paris, and New York, making a grand tour before returning home to Beijing, becoming one of the very few Chinese people to move back and forth between both sides of the Iron Curtain during the Cold War. Along the way, she had befriended many well-

A billboard advertising the Beijing Olympic Games in Wangfujing Street, 2008. From China's second bid for the Olympics in 1998 to the actual games a decade later, the traditional aesthetics of such art forms as Peking opera had become part of Beijing's rebranding as a metropolis and were crucial to national image and promotion.

Song became a bridge connecting an isolated China and the rest of the world.

travelled artists like herself, including Dolores Ling, T'ang Haywen, I. M. Pei, and Bernardo Bertolucci. This extraordinary path through life undoubtedly made her a world citizen.

In 1978, when she was an artist residing in Eastern Europe, Song had been invited to a symposium in Paris organised by the Taiwanese publication *Lion Arts Monthly*, joining artists and scholars like herself who were familiar with Zao Wou-Ki and other overseas Chinese artists. The topic of their discussion was 'Local Culture and Imported Culture'. At one point in the discussion, she remarked:

> Our personal circumstances have, for a long time, not been ordinary, and we have all absorbed many Western influences … [Zao Wou-Ki's] role in Western art goes without saying … Right now, I suspect it's still too early to talk about his influence on Chinese art.[7]

While other participants debated grand values, Song maintained a more detached attitude, but this reflected her natural sense of ease. Although she had undoubtedly been nourished by the West, she was confident in her own culture, and the result of the intermingling of these two currents became clear over time. This is also why, after her return to China, she had been able to move so effortlessly between her different roles. Song became a bridge connecting an isolated China and the rest of the world, drafting the blueprint for modern urban life, avant-garde art, fashion, modelling, Western cuisine, cinema, rock 'n' roll, and more. One can see her footprints on the paths along which these cultural forms developed, and she was a living example of what a modern Chinese woman could be. Towards the close of the 1990s, when China had become increasingly Westernised, she championed a traditional culture that was cosmopolitan rather than nationalistic.

Not long after Song's death, China was swept up in the tide of social media. Song's story has turned up periodically on different social media sites, and each time she appears in a different guise. There has been enthusiastic discussion of her marriage, as well as her relationships with film directors and movie stars. Alain Delon, John Lone, Leslie Cheung Kwok-wing, Tony Leung Ka-fai, Jiang Wen, Zhang Yimou, and Cui Jian are among those who considered her the 'Godmother of Fashion', whose blessing was a gold seal of approval.

One can never take interpersonal relationships for granted, and flourishing friendships like these must be built and maintained. But Song Huai-Kuei's actual life was completely different from those of contemporary Internet personalities who live their lives in the spotlight. To become Madame Song today, you would first have to be willing to leave home and stay away for years, all for the sake of love. You would have to be willing to live in Sofia, half a world away from home, where there were few Chinese people. Your two young children in tow, you would have to follow your husband from a socialist country to bustling Paris, making friends through your sincerity. Then, in middle age, you would resolutely set aside your artistic career and return to your home country, embarking on an entirely different path, trading the untrammelled life of brush and paint for the silent intoning of the names on the directory for the Chamber of Commerce and Industry, pouring all your mental energy into dealing with market and socio-political constraints. In the evening, while other people were enjoying quiet relaxation, you would pace and fret, loneliness invading every thread of your fine overcoat. The sky in the East would turn fish-belly white, and you would have to shrug off your clothing and get dressed again, heading out to start a new day. In your later years, you would invest your life savings to realise a dream. It would not be luck that would bring you so many pleasant vistas on your journey from humble origins, but rather your ability to overcome adversity through an unshakable combination of perseverance, passion, selflessness, and courage.

People might say it is a pity that the abundantly talented Song set aside her own artistic life and did not become a famous artist, especially since those around her left behind such outstanding oeuvres. Towards the end of her life, she commented:

> I studied art in Beijing for five years, and I continued my studies abroad. My early twenties was a perfect age for me to absorb so much rich knowledge. When I was a student, I certainly didn't lack for talent ... I worked very hard when I was a student. Now, whenever I see beautiful scenery, the desire to create wells up inside me. Maybe someday I'll go back to painting.[8]

This does not sound like a person turning their back on something; rather, it sounds like a choice. All of Song's major life decisions were linked to the ups

On 30 April 2008, a hundred singers from around greater China gathered at the Imperial Ancestral Temple to sing 'Beijing Welcomes You' a hundred days before the opening of the Olympic Games. Blending notions of tradition and nation, the Imperial Ancestral Temple is a site that exemplifies China's metropolitan national propaganda.

and downs of the lives of those around her, a reflection in microcosm of the history of art and visual culture. We see a generation of artists standing in the rubble of a war-torn country, yearning for new lives and modernisation, wanting to use tradition to remake themselves, to live peaceful lives with hearts at ease; we see modernism, we see the international communist movement and the movements in Asia, Africa, and Latin America brought to China, where they take on a life of their own and evolve in their own unique ways, leading to the development of Socialist Modernism; and we also see how the modernist logic of China differs from that of the West, rebelling against avant-garde popular culture and filtering it through collectivism in order to adopt what is good and discard what is not. In this sense, Song's rich and varied life at the confluence of Asian and Western culture can provide us with a map for an entirely different path towards modernism.

If life is a dynamic act of creation, and a person can only become themselves through their own actions, then who was able to turn their life into a work of art? Madame Song.

Qipao in Paris, Couture in Beijing: Madame Song and Cultural Identity in Fashion

Tanja Cunz

For centuries, applied artists and designers, including in fashion, have adopted stylistic elements from other cultures. The fascination for Chinese motifs and symbols has its own particular history,[1] and many Western fashion designers from Song Huai-Kuei's sphere, including Yves Saint Laurent, Gianfranco Ferré, Valentino, and John Galliano (b. 1960), drew inspiration from Chinese culture even before travelling to the country.[2] Ferré reportedly visited China during the throes of the Cultural Revolution in 1973,[3] but Pierre Cardin was the first Western designer to receive an official invitation to China, in late 1978, coinciding with the country's opening-up. Inspired by China's rich imagery and formal languages, he began to incorporate certain elements into his designs, notably borrowing from Chinese architecture with his so-called pagoda shoulders.[4]

Despite a certain 'anything goes' mentality that has persisted in fashion, and a possible interpretation of appropriation as an act of creative borrowing or even an expression of admiration, adopting elements from other cultures by Western designers has become an increasingly contested topic. Because many designs are based on personal fantasies and interpretations, the results are often romanticised and stylised to an extent that can distort their source material, perpetuate stereotypes, and invite charges of exoticism or orientalism. Cultural appropriation can thus reveal the underlying (political) power structures of the fashion industry, raise critical questions about authenticity, and prompt introspection about cultural, ethical, and political sensitivity (or lack thereof).[5]

However, transplanting and translating elements of other cultures is not a phenomenon exclusive to the West, despite inherent differences in historical circumstances. During the New Culture Movement in the early 1920s, for example, European tailoring techniques and silhouettes found their way into Chinese fashion and were used to signal a newfound modern identity—a tendency that would accelerate in the following decades before ending abruptly with the establishment of the People's Republic of China (PRC) in 1949. Consumers in China once again adopted Western styles and aesthetics in the 1980s and 1990s as the country modernised and opened up to international markets, albeit through state-controlled exchanges. In addition, these consumers began to understand fashion as a means of individual expression

Pierre Cardin visited China in late 1978 with a group of European journalists. After the trip, he began to incorporate such elements as pagoda shoulders into his designs. When he returned to China in 1979 with several models, he brought a few sets of pagoda-inspired ensembles with him.

Yves Saint Laurent had a profound interest in Asia. Some of his best-known Chinese-inspired designs are from his *Les Chinoises* Haute Couture Autumn/Winter 1977 collection. To coincide with the launch, Saint Laurent also created the perfume 'Opium'. The collection preceded his first visit to China in 1985 for his Beijing retrospective, where several ensembles of *Les Chinoises* were shown.

Ever since his first visit to China in 1973, a journey he recounted in his personal notes, Gianfranco Ferré had drawn on Chinese culture and imagery for inspiration, most obviously in his Ready-to-Wear Autumn/Winter 1992 collection. In 1993, together with Valentino and Pierre Cardin, he was invited to the inaugural Chinese International Clothing and Accessories Fair, where he presented an overview of his style and made his acquaintance with Song Huai-Kuei.

Even though Valentino only made it to China in 1993, for the first Chinese International Clothing and Accessories Fair, he had referenced Chinese patterns, motifs, and cuts much earlier in his work. The visit did, however, deepen his fascination with traditional Chinese aesthetics, informing his Haute Couture Autumn/Winter 1993/94 collection.

Wu Haiyan's career took off after she was awarded first prize at the inaugural Brother Cup Chinese International Young Fashion Designers Contest in 1993 for the *Heyday* collection. Today, she remains one of China's most influential contemporary designers. Since 2003, the contest has been known as the Hempel Award China International Young Fashion Designers Contest and takes place during China Fashion Week. It is considered an important platform for emerging Chinese designers.

Right

Guo Pei is part of the first generation of Chinese fashion designers to have emerged after the Cultural Revolution. With her label Rose Studio, which employs a team of several hundred skilled craftspeople, Guo has released a series of stunning couture collections, including *Legend of the Dragon* in 2012. She gained widespread recognition in the West when singer Rihanna wore one of her spectacular robes to the Met Gala in 2015. In the same year, Guo opened her second studio, in Paris, and received an invitation to present at Paris Haute Couture Week in the spring of 2016.

John Galliano's eclectic designs play
with different combinations of seemingly
paradoxical cultural and historical elements.
Chinese culture has been a recurring source
of inspiration for Galliano. His initial interest
in cinema also led him to research Chinese
painting, literature, and architecture. After
a weeks-long trip with his team in 2002 to
countries in Asia including China and Japan,
Galliano worked on his Haute Couture Spring/
Summer 2003 collection for Dior, which
contained overt stylistic references to his
journey. Song Huai-Kuei had accompanied
him for parts of the trip.

and incorporated foreign brands, such as
Louis Vuitton, Hermès, and Chanel, into their
lifestyles.[6] As a representative for Pierre Cardin
in China, Madame Song heralded this cultural
shift with her own predominately Western
wardrobe.

It was also in the context of reform and
opening-up in the 1980s that the Chinese fashion
system evolved. Apart from the establishment
of fashion magazines, fairs, and training courses
and competitions for designers and models,
the government actively created national
fashion trends with the goal of promoting
Chinese production and carving out a place
for Chinese fashion on the global market. By
the 1990s, the ensuing nexus of modernisation,
internationalisation, and national branding
provided the backdrop for the emergence of a
complex phenomenon known as 'Chineseness'.
In the earliest phase of this phenomenon,
many Chinese designers made explicit use
of traditional cultural symbols and motifs to
position their designs within a firmly Western-
determined global fashion system.[7] Madame

Song fed into this rediscovery of cultural
heritage in the mid-1990s with the *Five Dynasties*,
a travelling show intended to introduce a global
audience to traditional Chinese dress.[8]

While the enthusiasm for anything and
everything Chinese that accompanied the
country's reopening certainly bolstered the
strategy of the first generation of Chinese fashion
designers, few of them were able initially to
compete with the dominance of Western fashion.
Among those who attained a significant degree
of recognition were Wu Haiyan, whose Mogao
Caves–inspired collection won her first prize
at the 1993 Brother Cup Chinese International
Young Fashion Designers Contest, and Ma Ke,
who received the same prize in 1994 for her
collection inspired by the Terracotta Warriors.
Another example is Guo Pei, who quickly
became one of the most popular and sought-
after designers in the luxury segment in China
after founding her label Rose Studio in 1997 and
producing spectacular collections that fused
the cultural history of her native country
with the art of haute couture.[9]

Ma Ke won the second edition of the Brother Cup in 1994. Her breakthrough followed in 1996 when she co-founded the label EXCEPTION de Mixmind, which, unlike her earlier work, does not feature direct references to her native country's culture, heralding a new phase in contemporary Chinese fashion design.

Left

In 2008, after participating in Paris Fashion Week with *WUYONG/The Earth* the previous year, Ma Ke became the first Chinese designer to be invited to present at Paris Haute Couture Week. As a brand, WUYONG denotes a maverick attitude towards the fashion system. Known for recycling existing garments and leftover fabrics, WUYONG is also committed to preserving traditional Chinese craftsmanship. The brand's garments are therefore produced entirely by hand by a team of trained craftspeople in Zhuhai.

Nevertheless, the 'Made in China' label's reputation as the epitome of cheap products, denoting mere copies of Western designs, had a detrimental effect on the reception of Chinese fashion both inside and outside of the country. In the new millennium, however, the fashion system became increasingly globalised, and a rising generation of Chinese consumers called for a truly Chinese fashion identity. Also at this time, the PRC developed a new-found appreciation for fashion as a valuable creative and cultural good.[10]

In parallel, many fashion designers began to see their work as an outlet for creative expression rather than merely market-oriented production. In this environment, new articulations of 'Chineseness' took shape, and designers made subtler and more abstract allusions to their own cultural roots, presented in the form of a 'Chinese spirit' or with reference to traditional textiles, production techniques, or styles within a contemporary formal language.[11] Among the many examples are Ma Ke's subversively named haute couture line WUYONG, which translates into English as 'useless', and the designs by London-based Huishan Zhang, who effortlessly blends inspirations from his hybrid cultural background and his native country's traditional craftsmanship with influences from around the world.[12] Despite their different formal languages, such designers share a common aspiration to establish a new aesthetic in Chinese fashion, one that draws on the country's history and culture, yet speaks a modern, international language. Transcending cliché and stereotype, Chinese designers deploy this aesthetic of 'Chineseness' to establish themselves on a global stage.[13]

Tanja Cunz is Associate Curator of Design and Architecture at M+

Huishan Zhang belongs to a young generation of Chinese fashion designers who were born in China but trained in the West. His 2011 debut collection features six embroidered organza dresses in black and white. Zhang finds inspiration in his cultural heritage and traditional Chinese craftsmanship, which he interprets with a contemporary, global twist to redefine the meaning of 'Made in China'.

Afterword

Pi Li

I met Song Huai-Kuei only once, in the spring of 1997. I was working at the CourtYard Gallery, located just outside the East Gate of the Forbidden City in Beijing. My colleagues spoke of Song with great respect in discussions about a forthcoming exhibition we were planning. Her daughter, Boryana, had designed the logo and the print materials for our gallery. One afternoon, Song came to accompany Boryana home after work. Greeting her at the reception desk, I enquired as to why she was at the gallery. In the gentlest of voices, she replied, 'I'm Boryana's mother. I'm here to pick her up.' It was only then that I realised she was Song Huai-Kuei. The encounter left a deep impression on me.

In 2012, I came to Hong Kong from Beijing to work for M+. Aric Chen, who later joined the museum as a curator, brought me the news that Boryana wanted to donate to M+ her mother's fashion collection; artworks by her father, Maryn Varbanov; and the couple's archive. This became the museum's first collection project in which curators from the visual art team could collaborate with those from design and architecture. In late 2012, I returned to a heavily polluted Beijing, where levels of PM2.5 particulate matter were off the charts. I went to Boryana's apartment next to Ritan Park. As I opened sealed and dusty documents and photo albums, I began to notice how they reflected a cultural logic that was closely related to, yet completely different from, the '85 New Wave art movement of the 1980s 1 was familiar with. I decided on the spot to mount an exhibition on Chinese visual culture after the Cultural Revolution. In 2013, Beijing underwent large-scale urban redevelopment, and Song's archive could not escape the fate of forced relocation. Along with Aric Chen and Veronica Castillo, the current deputy director of collection and exhibition at M+, I went to the capital to conduct centralised cataloguing of Song's fashion collection and have the items shipped to M+'s warehouse. A year later, Beijing launched a crackdown on foreigners living and working in the city illegally. Boryana had to return to Paris owing to an expired resident visa. The M+ team went back to Beijing to select which of the remaining documents to ship to Hong Kong.

After the trials and tribulations of the preceding ten years, we finally started planning for the exhibition *Madame Song: Pioneering Art and Fashion in China* right around the time of M+'s grand opening, in Autumn 2021. We opened all the sealed documents, interviewed Song's family, friends, and colleagues, and worked with the conservation team to restore the items in her fashion collection. Approaching Song via her multiple identities—artist, entrepreneur, trendsetter, and lifestyle promoter—the exhibition depicts the profound changes in Chinese art, film, fashion, and lifestyle that occurred in the wake of the Cultural Revolution. With Song's biography as a point of departure, we elucidate Chinese artists' search for identity amid Western exoticisation and the rise of China's market economy and globalisation. The exhibition traces the developmental trajectory of Chinese visual culture from the years of the country's isolation to its opening-up in the second half of the twenty-first century.

This book eventually took on a life of its own, independent of the exhibition, and became a biography of Song. When I first started writing, I discovered that she had left no diaries or notes behind; even correspondence was scarce. Many who had worked with her had passed away, including, in 2020, Pierre Cardin. I made up for the lack of source material by borrowing the concept of *liu bai*, or 'leaving blank spaces', from Chinese ink painting. In other words, I tried to assist the reader in imagining her eventful life by describing the changes in her era and the fates of those around her. In my writing, I eschewed unfounded speculations and avoided excessive sentimentality, instead focusing on restoring who Song was and how she may have lived in her time. With the help of the odd essay, interview, or correspondence Song left behind and recollections from her friends, I tried my best to let Song's delicate and wilful voice shine through. At the same time, Wu Mo and Tanja Cunz fleshed out Song's image by conducting research into her life as an artist and her fashion collection, respectively.

That said, this book is not only about Song Huai-Kuei, but also about the trajectories of the lives of several generations of Chinese artists. The socialist revolution of the 1950s, the Cultural Revolution from the 1960s to the 1970s, the reform and opening-up of the 1980s, and the marketisation of the 1990s are all momentous developments in Chinese history. These massive changes shaped the creative environment in which Chinese artists worked and influenced those cultural figures overseas who maintained close ties to China, such as Song and Varbanov. Our research on Song brought to light a common misconception among historians: that ideology is static and makes an impact on society from the top. Reality is always more complex, as everyday occurrences accrue to become historical facts and phenomena, affecting and shaping our ways of thinking. Although many Chinese artists of the 1990s overtly criticised and ridiculed profit-oriented practices, the commercial model that Song represented had been fuelling the growth of avant-garde art since the 1980s. The expansion of commercial culture also kickstarted a lifestyle revolution that fostered the creativity of fifth-generation filmmakers and rock musicians.

This book takes a broad view that intertwines art history with the history of daily life. Song's multiple identities and endeavours open a window to new ideas and perspectives in visual culture and ways of living, allowing us to extend our gaze to developments in fashion, music, film, culinary experiences, and even social taboos in China from the twentieth century onwards. Her career exemplifies how ideas can spread, infiltrate, and reproduce, and how individuals may influence taste and mainstream aesthetics. I hope this publication will show readers that thought—artistic or otherwise—is never singular, and that it comprises a whole produced by the superimposition, montage, and juxtaposition of different, even contradictory, thoughts.

A concern for the place of the individual within a social structure runs throughout this publication. Chinese philosophical tradition, starting with the ancient *Records of the Grand Historian* (*Shiji*), had for centuries focused on portraying individuals who embody the spirit of their times. Historian Qian Mu (1895–1990) believed that this is where the value of Chinese historical studies lies. In his essay 'Chinese Historical Figures', Qian discusses the colossal influence of such individuals as Wen Tianxiang, arguing that leaving 'such a person in the annals of history makes a huge contribution and impact to China's future. A single incident, on the other hand, doesn't leave a mark in itself.' Qian also propagates the importance of the individual when it comes to documenting and analysing history: 'If facts are valued over people, it could lead to commendation of the blameworthy and discrediting of the commendable.' The charisma of the person is exactly what we wish to highlight in this book.

Owing to limited time and research materials, it was not possible to discuss all the questions that emerged during the writing process. Left unexplored were the experience of modernism offered by socialist avant-gardists during the Cold War, which differed from that of radical artists in the West, as well as the relationship between commerce and avant-garde culture in socialist China. Smaller topics were also left unexamined. How did fashion designer Yves Saint Laurent's exoticisation of China in the 1980s influence Chinese designers, and what was their awareness of cultural awakening? Why did the revival of traditional symbolism turn to Han and Tang styles in art and design, but favour the aesthetics of Republican China in film? How did the on-screen characters of Song's friends, such as Tony Leung Ka-fai in *The Lover*, Leslie Cheung in *Farewell My Concubine*, and John Lone in *M. Butterfly*, manifest a Western imagination of Chinese men? I hope this book will attract researchers to come and help open new paths for exploring Chinese visual culture.

This book was written during the Covid-19 pandemic. All those involved tried their best to finish their research despite travel restrictions. Nevertheless, I believe there will be imprecisions, even errors. As the lead author, I assume responsibility for all such mistakes. I also welcome colleagues far and wide to correct them with detailed studies, so that research in this area can reach new heights.

Notes

Introduction: Who is Madame Song?

1. The most renowned use was in relation to the three Soong sisters, especially the glorious, rebellious Madame Soong Ching-ling and Madame Soong Mei-ling, who had a profound impact on the course of Chinese history.

2. The term 'fifth-generation filmmakers' refers to directors, producers, and cinematographers who graduated from Beijing Film Academy in the 1980s, and who would have experienced the Cultural Revolution in their youth, such as Zhang Yimou, Chen Kaige, Tian Zhuangzhuang, and Gu Changwei. Richly allegoric and featuring new shooting styles and techniques, their films explore the scars of history and the Chinese psyche, creating a dramatic and historic image of China. Their works also won numerous awards at international film festivals in the 1990s, marking a new high point for Chinese cinema.

3. Luo Xin, 'The Contest of Forgetting', in *The Historian as Principled Rebel: Criticism, Doubt, and Imagination* (Shanghai: Joint Publishing, 2019), 27.

Chapter One
1950s: A Window of Freedom in Beijing

1. Dong Xiwen, 'My Experience Creating the Oil Painting *The Founding of the Nation*', *New Observer*, no. 21 (1953), 24.

2. Quoted in Dong Yisha, 'My Father Dong Xiwen's Years at Dayabao', in *No.2A Dayabao Hutong—The Legend of 20th Century Chinese Art*, ed. Liu Ying (Beijing: China Youth Press, 2020), 258.

3. Song Huai-Kuei, 'The Bond between Teacher and Student: Remembering My Teacher Mr Dong Xiwen', in *Endless Memory: In Honour of the 80th Anniversary of Mr Dong Xiwen's Birth*, ed. Li Yuchang and Xie Shanxiao (Beijing: International Culture Publishing Co., 1994), 157.

4. Guo Moruo, 'Out with Counter-Revolutionary Art', *Literature and Art for the Masses*, no. 1 (1948), 19.

5. Shen Congwen, 'Everything Starts with Love and Understanding', in *Collected Works of Shen Congwen: Border Town Collection* (Hunan: Yuelu Publishing House, 2005), 22–23.

6. *Ibid.*

7. Song, 'Remembering My Teacher Mr Dong Xiwen', 158.

8. Wang Qi, 'Remembering Siqueiros', *Meishu*, vol. 9 (1994), 12.

9. Song, 'Remembering My Teacher Mr Dong Xiwen', 156.

Chapter Two
1958–1974: A New World in Sofia

1. Song Huai-Kuei, 'The Bond between Teacher and Student: Remembering My Teacher Mr Dong Xiwen', in *Endless Memory: In Honour of the 80th Anniversary of Mr Dong Xiwen's Birth*, ed. Li Yuchang and Xie Shanxiao (Beijing: International Culture Publishing Co., 1994), 271.

2. For more on Maryn Varbanov's pedagogical practice and contributions, see Assadour Markarov, 'At the Confluence of Multiple Cultures: A Critical Biography of Maryn Varbanov', unpublished PhD thesis, China Academy of Art, 2015, 113–124.

3. 'China's Population Growth and Demographic Change Will Have Far-Reaching Influences on China's Development', 23 October 2008, www.gov. cn/wszb/zhibo275/content_1128989.htm, accessed 8 June 2022.

4. Eric J. Hobsbawm, 'Socialism and the Avantgarde in the Period of the Second International', *Le Mouvement social*, no. 111 (1980), 189–199.

5. Vladimir Lenin, 'Party Organization and the Party Publications', November 1905, www.marxists.org/ chinese/lenin/06.htm, accessed 8 June 2022.

6. Quoted in Clara Zetkin, 'Remembering Lenin', in *Remembering Lenin, Volume 5*, trans. Shanghai Institute of Foreign Languages, Research Office for the Translation of Lenin's Writings (Beijing: People's Publishing House, 1982), 8.

7. Markarov, 'At the Confluence of Multiple Cultures', 113–124.

8. *Ibid.*, 51–52.

9. The Soviet Union had created an organisation for the socialist bloc called the Council for Mutual Economic Assistance (COMECON), which held regular conventions on socialist dress. Intended to demonstrate the level of light-industry production in socialist countries, the conventions included discussions and exhibitions about the clothing designed by the different nations, together with exhibits related to textile technology. Bulgaria's Centre for New Goods and Fashion was among the attendees. China sent representatives in the capacity of observers, but after the Sino-Soviet split of 1961, China stopped participating in COMECON activities. See Djurdja Bartlett, *FashionEast: The Spectre that Haunted Socialism* (Cambridge, MA: MIT Press, 2010), 286.

10. For a detailed discussion of these works, see the essay by Wu Mo included in the present volume, 'Like a Butterfly: Revisiting Madame Song the Artist', pages 96–103.

11. Among the figures in the original painting who were removed during various political campaigns were Gao Gang, former vice-chair of the Central People's Government; Liu Shaoqi, former president of the PRC; and Lin Boqu, a former member of the Central Committee of the CPC. The third revision of the painting was made to the copy of the work produced by Dong Xiwen's student Jin Shangyi and artist Zhao Yu. It wasn't until 1978 that the National Museum of China suggested that *The Founding of the Nation* be restored to its original appearance. However, Dong's family was opposed to seeing any more changes made to his original composition, and, in the end, the version put on display was the copy made by Jin and Zhao. Dong's original painting was put into long-term storage.

Chapter Three
1975–1981: Adrift in Paris, Rooted in Beijing

1. Assadour Markarov, 'At the Confluence of Multiple Cultures: A Critical Biography of Maryn Varbanov', unpublished PhD thesis, China Academy of Art, 2015, 111.

2. *Ibid.*, 110.

3. Quoted in 'A Few Quotes on Zao or by Zao', *Asian Art*, www.asianart.com/exhibitions/zao/quotes. html, accessed 1 August 2022.

4. Quoted in Deng Xiaoping, 'The Need to Strongly Develop Civil Aviation and Tourism', in *Deng Xiaoping on Tourism*, ed. CPC Central Committee Party Literature Research Center and China National Tourism Administration (Beijing: Central Party Literature Press, 2000), 2.

5. International hotels were an important venture, both architecturally and in terms of urban planning, during the reform and opening-up era. For a detailed discussion of this subject, see Cole Roskam, 'International Hotels and Architectural and Economic Experimentation in the Early Reform and Opening Period in China', trans. Chan Man Ha Sylvia, *Architectural Journal*, no. 12 (2018), 56–62.

6. Christopher S. Wren, 'I. M. Pei's Peking Hotel Returns to China's Roots', *New York Times*, 25 October 1982, 13.

7. Chinese vernacular style was a topic of heated debate after 1949. For a detailed treatment, see Chen Shimin, 'Chinese National Form and Architectural Style', *Architectural Journal*, no. 2 (1980), 36–41.

8. Quoted in Zhang Qinzhe, 'I. M. Pei Discusses Creating Chinese Architecture', *Architectural Journal*, no. 6 (1981), 11–12.

9. Gu Mengchao, 'Symposium on the Architectural Design of the Fragrant Hill Hotel in Beijing', *Architectural Journal*, no. 3 (1983), 57–64.

10. *Ibid.*, 58.

11. Huang Mo, 'Pros and Cons of the Design of the Fragrant Hill Hotel', *Architectural Journal*, no. 4 (1983), 69.

12. The expression 'blue ant' originated with the French reporter Robert Guillain, appearing in his book *The Blue Ants: 600 Million Chinese Under the Red Flag* (1957). The phrase went on to be widely adopted by Western media and was a stereotypical description of Chinese sartorial aesthetics.

13. Frank J. Prial, 'China Names Cardin as Fashion Consultant', *New York Times*, 8 January 1979, 2.

14. Quoted in Richard Morais, *Pierre Cardin: The Man Who Became a Label* (London: Bantam, 1991), 194.

15. 'Proper Treatments of the Human Figure in Art: A Discussion of the Portrayal of the Human Body in Sculpture and Painting', *Meishu*, no. 6 (1980), 43.

16. Quoted in Wu Jijin, 'The Artistic Incident that Shook the Nation in the Early Days of the Reform and Opening Era', October 2018, www.zgdsw.com/ article/700.html, accessed 18 June 2022.

17. Peter Dunn Siu-Yue, 'Not Exactly about Pierre Cardin in Beijing', *City Magazine*, no. 1 (1982), 27–33.

18. *Ibid.*

Like a Butterfly: Revisiting Madame Song the Artist

1. The parable is taken from *Zhuangzi*, a classic work of Daoist thought composed during the Warring States period (475–221 BCE). In it, Zhuang Zhou dreams that he has become a butterfly, dancing freely and happily. When he wakes up, however, he is confused and, for a while, cannot tell if he is Zhuang Zhou or a butterfly. The parable is a metaphor for the blurred boundaries between reality and illusion, between human beings and all other things.

2. Judy Chicago (b. 1939) is a pioneer of feminist art, and *The Dinner Party* is her most celebrated

installation. The work consists of three long tables arranged in a triangular shape, with thirty-nine seats paying tribute to thirty-nine female figures in cultural history. On top of the embroidered napkins, representing female labour, are porcelain plates decorated with motifs of female genitalia. The work was considered too vulgar and provocative for the male-dominated art world of the time. Today, however, *The Dinner Party* is regarded as one of the most significant works of the feminist art movement.

3. See the interview with Cui Jian in the present volume, pages 208–211.

Chapter Four
1982–1989: Striving in Hangzhou and Beijing

1. Peter Dunn Siu-Yue, 'Woman in Transit: Song Huaigui', *City Magazine*, vol. 3 (1984), 20.
2. Quoted in *ibid*.
3. The term 'yellow music' was presumably borrowed from the concept of 'yellow journalism', which had become widely known following its adoption by state media in the United States in the 1950s. In the same decade, the People's Music Publishing House issued a collection of essays titled *How to Identify Yellow Music*, denouncing a number of pop songs from Hong Kong and Taiwan—such as those by Teresa Teng—as vulgar, liberal pollution emitted by a capitalist society that aimed only to profit from love and demoralise the youth. Meanwhile, avant-garde artists in southern China saw such pop-cultural artefacts as Teng's music as sources of inspiration. For more on this subject, see the documentary *From Jean-Paul Sartre to Teresa Teng: Cantonese Contemporary Art in the 1980s* (2010), written, directed, and produced by Asia Art Archive.
4. Deng Xiaoping, 'The Party's Urgent Tasks on Organisational and Ideological Fronts', in *Selected Works of Deng Xiaoping, Volume III* (Beijing: People's Publishing House, 2009), 40–41.
5. Hou Hanru, 'Preface of *Exhibition by Beijing Artistic Tapestry Center*', November 1985, https://aaa.org.hk/en/collections/search/archive/wang-youshen-archive--1985-exhibition-by-beijing-artistic-tapestry-center--beijing/object/preface-and-artist-biographies-of-exhibition-by-beijing-artistic-tapestry-center, accessed 27 June 2022.
6. 'Hou Hanru: Rauschenberg Praised Varbanov's Soft Sculptures', art.ifeng.com, 6 January 2016, https://mp.weixin.qq.com/s/ruxoke15tVAreplON57KRQ, accessed 27 June 2022.
7. Hou Hanru, 'Varbanov's Art', *Meishu*, vol. 10 (1989), 55–58.
8. 'Conversation between Liang Shaoji and Assadour Markarov', ShanghART gallery, June 2016, www.shanghartgallery.com/galleryarchive/texts/id/10011, accessed 27 June 2022.
9. Tony Rayns, 'Model Citizen: Bernardo Bertolucci on Location in China', *Film Comment*, vol. 23, no. 6 (November 1987), 35.
10. Hao Jian, 'Forbidden City's Bright Yellow Silk, Revolutionary Red Flag, and Bertolucci's Film World', BBC China, 30 November 2018, www.bbc.com/zhongwen/trad/chinese-news-46397213, accessed 27 June 2022. The film-production contract was only two pages long, but every time Bertolucci's name was mentioned, the words 'member of the Italian Communist Party' would appear. See Rayns, 'Model Citizen', 35.

11. 'Malicious Intentions and Despicable Means: A Critique of Antonioni's Anti-China Film *Chung Kuo, Cina*', *People's Daily*, 30 January 1974, 2nd edition.
12. Quoted in Rayns, 'Model Citizen', 35.
13. Zhong Chengxiang quoted in Wang Xiaolu, '*The Troubleshooters* and Mi Jiashan', *Economic Observer*, 25 January 2014, http://finance.sina.com.cn/roll/20140125/001018078791.shtml, accessed 9 November 2022.

Chapter Five
1989–2006: A Global Life and Legacy

1. 'Maryn Varbanov Timeline', in *Maryn Varbanov*, ed. Chen Tong and Song Huai-Kuei (Hangzhou: China Academy of Art Press, 2001), 238.
2. Established in 1987, this was a joint venture undertaken by a consortium that included the Tianjin Textile Group, CITIC Group Corporation Ltd., and the Italian GFT Group.
3. Djurdja Bartlett, *FashionEast: The Spectre that Haunted Socialism* (Cambridge, MA: MIT Press, 2010), 231.
4. Svetla Kazalarska, 'Fashioning Fashion in Socialist Bulgaria', *Centre for Advanced Study Sofia Working Paper Series*, no. 6 (2014), 20.
5. See the essay 'Qipao in Paris, Couture in Beijing: Madame Song and Cultural Identity in Fashion' by Tanja Cunz in the present volume, pages 240–247.
6. Meng Xianli, 'Fashion Performance on a Grand Scale: *Five Dynasties* Comes to Macau', *People's Daily*, 17 December 1999, 4.
7. Quoted in 'Local Culture and Imported Culture (Paris Symposium)', *Lion Arts Monthly*, no. 96 (1979), 70.
8. Quoted in Wang Baoju, 'Song Huai-Kuei: A Blossom that Doesn't Wither', *China Foreign Service*, no. 7 (2002), 87.

Qipao in Paris, Couture in Beijing: Madame Song and Cultural Identity in Fashion

1. On the origins and evolution of chinoiserie, see, among others, Dawn Jacobson, *Chinoiserie* (London: Phaidon Press, 1999), and David L. Porter, 'Monstrous Beauty: Eighteenth-Century Fashion and the Aesthetics of the Chinese Taste', *Eighteenth-Century Studies*, vol. 35, no. 3 (Spring 2002), 395–411.
2. Cf. Aurélie Samuel, ed., *Yves Saint Laurent: Dreams of the Orient* (London: Thames & Hudson, 2018); www.valentinogaravanimuseum.com/features/1316/china-through-the-looking-glass and www.valentinogaravanimuseum.com/features/1222/beijing, both accessed 9 June 2022; and 'John Galliano in Conversation with Andrew Bolton', in Andrew Bolton et al., eds, *China: Through the Looking Glass*, exhib. cat. (New Haven, CT/London: Yale University Press, 2015), 230–237.
3. Cf. Gianfranco Ferré, 'Notes: China', www.fondazionegianfrancoferre.com/home/appunti.php?lang=en#4, accessed 9 June 2022.
4. Cf. Richard Morais, *Pierre Cardin: The Man Who Became a Label* (London: Bantam, 1991), 191–196, and Elisabeth Längle, *Pierre Cardin: Fifty Years of Fashion and Design* (New York: Vendome Press, 2005), 28.
5. On (cultural) appropriation in fashion and related discourses, see, among others, *Fashion, Style & Popular Culture*, vol. 4, no. 2 (2017) [special issue: 'Fashion and Appropriation']; Djurdja Bartlett, ed., *Fashion and Politics* (New Haven, CT/London: Yale University Press, 2019); Adam Geczy, *Fashion and Orientalism: Dress, Textiles and Culture from the*

17th to the 21st Century (London: Bloomsbury, 2013); and Barbara Pozzo, 'Fashion between Inspiration and Appropriation', *Laws*, vol. 9, no. 1 (February 2020) [special issue: 'The New Frontiers of Fashion Law'], doi: 10.3390/laws9010005.
6. Cf. Bao Mingxin, 'Shanghai Fashion in the 1930s', in Jo-Anne Birnie Danzker et al., eds, *Shanghai Modern 1919–1945*, exhib. cat. (Ostfildern-Ruit: Hatje Cantz, 2004), 318–330. For a comprehensive overview of the evolution of Chinese fashion and the country's fashion industry, see, among others, Antonia Finnane, *Changing Clothes in China: Fashion, History, Nation* (New York: Columbia University Press, 2008); Wu Juanjuan, *Chinese Fashion: From Mao to Now* (Oxford/New York: Berg, 2009 [from the series *Dress, Body, Culture*]; and Zhao Jianhua, *The Chinese Fashion Industry: An Ethnographic Approach* (London: Bloomsbury, 2013).
7. Cf. Jin Yating, 'A Mechanism of the Chinese Fashion System', *Fashion Theory*, vol. 26, no. 5 (2020), 595–621, doi: 10.1080/1362704X.2020.1736813; Li Xiaoping, 'Fashioning the Body in Post-Mao China', in Anne Brydon and Sandra Niessen, eds, *Consuming Fashion: Adorning the Transnational Body* (Oxford/New York: Berg, 1998), 71–89 [from the series *Dress, Body, Culture*]; Simona Segre Reinach, 'The Identity of Fashion in Contemporary China and the New Relationship with the West', *Fashion Practice*, vol. 4, no. 1 (2012), 57–70; and Christine Tsui, 'From Symbols to Spirit: Changing Conceptions of National Identity in Chinese Fashion', *Fashion Theory*, vol. 17, no. 5 (2013), 597–604.
8. For more on the *Five Dynasties* show, see pages 228–233 of the present volume.
9. Cf. Tsui, 'From Symbols to Spirit', 583, 584–586, and 602; and www.bbc.com/culture/article/20220422-meet-guo-pei-the-worlds-most-fantastical-fashion-designer, accessed 13 June 2022.
10. Cf. Gu Xin and Lu Min, 'Re-negotiating National Identity Through Chinese Fashion', *Fashion Theory*, vol. 25, no. 7 (2021), 901–915. See also Jin, 'A Mechanism of the Chinese Fashion System'; Segre Reinach, 'The Identity of Fashion in Contemporary China'; and Tsui, 'From Symbols to Spirit'.
11. *Ibid*.
12. Cf. Tsui, 'From Symbols to Spirit', 584, and www.tatlerasia.com/style/fashion/hk-huishan-jang-chinese-fashion-designer, accessed 13 June 2022.
13. Cf. Segre Reinach, 'The Identity of Fashion in Contemporary China', and Tsui, 'From Symbols to Spirit'.

1937 1938 1939 1940

CHINA AND THE WORLD

1937	1938	1939	1940
On 7 July, the Second Sino-Japanese War breaks out with the conflict on Marco Polo Bridge.		On 1 September, Germany invades Poland, marking the start of the Second World War in Europe.	

SONG HUAI-KUEI

1937	1938	1939	1940
Song Huai-Kuei is born in Beijing on 7 December.	Song Huai-Kuei leaves Beijing with her mother, Li Jingfang.		Song Huai-Kuei is reunited with her parents in Jiangxi.

PEOPLE AROUND SONG

1937	1938	1939	1940
		Dong Xiwen graduates from the National College of Art (predecessor of the Zhejiang Academy of Fine Arts, now the China Academy of Art) in the summer and goes to study at École des Beaux-Arts de l'Indochine in Hanoi, Vietnam.	

1941

1944

1945

The surrender of Imperial Japan is announced by Emperor Hirohito on 15 August and formally agreed on 2 September. The Second World War ends.

Le Chambre Syndicale de la Haute Couture, the governing board of French couture designers, sets out rigorous rules for any fashion house wishing to produce haute couture. Among other stipulations, a couture house must design made-to-measure pieces for private clients, and present a collection of day and evening wear every fashion season.

1946

During June and July, the second phase of the Chinese Civil War breaks out between the Kuomintang-led government of the Republic of China (ROC) and forces of the Communist Party of China (CPC).

Christian Dior establishes the House of Dior at 30 Avenue Montaigne, Paris. The first *New Look* collection debuts on 12 February 1947 and marks a return to opulence after the Second World War. That same year, Pierre Cardin is appointed as the head of the Dior Studio. He leaves Dior in 1950 to establish his own fashion house.

Zao Wou-Ki graduates from the National College of Art and stays on as a teacher.

Inspired by copies of the Dunhuang murals made by Chang Shuhong, Dong Xiwen joins the National Dunhuang Art Institute (now the Dunhuang Academy), of which Chang is the founding director.

Dong Xiwen starts teaching at the National Beijing Art College, now the Central Academy of Fine Arts (CAFA).

Shen Congwen publishes *A Memory of Beijing*, which recounts the Japanese invasion of Beijing in 1937.

1947

1948

1949

On 12 March, US President Harry S. Truman delivers his State of the Union address to Congress. Later known as the Truman Doctrine, his speech declares the containment of communism on a global scale is at the core of American ideology and foreign policy. Truman's address has a profound impact on the post-war political landscape and marked the beginning of the Cold War.

On 1 October, Mao Zedong formally proclaims the founding of the People's Republic of China (PRC). In December, the ROC government retreats from mainland China to the island of Taiwan, marking the end of the second phase of the Chinese Civil War.

In Bulgaria, Valko Chervenkov (1900–1980) takes power and becomes general secretary of the Central Committee of the Bulgarian Communist Party. The country industrialises rapidly.

Returning to Beijing with her family, Song Huai-Kuei enrols at Peiyuan Elementary School (now Beijing No. 166 High School).

On 26 February, after teaching at the Hangzhou Academy of Fine Arts for five years, Zao Wou-Ki moves to Paris with his wife, Lanlan (Xie Jinglan), and becomes a full-time artist.

T'ang Haywen arrives in Paris and starts taking drawing lessons at the Académie de la Grande Chaumière.

Following criticism from Guo Moruo and others, Shen Congwen declares on 31 December 1948 that he will stop writing. In March 1949, he attempts suicide. Later that year, in August, Shen starts working at the Beijing Museum of History, now the National Museum of China (NMC). He is assigned to the team in charge of giving tours and registering and labelling artefacts. He focuses on historical research, specialising in ancient Chinese costumes.

1950

On 19 April, the Central Committee of the CPC issues the 'Decision on the Commencement of Criticism and Self-Criticism in Newspapers and Publications', beginning the ideological reformation campaign that targets intellectuals. Between March and May, the film *Sorrows of the Forbidden City* (1948) is released in Beijing, Shanghai, and other cities. It is immediately condemned by Mao Zedong for promoting 'treason' owing to its positive depiction of the Qing Emperor.

1951

Song Huai-Kuei begins to study painting at the Working People's Cultural Palace (formerly the Imperial Ancestral Temple) in Beijing.

From 13 November 1951 to 20 February 1952, Shen Congwen travels to southern Sichuan to participate in the land reform movement. This is a key part of the ideological reformation of artists, intellectuals, and cultural figures, directing them to serve the proletariat with their creative work.

1952

Chilean artist José Venturelli arrives in Beijing, becoming the first Latin American artist to visit China since the founding of the PRC. He settles in China with his family and stays for eight years, teaching at CAFA; there, he develops deep friendships with Chinese artists Xu Beihong and Qi Baishi, and the poet Ai Qing. He visits China from time to time after 1960.

1953   1954   1955

CHINA AND THE WORLD

1953

Joseph Stalin, leader of the Soviet Union, dies on 5 March in Moscow. In the years that follow, the socialist countries of Eastern Europe start dismantling the repressive social systems that Stalin and his acolytes had put in place.

1955

From 18 to 24 April, the Asian–African Conference is held in Bandung, Indonesia, to promote economic and cultural exchange within the Third World. The conference aims to foster political alliances between countries outside the Western and Soviet blocs, thereby presenting opportunities for Chinese diplomacy.

On 14 May, the Warsaw Pact is signed in Poland by most of the socialist countries of Eastern Europe. It is a political–military alliance of communist states against the North Atlantic Treaty Organization (NATO) spearheaded by the United States.

In July, the CPC launches the nationwide Campaign to Eradicate Hidden Counter-Revolutionaries, also known as the Sufan Movement.

SONG HUAI-KUEI

1954

In September, Song Huai-Kuei is admitted to CAFA and becomes a student in the oil painting department. Maryn Varbanov is also admitted and majors in silk weaving and pattern design while taking introductory art courses.

PEOPLE AROUND SONG

1953

In 1952, the Central Revolution Museum (now NMC) had commissioned CAFA to create a work marking the founding of the PRC. Dong Xiwen accepted the assignment, producing the oil painting *The Founding of the Nation*. The first version of the work is exhibited in May 1953 at Huairen Hall in Zhongnanhai. Mao Zedong praises the painting for its 'unique national form'. On 27 September, *People's Daily* features the painting prominently on its front page. The People's Art Publishing House also reproduces the work as a New Year painting and as art prints, distributing more than a million copies. *The Founding of the Nation* is included in primary and secondary school textbooks and becomes one of the most popular artworks in the country.

1955

Song Liquan's professional history as a civil servant under the Kuomintang government is investigated during the Campaign to Eradicate Hidden Counter-Revolutionaries.

Pressured by criticism of his attempt to launch a power struggle, Gao Gang, former vice-chair of the Central People's Government, commits suicide in the summer of 1954 and is formally expelled from the CPC in April 1955. Dong Xiwen is ordered to remove Gao from *The Founding of the Nation*, replacing the politician with a pot of flowers.

Varbanov transfers to the newly founded Central Academy of Arts & Design (now the Academy of Arts & Design, Tsinghua University) to continue his studies in dyeing and pattern design under Chai Fei.

1956

1957

1958

The CPC launches the Great Leap Forward, a primarily economic and social campaign from 1958 to 1962 that has a tremendous impact on art and literary circles in China. The Great Leap Forward leads to the Great Chinese Famine from 1959 to 1961, resulting in a large number of deaths and greatly affecting China's literary and art circles.

To obtain a licence for her marriage to Maryn Varbanov, Song Huai-Kuei writes to Zhou Enlai, premier of the PRC, asking for his endorsement. The couple officially register their marriage on 26 November, with their marriage certificate issued by the Bulgarian Embassy in China. Jiang Feng, the interim director of CAFA, officiates the wedding ceremony. This is the first international marriage since the founding of the PRC.

In July, Song Huai-Kuei's daughter, Boryana, is born. Song and Varbanov move to A2 Dayabao hutong, where many renowned Chinese artists live.

In November, the Varbanov family moves to Sofia, Bulgaria. Song Huai-Kuei continues to study oil painting at the National Academy of Art under Ilya Petrov.

Shen Congwen is invited to become a guest lecturer at the Central Academy of Arts & Design. There, he gives a lecture on the history of Chinese patterns, discussing the formation and development of decorative styles across dynasties.

David Alfaro Siqueiros visits China and presents a slideshow at CAFA introducing works by fellow Mexican muralists, including José Clemente Orozco and Diego Rivera. In the same period, *Exhibition of Oil Painting and Printmaking* by the Mexican National Front of Plastic Arts is held at the Working People's Cultural Palace, where Siqueiros's *Our Present Image* (1947) is shown.

Maryn Varbanov visits Jean Lurçat's exhibition at CAFA and is inspired by the French artist's tapestry works. He decides to dedicate himself to tapestry art and starts researching traditional *kesi* weaving techniques in China.

In July, Jiang Feng, the interim director of CAFA who presided over the wedding of Song Huai-Kuei and Varbanov, is labelled a rightist and removed from his post. Yuan Yunsheng, Song's classmate, is also labelled a rightist. Both are sent to Shuangqiao Farm in Beijing (Jiang in 1958, Yuan in 1960) to undergo reform through labour. They become roommates during their time there.

In early 1958, Dong Xiwen creates the propaganda image *Diligence and Frugality in Housekeeping* with Song as his model. He had been penalised by the CPC during the Anti-Rightist Campaign.

In June, Maryn Varbanov graduates from the Central Academy of Arts & Design.

	1959	**1960**	**1961**	**1962**
CHINA AND THE WORLD			On 13 August, construction of the Berlin Wall begins amid fierce Cold War conflict between the American and Soviet camps.	
SONG HUAI-KUEI		Song Huai-Kuei and her family return to Beijing briefly so that Maryn Varbanov can research art tapestry education in China.		In March, Song Huai-Kuei finishes her study at the National Academy of Art in Sofia. In July, Song's son, Phénix, is born. In October, the Bulgarian film *The Sun and the Shadow* is released. Song plays an East Asian dancer from a troupe of vagrant artists.
PEOPLE AROUND SONG	The Malchika Textile Factory in Sofia employs Maryn Varbanov as lead designer. In the same year, he holds his first solo exhibition, also in Sofia. Pierre Cardin launches his first ready-to-wear collection, a pioneering move that leads to his temporary expulsion from the Chambre Syndicale de la Haute Couture. Cardin is later reinstated but leaves on his own accord in 1966.	In April, Shen Congwen writes a letter to his elder brother, revealing his plan to compile a history of ancient Chinese costumes.	Maryn Varbanov resigns from the Malchika Textile Factory and is appointed as a lecturer at the National Academy of Art in Sofia. There, he submits a written proposal to establish a textiles department.	In Switzerland, Jean Lurçat co-founds the Lausanne International Tapestry Biennial with Pierre Pauli. Varbanov is promoted to assistant professor at the National Academy of Art in Sofia.

1963

In December, with the approval of Zhou Enlai, the National Museum of Chinese History (now NMC) starts preparing for the publication of *A Study of Ancient Chinese Costumes*. Shen Congwen is appointed as chief editor.

1964

Song Huai-Kuei starts working at the Centre for New Goods and Fashion (CNGF) in Bulgaria.

In September, Shen Congwen completes the first draft of *A Study of Ancient Chinese Costumes*. However, with political turmoil looming on the horizon, the publication cannot be released ahead of National Day and is further delayed.

1966

Mao Zedong launches the Cultural Revolution in China. The revolution lasts for ten years.

1968

The Prague Spring, a movement to democratise the Czechoslovak Socialist Republic, starts on 5 January and is crushed in August by the armed invasion of the Soviet Union and other Warsaw Pact members.

Song Huai-Kuei and Maryn Varbanov meet Jean Beaulieu, cultural attaché at the French Embassy in Bulgaria, and his wife, Dolores Ling.

In Sofia, Song and Varbanov meet Georges Heckly, president of the gallery Art-Dialogue, who later becomes the major collector of their work.

	1969	**1970**	**1971**	**1972**
CHINA AND THE WORLD			On 13 September, Lin Biao, vice-chair of the CPC and Mao Zedong's designated successor, dies with his family in a plane crash in Outer Mongolia. The incident casts doubt on the unity of CPC leadership under Mao.	US President Richard Nixon visits Beijing, Hangzhou, and Shanghai from 21 to 28 February at the invitation of Zhou Enlai, the then premier of the PRC. The visit is widely regarded as an important step in the normalisation of diplomatic relations between China and the United States during the Cold War.
SONG HUAI-KUEI	In August, the Bulgarian television series *Every Kilometre* (1969–1971) is released. Song Huai-Kuei plays a Japanese woman in one of the episodes.	Song Huai-Kuei is promoted to full-time fashion designer at CNGF.	Song Huai-Kuei and Maryn Varbanov participate in the 5th Lausanne International Tapestry Biennial with their collaborative work *Composition 2001*.	Song Huai-Kuei starts to plan and produce *Dream of Zhuangzi* (or *Butterfly*), the major tapestry series of her career as an artist.
PEOPLE AROUND SONG	Dong Xiwen is sent to the Beijing Steel Factory to undergo labour reform. In the winter, Shen Congwen is sent to a rural area in Hubei province to undergo labour reform.	T'ang Haywen visits Sofia. Song shows him around the city with Varbonov and friends.	As Liu Shaoqi, former president of the PRC, is overthrown at the beginning of the Cultural Revolution, Dong Xiwen is ordered to remove Liu from *The Founding of the Nation* and replace him with Dong Biwu. Despite being severely ill with cancer, Dong Xiwen executes the revision himself.	Lyudmila Todorova Zhivkova joins the Committee for Arts and Culture in Bulgaria as assistant president. Over time, she becomes the de facto leader of Bulgarian cultural and artistic affairs. In 1975, she becomes the president of the committee but passes away six years later, in 1981. During her time in office, she actively promoted a relatively liberal arts and cultural policy while preserving indigenous Bulgarian culture. Shen Congwen makes a request to go back to Beijing to complete *A Study of Ancient Chinese Costumes*. He manages to return on 4 February, and in May the following year finishes a 240,000-word draft of the treatise.

1972

In 1972, Italian director and communist Michelangelo Antonioni is invited by Zhou Enlai to visit China during the Cultural Revolution. Antonioni makes the documentary *Chung Kuo, Cina*. The film is later criticised for being 'anti-Chinese' and 'anti-communist', and its release in China is banned.

Dong Xiwen receives a third order to update *The Founding of the Nation*. This time, it is to remove Lin Boqu, former member of the Central Committee of the CPC. Since Dong is too ill to revise the painting himself, his student Jin Shangyi and artist Zhao Yu create a copy of the original and make changes to the replica.

Zao Wou-Ki returns to China to visit his family for the first time since moving to Paris twenty-four years earlier.

1973

At the beginning of the Cultural Revolution, Deng Xiaoping was forced to retire from all his positions. He and his family were sent to Jiangxi to work as regular workers. In February 1973, with the support of Zhou Enlai, Deng returns to Beijing and resumes his duties as vice-premier of the State Council.

On 21 February, Song Huai-Kuei is accepted as a member of the Union of Bulgarian Artists.

Song and Varbanov participate in the 6th Lausanne International Tapestry Biennial with their collaborative work *Aporia* (1972).

On 8 January, Dong Xiwen dies.

1974

In June, Song Huai-Kuei and Maryn Varbanov travel to Paris for Varbanov's solo show at the Bulgarian Embassy. They also participate in a group exhibition with Bulgarian artist Letchko Ochavkov at Galerie Etienne de Causans. Song exhibits three works from her *Dream of Zhuangzi* series.

In September, Song returns to Beijing with her children upon the invitation of the Chinese government. She meets Zao Wou-Ki during her journey.

Song and Varbanov receive an official invitation to become resident artists at the Cité Internationale des Arts in Paris.

With Lyudmila Todorova Zhivkova's support, Varbanov holds his first retrospective at the Union of Bulgarian Artists in Sofia, which also tours to the Bulgarian Embassy in France the same year.

I. M. Pei visits China as part of a delegation from the American Institute of Architects.

	1975	**1976**	**1977**	**1978**
CHINA AND THE WORLD		On 9 September, Mao Zedong dies in Beijing. The Gang of Four, a Maoist faction that rose to power during the Cultural Revolution, disbands. The Cultural Revolution ends.		Universities in China resume admissions. Many students who were unable to receive higher education during the Cultural Revolution enrol. From 18 to 22 December, the Third Plenary Session of the 11th Central Committee of the CPC launches the economic reform policy backed by Deng Xiaoping, now restored to power.
SONG HUAI-KUEI	On 1 April, Song Huai-Kuei and Maryn Varbanov receive a letter from Luydmila Todorova Zhivkova approving their residency at the Cité Internationale des Arts for two years to research tapestry art. The family settles down in Paris the following year. Their residency is later extended until the early 1980s. Song participates in an international exhibition at Jacques Baruch Gallery in Chicago.			
PEOPLE AROUND SONG		Maryn Varbanov participates in a tapestry exhibition at Musée Ingres in Montauban, France, staged by Galerie La Demeure.	Maryn Varbanov is introduced to art dealer Hervé Odermatt by Bulgarian art historian and critic Dora Vallier. He is subsequently represented by Galerie Hervé Odermatt in Paris. Despite having never been to China, Yves Saint Laurent creates his famous *Les Chinoises* Haute Couture Autumn/ Winter 1977 collection and the perfume 'Opium'.	Supported by the French Ministry of Culture, Maryn Varbanov's solo exhibition *Varbanov Tapisseries* opens at Galerie Hervé Odermatt on 26 October and runs until 30 November. Dora Vallier writes the preface to the exhibition catalogue. Dolores Ling travels to Paris from Chicago with her husband, Jean Beaulieu. In the winter, Pierre Cardin receives an official invitation to visit China with a group of European journalists. I. M. Pei visits China for a second time and gives a speech on planning and architecture. The Chinese government invites him to start an architectural project in Beijing, and he returns in late 1978. He decides to build a hotel on Fragrant Hill after a site visit.

1979

On 4 May, Margaret Thatcher becomes the first female prime minister of the United Kingdom. In the 1980s, her policies will shift Britain towards neoliberalism.

On 15 July, the Central Committee of the CPC and the State Council decide to set up special economic zones in Shenzhen, Zhuhai, Shantou, and Xiamen on a trial basis.

In January, with the help of several assistants, the manuscript and illustrations for Shen Congwen's *A Study of Ancient Chinese Costumes* are completed.

Pierre Cardin is invited by the Chinese government to return to Beijing and stage a fashion show at the Cultural Palace of Nationalities featuring more than two hundred of his garments. Only officials from the Ministry of Foreign Trade and the textile industry are allowed entry. Among the participating models is Wang Guihua, who will later become one of China's first celebrity models.

Maryn Varbanov is commissioned to create an enormous public artwork, *1300 Years of Bulgaria*, at the National Palace of Culture in Sofia.

On 26 September, at Beijing Capital International Airport, a group of murals by different artists is revealed to the public. Two female nudes in Yuan Yunsheng's *Water-Splashing Festival: Ode to Life* become widely controversial.

Amid calls by Deng Xiaoping's administration to correct the fallacies of the Cultural Revolution and reinstate social order, the National Museum of Chinese Revolution and History (now NMC) decides to restore *The Founding of the Nation* to its original form. Dong Xiwen's family opposes any further adjustments being made to the original work, so young artists Yan Zhenduo and Ye Wulin are commissioned to make changes to the 1972 replica.

1980

In April, Foreign Trade Publishing House launches the quarterly *Fashion*, China's first fashion magazine after the Cultural Revolution. Distributed in China and overseas, *Fashion* includes the latest trends in both China and abroad, as well as international industry news.

In October, Galerie Hervé Odermatt shows Maryn Varbanov's work at the annual Foire Internationale d'Art Contemporain (FIAC) at the Grand Palais, Paris. Pierre Cardin acquires six works by Varbanov, meeting Song Huai-Kuei and Varbanov in the process.

In December, Varbanov's solo exhibition opens at Espace Pierre Cardin in New York, the fashion designer's new arts venue.

1981

1982

1983

CHINA AND THE WORLD

In January, the Ministry of Public Security and the Ministry of Culture draft a document entitled 'On the Spirit of Banning Commercial Dancing and Discouraging Social Dancing', which deters dance parties in private establishments.

On 8 February, Hu Yaobang, the then general secretary of the CPC, visits the Shenzhen Special Economic Zone and encourages party cadres to wear Western suits.

From March to December, the CPC implements the Anti-Spiritual Pollution Campaign to diminish the popularity of bourgeois lifestyle and culture.

In September, with the support of Deng Xiaoping, the 'Strike Hard Against Crime' campaign, commonly known as the 1983 Strict Crackdown, is launched in China and lasts for three years.

SONG HUAI-KUEI

In March, Song Huai-Kuei returns to Beijing. She is appointed by Pierre Cardin as the brand's chief representative in China.

Song makes a brief visit to Paris before returning to Beijing on 21 November to assist Pierre Cardin with the opening of his new showroom and latest fashion show. The showroom is in the Palace of Abstinence at the Temple of Heaven, while the fashion show is to be held at the Beijing Hotel. The latter, for which Song employs the first group of Chinese models, marks the country's first high-profile fashion show and underscores the opening-up of the country.

On 13 December, Pierre Cardin and Beijing Tourism Group sign a contract in Paris to establish the first Maxim's restaurant in China. Song Huai-Kuei is appointed manager of the restaurant.

Early in the year, Song Huai-Kuei is reunited with Boryana, who comes to help her with the establishment of Maxim's in Beijing.

On 26 September, Maxim's opens after nine months of construction.

In September, Song helps to organise the first Pierre Cardin International Products Fair at the Cultural Palace of Nationalities in Beijing. She is assisted by the Beijing branch of the China National Textiles Import and Export Corporation and the Beijing Fashion Manufacturing Corporation.

PEOPLE AROUND SONG

In May, Pierre Cardin takes ownership of Maxim's de Paris.

In September, *A Study of Ancient Chinese Costumes* is published by the Hong Kong branch of Commercial Press. The book contains 700 illustrations and 250,000 words.

Fragrant Hill Hotel opens. On display in the lobby are ink paintings by Zao Wou-Ki specially commissioned by I. M. Pei.

Li Han-hsiang begins shooting *The Burning of Imperial Palace* and *Reign behind a Curtain*—the first two films of his *Qing Palace Trilogy*—in Beijing.

Jerry Zhang graduates from the Beijing Institute of Fashion Technology and is assigned to work at the Beijing Textile Bureau. Inspired by the Pierre Cardin fashion show during the brand's International Products Fair at the Cultural Palace of Nationalities in Beijing, Zhang starts putting together a fashion show unit at the bureau.

Artist Xiao Feng, the husband of Song Ren, one of Song Huai-Kuei's classmates at CAFA, is appointed director of the Zhejiang Academy of Fine Arts (ZAFA).

In November, David Tang Wing-cheung holds his wedding reception at Maxim's Beijing.

1984

In October, many avant-garde, abstract, and non-realist artworks are considered 'spiritual pollution' and rejected by the *Sixth National Fine Art Exhibition*. This eventually gives rise to the '85 New Wave art movement.

On 19 December, the Sino-British Joint Declaration is signed between Zhao Ziyang, the premier of the PRC, and British Prime Minister Margaret Thatcher. Under the principle of 'one country, two systems', the UK will hand Hong Kong over to China on 1 July 1997.

At a cocktail party at Maxim's, Pierre Cardin and Song Huai-Kuei propose to Yang Bo, minister of light industry, that Chinese models should be allowed to participate in Pierre Cardin's fashion show during Paris Haute Couture Week.

In July, Song assists Cardin with the opening of Minim's in Beijing, a restaurant selling upmarket fast food.

In October, Jiang Zemin, at that time the minister of industry and electronics, takes part in the celebrations marking the first anniversary of Maxim's in Beijing.

Maryn Varbanov attends the ceremony marking the collaboration between Cité Internationale des Arts in Paris and ZAFA in Hangzhou. There he meets artists Cai Liang and Xiao Feng.

Bernardo Bertolucci visits China for the first time, bringing two film proposals: an adaptation of Georges André Malraux's *Man's Fate*, and *The Last Emperor*, based on the life of Aisin-Gioro Puyi. The Chinese government chooses the latter.

1985

In July, after receiving approval from Yang Bo, Song Huai-Kuei brings eight Chinese models to France for the 1985 Autumn/Winter Pierre Cardin show, marking the first appearance of Chinese models during Paris Haute Couture Week.

In May, Zao Wou-Ki holds a month-long painting workshop at his alma mater, ZAFA. The workshop is attended by twenty-seven 'progressive teachers and students' from nine art schools across China.

In May, Yves Saint Laurent visits Beijing. A retrospective exhibition exploring his twenty-five-year career as a fashion designer is held at the National Art Museum of China (NAMOC) from 7 May to 10 July.

Exhibition by Beijing Artistic Tapestry Center, organised by Maryn Varbanov and featuring work by Han Meilun, Mu Guang, and Zhao Bowei, opens at NAMOC in November. The curator is Hou Hanru, an MA student from CAFA. *Rauschenberg Overseas Culture Interchange* (*ROCI*) is shown concurrently at the same venue.

1986

Dissatisfied with the Chinese government's lack of political reform, students organise demonstrations in such areas as Anhui, Hubei, and Shanghai from December 1986 to mid-January 1987. Known as the 1986 Chinese student demonstrations, the protests cause Hu Yaobang to resign from his position of general secretary of the CPC under pressure from conservative party leaders. He is succeeded by Zhao Ziyang.

Song Huai-Kuei stars as Empress Dowager Longyu in *The Last Emperor* and meets John Lone, who plays Puyi.

With the financial support of Georges Heckly, Song and Varbanov become sponsors of a studio at Cité Internationale des Arts and place it under the management of ZAFA.

On 9 May, rock singer Cui Jian performs 'Nothing to My Name' for the first time at the 100-Singer Concert of Year of International Peace at Beijing Workers' Stadium.

In September, Varbanov establishes and becomes director of the Institute of Art Tapestry Varbanov (IATV) at ZAFA.

1987

1988

1989

CHINA AND THE WORLD

In direct response to the 1986 Chinese student demonstrations, conservatives in the CPC launch the Anti-Bourgeois Liberalisation campaign in early 1987 with Deng Xiaoping's support. The movement to criticise and oppose capitalism gradually ends in mid-1987.

In February, the Polish Solidarity union is legitimised in an election, leading the coalition government towards a democratic transition and marking the beginning of dramatic changes in Eastern Europe. The socialist countries of Eastern and Central Europe see rapid political change as more communist regimes are overthrown.

On 15 April, Hu Yaobang dies in Beijing. A large student-led protest against corruption breaks out, with students occupying Tiananmen Square for several weeks. In the early hours of 4 June, troops from the People's Liberation Army enter the city to drive out protesters,

SONG HUAI-KUEI

The IATV organises the *Contemporary China Tapestry Exhibition* at the Shanghai Exhibition Centre. Jiang Zemin, at that time mayor of Shanghai, attends the opening ceremony accompanied by Song Huai-Kuei and Varbanov.

In Hangzhou, Song attends the celebration marking the first anniversary of the IATV.

Song facilitates Christian Dior's sponsorship of make-up products used in the film *The Troubleshooters*, directed by Mi Jiashan.

Song helps Pierre Cardin secure a licensing deal with Jin Tak Garment Company Ltd in Tianjin. The company becomes the first in China to manufacture and sell Pierre Cardin's menswear.

Through Song Huai-Kuei, Pierre Cardin is invited to design the uniforms for Air China's flight attendants.

In October, *New Direction in Contemporary Chinese Tapestry* opens at Pao Gallery, Hong Kong Arts Centre. Song's *Pink Perception* is among the artworks on show.

Maxim's is forced to close its doors from the summer until November because Beijing is under martial law. During that time, Song Huai-Kuei focuses on taking care of Varbanov, who is seriously ill. He dies in Beijing on 10 July.

PEOPLE AROUND SONG

On 14 January, Cui Jian performs a cover version of the revolutionary classic 'Nanniwan' at Beijing's Capital Indoor Stadium, which leads to Cui's music being banned.

On 11 April, *The Last Emperor* wins nine awards at the 60th Academy Awards ceremony, including Best Director and Best Picture, making it the biggest winner of the night.

In June, three works by IATV artists Gu Wenda, Liang Shaoji, and Shi Hui and Zhu Wei are selected for the 13th Lausanne International Tapestry Biennial.

On 10 May, Shen Congwen dies in Beijing.

On 17 September, José Venturelli dies in Beijing.

The Troubleshooters, directed by Mi Jiashan, is released. The film receives multiple nominations at the 1989 China Golden Rooster Awards.

On 10 October, *Red Sorghum*, directed by Zhang Yimou, is released. The film wins multiple domestic and international film awards and nominations.

The first Chinese issue of French magazine *Elle* is published. It is the first international fashion magazine to enter the Chinese market.

On 5 February, *China/Avant-Garde* opens at the National Art Museum of China. It is the first contemporary art exhibition organised by artists and critics at a national art institution in China, and features a total of 186 artists. About two hours into the opening, the exhibition is suspended as artist Xiao Lu fires a gun at her own work *Dialogue*, an installation consisting of two telephone booths, as part of a performance. The exhibition reopens five days later but closes again soon after. Among the artists included in the exhibition are two of Varbanov's students, Gu Wenda and Liang Shaoji.

1989

resulting in injuries and fatalities among students, protesters, and soldiers. This event becomes known as the Tiananmen Incident or the June Fourth Incident.

From 23 to 24 June, the Central Committee of the CPC decides to dismiss Zhao Ziyang's administrative duties, while Jiang Zemin is elected general secretary of the Central Committee.

Jerry Zhang founds the state-run China Fashion Show Group and becomes its director. In October, Zhang organises the inaugural Best Fashion Models Competition of China in Guangzhou, with Ye Jihong winning the title. The competition is the predecessor of the New Silk Road Model Contest.

1990

From 22 September to 7 October, Beijing hosts the 11th Asian Games.

Shanghai and Shenzhen set up stock exchanges as part of a trial to reform the shareholding system.

In September, during the Asian Games, Song Huai-Kuei organises five Pierre Cardin fashion shows, one of which takes place at the Imperial Ancestral Temple. The show features more than two hundred garments designed by Cardin and shipped over from France. Other shows are held at such venues as the Beijing Exhibition Center and the Capital Hotel in Tianjin.

In April, *Ju Dou*, directed by Zhang Yimou, is released.

1991

On 25 December, Mikhail Gorbachev resigns from his position as president of the USSR. The following day, the Soviet Union is formally dissolved, marking the end of the Cold War.

In March, Song Huai-Kuei oversees the production of Varbanov's unfinished work *Harmony*. With sponsorship from Amway International in Hong Kong, she installs the gigantic tapestry work on the wall of the Hong Kong Cultural Centre in Tsim Sha Tsui as a tribute to her late husband.

In October, Song helps to judge the Supermodel Competition of the World China Division & the 2nd Best Fashion Models Competition of China, asking Loletta Chu and Ellen Liu to join her. Chen Juanhong wins first place.

Song and Pierre Cardin set up Paris Maxim's Clothing (China) Co. Ltd with David Edison Company from Hong Kong and Zhukuan Group from Zhuhai to showcase Cardin's Maxim's line in the mainland Chinese market.

On 8 September, David Tang Wing-cheung opens China Club in the old Bank of China building in Central, Hong Kong.

On 9 September, T'ang Haywen dies in Paris.

On 10 September, *Raise the Red Lantern*, directed by Zhang Yimou, is released.

	1992	**1993**	**1994**	**1996**
CHINA AND THE WORLD	From 18 January to 21 February, Deng Xiaoping tours Shenzhen, Zhuhai, Guangzhou, and Shanghai in southern China and gives speeches to reiterate the necessity of China's opening-up policy, further providing political legitimacy for the country's economic reform.	On 24 September, the International Olympic Committee (IOC) announces that Sydney has been awarded the right to host the 27th Olympic Games in 2000, leaving China's first bid for the games unsuccessful.		
SONG HUAI-KUEI	Song Huai-Kuei and Jerry Zhang accompany Chen Juanhong to Los Angeles where Chen participates in the twelfth Supermodel of the World competition. The second Maxim's in Beijing opens at China World Trade Center.	During the first Chinese International Clothing and Accessories Fair (CHIC), Song Huai-Kuei is received by President Jiang Zemin at Zhongnanhai with European fashion designers Pierre Cardin, Gianfranco Ferré, and Valentino. Song starts planning and designing the concept and costumes for the *Five Dynasties* show.		Song Huai-Kuei invites costume designer Shi Yanqin, who is working at the China National Garment Research and Design Center, to co-design the costumes for the *Five Dynasties* show.
PEOPLE AROUND SONG	The China Fashion Show Group is renamed New Silk Road Model Inc.	Arranged by governmental organisations and state-owned enterprises, CHIC takes place at China World Trade Center in Beijing. In May, the Brother Cup Chinese International Young Fashion Designers Contest is founded and sponsored by Japan's Brother Industries Ltd. Wu Haiyan is awarded first prize with a collection inspired by the Dunhuang Grottoes. On 10 September, *Farewell My Concubine*, directed by Chen Kaige, is released. The film receives national and international film awards and nominations, including the Palme d'Or at the Cannes Film Festival.	David Tang Wing-cheung founds luxury Hong Kong fashion house Shanghai Tang. A year later, he opens China Club at Sichuan Restaurant, a Qing Dynasty courtyard house not far from Maxim's Beijing. Ma Ke wins the golden medal at the second edition of the Brother Cup Chinese International Young Fashion Designers Contest with a collection inspired by the Terracotta Warriors.	Zhang Yimou receives an invitation from Florentine Opera in Italy to direct the 70th-anniversary performance of Puccini's *Turandot*. Ma Ke co-founds the label EXCEPTION de Mixmind with Mao Jihong and becomes its design director.

1997

On 19 February, Deng Xiaoping dies in Beijing.

On 1 July, Hong Kong is formally handed over from Britain to China.

Song Huai-Kuei's *Five Dynasties* show is launched at fashion festivals in Dalian and Ningbo.

1998

China prepares its bid to host the 2008 Summer Olympics in Beijing, its second attempt at hosting the Olympic Games. The promotional slogan is 'New Beijing, New Olympics'.

A branch of Maxim's opens in the new Shanghai Grand Theatre. Song Huai-Kuei oversees the management of the branch.

Jerry Zhang and Chen Juanhong co-found the Galaxy Model Management Company.

From 5 to 13 September, *Turandot* is staged at the Working People's Cultural Palace in Beijing.

1999

On 20 December, Macau is formally handed over from Portugal to China.

On 14 December, the first *Five Dynasties* show to be staged outside mainland China takes place at Senado Square in Macau to celebrate the handover of the city.

Dolores Ling dies in Paris.

2000

Five Dynasties is staged in Sydney, Australia, as part of the Overseas Chinese Cultural Festival.

On 31 August, the promotional video for Beijing's Olympic bid, directed by Zhang Yimou, is released.

CHINA AND THE WORLD

2001

On 13 July, the IOC announces that Beijing will host the 2008 Summer Olympics.

On 11 December, China joins the World Trade Organization, signalling the entry of the country's workforce of hundreds of millions of people into the global economic system. China's low labour costs and stable internal environment make it a key player in the world economy.

SONG HUAI-KUEI

2001

A catalogue of Maryn Varbanov's work is published in his memory, with Song Huai-Kuei as one of the editors.

2002

Five Dynasties is staged in São Paulo, Brazil, as part of the Chinese Cultural Festival.

2003

Five Dynasties is staged in Bangkok, Thailand, from 1 to 7 February. Two of the shows are arranged especially for the Thai royal family.

In September, Song Huai-Kuei compiles and publishes *The Golden Times of Maxim's China*, a record of the celebrities who had frequented the restaurant in the twenty years since its opening.

On 24 October, Song Huai-Kuei wins the Lycra In Style Achievement Award.

2004

Five Dynasties is staged in Paris as part of L'Année de la Chine en France (the Sino-French Culture Year).

PEOPLE AROUND SONG

2001

In October, *Peony Pavilion*, directed by Yonfan, is released.

2002

After a weeks-long trip to Asia, John Galliano designs his Haute Couture Spring/Summer 2003 collection for Dior. It is partially inspired by his meeting with Song Huai-Kuei, who looked after Galliano and his colleagues during their time in China.

From 8 to 24 August, the 29th Olympic Games is held in Beijing.

Song Huai-Kuei is diagnosed with cancer.

On 21 March, Song Huai-Kuei dies in Beijing.

Ma Ke founds the label and studio WUYONG and becomes its design director.

In February, *WUYONG/The Earth* is presented at Paris Fashion Week. Ma Ke's innovative incorporation of traditional Chinese craftsmanship and leftover or recycled fabrics gains much acclaim within art and fashion circles. A year and a half later, Ma returns to Paris with her new collection *Luxurious Qing Pin*, making her the first Chinese designer to show at Paris Haute Couture Week.

Biographies

A

ANTONIONI, Michelangelo
1912–2007
born Italy
Film director. Directed the documentary *Chung Kuo, Cina* (1972).

B

BEAULIEU, Jean
Husband of Dolores Ling and cultural attaché at the French Embassy in Sofia. Met Song Huai-Kuei and Maryn Varbanov in 1968 at Bulgaria's *National Decorative Arts Exhibition*, in which Varbanov won first prize. Impressed by his work, Beaulieu organised Varbanov's first visit to France in 1970.

BERTOLUCCI, Bernardo
1941–2018
born Italy
Film director and screenwriter. Directed *The Last Emperor* (1987), which won nine awards at the 60th Academy Awards held in April 1988, including Best Picture and Best Director.

BUIĆ, Jagoda
born 1930, Yugoslavia (now Croatia)
Artist best known for monumental fibre-art installations and tapestries. Head of the tapestry studio at Cité Internationale des Arts in Paris when Song Huai-Kuei and Maryn Varbanov started their residency there in 1975.

C

CAI Liang
1932–1995
born Fujian
Artist and art educator. Began tenure as professor at Zhejiang Academy of Fine Arts (now China Academy of Art) in 1981. Visited Cité Internationale des Arts in Paris in 1984 with Xiao Feng. There, they met Maryn Varbanov and discussed artistic exchange between China and France.

CARDIN, Pierre
1922–2020
born Italy
Fashion designer. Met Song Huai-Kuei in 1980 and recruited her as his chief representative in China. He was the first Westerner of his profession to enter the Chinese market after the Cultural Revolution.

CHAI Fei
1903–1972
born Zhejiang
Maryn Varbanov's professor at Central Academy of Arts & Design in Beijing, where he taught textile design, dyeing, and weaving.

CHAN, Jackie
born 1954, Hong Kong
Actor, fight choreographer, singer, director, screenwriter, and film producer. Participated in activities of the China Tai Chi Kung Fu Troupe established by Song Huai-Kuei.

CHEN Juanhong
born 1969, Zhejiang
Model. Winner of the Supermodel Competition of the World China Division & the 2nd Best Fashion Models Competition of China, October 1991.

CHEN Kaige
born 1952, Beijing
Director. Awarded the Palme d'Or at the 1993 Cannes Film Festival for *Farewell My Concubine*.

CHEUNG Kwok-wing, Leslie
1956–2003
born Hong Kong
Actor, singer, and songwriter. Frequent patron of Maxim's and good friend of Song Huai-Kuei.

CHIANG Ching-kuo
1910–1988
born Zhejiang
Politician and eldest son of Chiang Kai-shek, former president of the Republic of China (ROC). As his father's successor, he served as the president of the ROC from 1978 to 1988. During the Second Sino-Japanese War, Chiang was appointed commissioner of Gannan, Jiangxi province. Song Liquan, Song Huai-Kuei's father, also worked for the Nationalist government in Jiangxi.

CHRISTO AND JEANNE-CLAUDE
Christo Vladimirov Javacheff
1935–2020
born Bulgaria
Jeanne-Claude Denat de Guillebon
1935–2009
born Morocco
Artist duo known for their large-scale, site-specific environmental installations. Met Song Huai-Kuei and Maryn Varbanov at the latter's solo exhibition at Espace Cardin in New York through Anani, Christo's brother, and his wife.

CHU, Loletta
born 1958, Burma (now Myanmar)
Actress and model. Jury member of the Supermodel Competition of the World China Division & the 2nd Best Fashion Models Competition of China, October 1991.

CORNUCHÉ, Eugène
1867–1926
born France
The second owner of Maxim's de Paris.
Renovated the restaurant in the style
of Art Nouveau.

CRESSON, Édith
born 1934, France
Former French prime minister (1991–1992).
Visited Maxim's during her visit to China
in 1985.

CUI Jian
born 1961, Beijing
The father of rock music in mainland
China. Performed at Maxim's on several
occasions in mid- to late 1980s.

D

DELON, Alain
born 1935, France
Actor and close friend of Song Huai-Kuei.
Held a press conference for his fiftieth
birthday at Maxim Beijing's in 1985.

DENG Lin
born 1941, Hebei
Ink artist. Daughter of Deng Xiaoping
and an alumnus, like Song Huai-Kuei,
of Central Academy of Fine Arts.

DES LYONS DE FEUCHIN, Humbert
born in France
The first French manager of Maxim's
in Beijing.

DONG Xiwen
1914–1973
born Zhejiang
Artist and art educator. Song Huai-Kuei's
professor at Central Academy of Fine Arts.

DUNN Siu-Yue, Peter
born 1951, Hong Kong
Co-founder and editor of *City Magazine*.
Friend of Song Huai-Kuei.

F

FANG Fang
born 1969, Beijing
Song Huai-Kuei's assistant in the
1990s. Pierre Cardin's current chief
representative in China.

FERRÉ, Gianfranco
1944–2007
born Italy
Fashion designer. Ferré was received
with Song Huai-Kuei, Pierre Cardin,
and Valentino by Jiang Zemin, former
president of the People's Republic of
China, in Zhongnanhai, Beijing, 1993.

FORD, Eileen
1922–2014
born New York, United States
American modelling-agency executive
and co-founder of Ford Modeling
Agency (now known as Ford Models)
in 1946. Ford Models co-organised the
Supermodel Competition of the World
China Division & the 2nd Best Fashion
Models Competition of China in 1991,
at which Song Huai-Kuei served as
a jury member.

G

GALLIANO, John
born 1960, Gibraltar
Gibraltarian-Spanish fashion designer.
Song Huai-Kuei accompanied Galliano
and his team on parts of their 2002 trip
to Asia. He and his team also visited
Maxim's in Beijing.

**GARAVANI, Valentino Clemente
Ludovico**
born 1932, Italy
Fashion designer, usually known as
Valentino. Together with Song Huai-Kuei,
Pierre Cardin, and Gianfranco Ferré,
he was received by Jiang Zemin, former
president of the People's Republic of
China, in Zhongnanhai, Beijing, 1993.

GASPARD, Maryse
born 1947, France
Model and director of haute couture
for Pierre Cardin.

GONG Li
born 1965, Shenyang
Actress. A frequent guest at Maxim's in
Beijing and Song Huai-Kuei's close friend.

GU Wenda
born 1955, Shanghai
Artist. Student of Maryn Varbanov at
the Institute of Art Tapestry Varbanov,
Zhejiang Academy of Fine Arts (now
China Academy of Art).

H

HAN Meilun
born 1957, Beijing
Artist. Participated in the *Exhibition by
Beijing Artistic Tapestry Center* organised
by Maryn Varbanov at the National Art
Museum of China in 1985.

HECKLY, Georges
Art collector. President of Art-Dialogue
gallery in Paris. Major collector of Song
Huai-Kuei and Maryn Varbanov's works.

HOU Hanru
born 1963, Guangdong
Curator and art critic. Curated the
*Exhibition by Beijing Artistic Tapestry
Center* at the National Art Museum of
China organised by Maryn Varbanov
in 1985.

HU Yaobang
1915–1989
born Hunan
Politician and senior member of the Communist Party of China, in which he served as chairman (1981–1982) and then general secretary (1982–1987).

HUANG Yongyu
born 1924, Hunan
Artist and art educator. Song Huai-Kuei and Maryn Varbanov's neighbour when they were living in Dayabao hutong and the family's lifelong friend.

J

JIANG Feng
1910–1983
born Shanghai
Artist and art educator. While interim director of the Central Academy of Fine Arts, Jiang officiated Song Huai-Kuei and Maryn Varbanov's wedding ceremony in 1956.

JIANG Wen
born 1963, Hebei
Actor and film director. A frequent guest at Maxim's in Beijing and Song Huai-Kuei's close friend.

JIANG Zemin
1926–2022
born Jiangsu
Politician. Jiang served as general secretary of the Communist Party of China from 1989 to 2002 and president of the People's Republic of China from 1993 to 2003. He visited Maxim's in 1984 and the *Contemporary China Tapestry Exhibition* organised by the Institute of Art Tapestry Varbanov. He also received Song Huai-Kuei, Pierre Cardin, Valentino, and Gianfranco Ferré in Zhongnanhai in 1993.

K

KING, Alice
born 1940, Shanghai
Art collector and gallerist. A friend of Song Huai-Kuei and Maryn Varbanov. Organised the exhibition *New Direction in Contemporary Chinese Tapestry* at Hong Kong Arts Centre in 1988.

L

LEE, Michel
Fashion brand representative. A close friend of Song Huai-Kuei in Paris. Met T'ang Haywen in the early 1970s through Song.

LEUNG Ka-fai, Tony
born 1958, Hong Kong
Actor. Met Song Huai-Kuei in 1983 in Beijing during the shooting of *The Burning of Imperial Palace* and *Reign behind a Curtain*, both directed by Li Han-hsiang.

LI Han-hsiang
1926–1996
born Liaoning
Film director. Li's best-known work in China is the *Qing Palace Trilogy*, which describes the court politics of the Qing Dynasty.

LI Jingfang
1904–1980
born Hubei
Song Huai-Kuei's mother.

LIANG Heping
born 1954, Heilongjiang
Musician. A pioneering figure in Chinese rock music. Song Huai-Kuei's guest at Maxim's in Beijing.

LIANG Shaoji
born 1945, Shanghai
Artist. Student of Maryn Varbanov at the Institute of Art Tapestry Varbanov, Zhejiang Academy of Fine Arts (now China Academy of Art).

LIN Fengmian
1900–1991
born Guangdong
Artist and art educator. Met with Song Huai-Kuei and Maryn Varbanov in Hong Kong for the exhibition *New Direction in Contemporary Chinese Tapestry* in 1988.

LING, Dolores
1932–1999
born Austria
Artist, actress, and singer. Met Song Huai-Kuei in Sofia in 1968, after which the two became best friends.

LING Zifeng
1917–1999
born Beijing
Film director and Song Huai-Kuei's friend. Song visited Ling on location when he was shooting *Chun Tao: A Woman for Two* in 1988.

LIU, Ellen
1944–2019
British Malaya (now Malaysia)
Model based in Hong Kong. Jury member for the Supermodel Competition of the World China Division & the 2nd Best Fashion Models Competition of China, October 1991.

LIU Xiaoqing
born 1955, Chongqing
Actress and businesswoman. A frequent guest at Maxim's and Song Huai-Kuei's close friend.

LIU Yuan
born 1960, Beijing
Musician. A leading figure in Chinese jazz and a key member of Cui Jian's band.

LONE, John
born 1952, Hong Kong
Actor. Met Song Huai-Kuei when he starred as Aisin-Gioro Puyi in *The Last Emperor* (1987). A frequent guest at Maxim's and Song Huai-Kuei's close friend.

LURÇAT, Jean
1892–1966
born France
Artist and pioneer of tapestry art. Co-founder of the Lausanne International Tapestry Biennial with Pierre Pauli. His works were a lifelong inspiration for Maryn Varbanov.

M

MA Ke
born 1971, Jilin
Fashion designer. Founder of two clothing labels, EXCEPTION de Mixmind in 1996 and WUYONG in 2006.

MARKAROV, Assadour
born 1961, Bulgaria
Artist, curator, and art educator. Maryn Varbanov's student at Institute of Art Tapestry Varbanov, Zhejiang Academy of Fine Arts (now China Academy of Art), in the 1980s.

MATHIEU, Mireille
born 1946, France
Singer. Visited China and Maxim's Beijing in 1986 at the invitation of the Chinese Ministry of Culture.

MI Jiashan
born 1947, Shanxi
Film director. Mi's comedy *The Troubleshooters* (1988) received sponsorship from Christian Dior with Song Huai-Kuei's help.

MU Guang
born 1945
Artist. Participated in the *Exhibition by Beijing Artistic Tapestry Center* at the National Art Museum of China organised by Maryn Varbanov in 1985.

MURDOCH, Rupert
born 1931, Australia
Businessman, media tycoon, and investor. Helped the Beijing government redevelop its public relations plan for China's Olympic bid in 1998.

O

ODERMATT, Hervé
born 1927, France
Art dealer and gallerist. Founder of Galerie Hervé Odermatt in Paris, which represented Maryn Varbanov.

P

PEI, Ieoh Ming
1917–2019
born Guangdong
Architect. Designed the Fragrant Hill Hotel, which opened in Beijing in 1982.

PETROV, Ilya
1903–1975
born Bulgaria
Artist and art educator. Song Huai-Kuei's teacher at the National Academy of Art in Sofia.

POMPIDOU, Claude Jacqueline
1912–2007
born France
Wife of French president Georges Pompidou, philanthropist, and patron of modern art. Visited Maxim's in 1983 during a trip to China.

R

RAUSCHENBERG, Robert
1925–2008
born Texas, United States
Artist. Visited China in 1985 and held the *Rauschenberg Overseas Culture Interchange* (*ROCI*) show at the National Art Museum of China in Beijing. The show ran concurrently with the *Exhibition by Beijing Artistic Tapestry Center* organised by Maryn Varbanov at the same venue.

RONG Gaotang
1912–2006
born Hebei
Former leader of the General Administration of Sport in the People's Republic of China and Olympic medallist. Student of Song Huai-Kuei's mother.

S

SAINT LAURENT, Yves
1936–2008
born France
Fashion designer. Visited China in 1985 and held a retrospective exhibition at the National Art Museum of China in Beijing. Boryana Varbanov, Song Huai-Kuei's daughter, acted as his interpreter.

SHEN Congwen
1902–1988
born Hunan
Novelist, literary critic, and historian. Teacher of Song Huai-Kuei and Maryn Varbanov in the 1950s.

SHI Hui
born 1955, Shanghai
Artist. Student of Maryn Varbanov at the Institute of Art Tapestry Varbanov, Zhejiang Academy of Fine Arts (now China Academy of Art).

SHI Peipu
1938–2009
Peking opera singer. Met Song Huai-Kuei around 1982. Arrested in 1983 with his partner, the French diplomat Bernard Boursicot, for spying for China in France.

SHI Yongxin
born 1965, Anhui
Abbot of the Shaolin Temple. Attended banquet at Maxim's.

SONG Huaibing
born 1948, Beijing
Song Huai-Kuei's youngest brother.

SONG Liquan
1903–1991
born Beijing
Song Huai-Kuei's father.

T

TAKATA, Yoshi
1916–2009
born Japan
Photographer. Met Pierre Cardin in 1954 and became his lifelong collaborator and close friend. Frequent visitor, with Cardin, to China and Maxim's in Beijing.

T'ANG Haywen
1927–1991
born Fujian
Artist. Met Song Huai-Kuei through Dolores Ling and became close friends with Song.

TANG Wing-cheung, David
1954–2017
born Hong Kong
Businessman, philanthropist, and socialite. Founder of fashion brand Shanghai Tang and the China Club. Held his wedding reception at Maxim's in Beijing in 1983.

TARANTINO, Quentin
born 1963, Tennessee, United States
Film director. Visited Maxim's in Beijing in 2002 during the shooting of parts of *Kill Bill* in China.

TENG, Teresa
1953–1995
born Yunlin
Singer, actress, musician, and philanthropist. Met Song Huai-Kuei in the early 1990s.

TIAN Jiyun
born 1929, Shandong
Former vice-premier of the State Council of the People's Republic of China. Presenter of the winner's crown at the Supermodel Competition of the World China Division & the 2nd Best Fashion Models Competition of China in 1991.

TSUI Hark
born 1950, Hong Kong
Film director, producer, and screenwriter. Visited Maxim's in Beijing in 1992 while shooting part of his film *Once Upon a Time in China III* in the restaurant.

V

VALLIER, Dora
1921–1997
born Bulgaria
Art historian and critic. Introduced Maryn Varbanov to Galerie Hervé Odermatt and wrote the preface for the catalogue of his 1978 solo exhibition there.

VARBANOV, Boryana
born 1957, Beijing
Song Huai-Kuei's daughter.

VARBANOV, Maryn
1932–1989
born Bulgaria
Song Huai-Kuei's husband.

VARBANOV, Phénix
born 1962, Bulgaria
Song Huai-Kuei's son.

W

WU Haiyan
born 1958, Shanghai
Fashion designer and winner of the first Brother Cup Chinese International Young Fashion Designers Contest held in 1993.

X

XIAO Feng
born 1932, Jiangsu
Artist and art educator. Director of Zhejiang Academy of Fine Arts (now China Academy of Art) from 1983 to 1996. Visited Cité Internationale des Arts in Paris in 1984 with Cai Liang. There, they met Maryn Varbanov and discussed artistic exchange between China and France.

Y

YANG Bo
1920–2016
born Shandong
Former minister of light industry in China. Showed governmental support for the 1985 trip of Chinese models to Paris.

YANG Lan
born 1968, Beijing
Media proprietor and journalist. Participated in events wearing Pierre Cardin haute couture borrowed from Song Huai-Kuei.

YONFAN
born 1947, Hubei
Film director, producer, screenwriter, production designer, writer, and photographer. Met Song Huai-Kuei in Paris in the 1970s and became a close friend. A frequent guest at Maxim's.

YUAN Yunsheng
born 1937, Jiangsu
Artist and professor at the Central
Academy of Fine Arts (CAFA). Graduate
of Dong Xiwen's class in the oil painting
department at CAFA. His 1979 mural
for Beijing Capital International Airport,
Water-Splashing Festival: Ode to Life,
became widely controversial for featuring
two female nudes.

Z

ZAO Wou-Ki
1920–2013
born Beijing
Diasporic Chinese artist based in
Paris. Met Song Huai-Kuei in 1974
when he returned to Beijing for the
25th anniversary of the founding of the
People's Republic of China. They became
friends upon their return to Paris.

ZHANG, Jerry
born 1959, Beijing
Founder of the Beijing Textile Bureau's
fashion show unit in the mid-1980s.
Zhang met Song Huai-Kuei around 1985,
becoming a frequent guest at Maxim's,
and organised modelling competitions
from 1989. He founded the China Fashion
Show Group in 1989 (renamed New Silk
Road Model Inc. in 1992) and the Galaxy
Model Management Company with
Chen Juanhong in 1998.

ZHANG Yimou
born 1950, Shanxi
Film director, producer, writer, actor,
and former cinematographer. Friend of
Song Huai-Kuei. Directed a production of
Puccini's opera *Turandot* at the Imperial
Ancestral Temple in Beijing in 1998.

ZHAO Bowei
born 1957, China
Artist. Took part in the *Exhibition by
Beijing Artistic Tapestry Center* organised
by Maryn Varbanov at the National Art
Museum of China in 1985.

ZHENG Shengtian
born 1938, Henan
Artist, critic, curator, and art educator.
Taught in the oil painting department
at Zhejiang Academy of Fine Arts (now
China Academy of Art) for more than
thirty years.

ZHIVKOV, Todor Hristov
1911–1998
born Bulgaria
Bulgarian Party general secretary
from 1954 to 1989.

ZHIVKOVA, Lyudmila Todorova
1942–1981
born Bulgaria
Assistant president (1972–1973), vice-
president (1973–1975), and president
(1975–1981) of the Committee for Arts
and Culture in Bulgaria. Daughter of
Todor Hristov Zhivkov and patron of
Song Huai-Kuei and Maryn Varbanov.

ZHOU Enlai
1898–1976
born Jiangsu
Chinese politician who served in various
prominent positions, including premier
of the State Council and chairman of the
Chinese People's Political Consultative
Conference.

ZHU Wei
born 1966, Wuxi
Artist, art educator, and member of
the Institute of Art Tapestry Varbanov.
Participated in the *Contemporary China
Tapestry Exhibition* in Shanghai in 1987
and the 13th Lausanne International
Tapestry Biennial with the work *Longevity*
(1986), a collaboration with Shi Hui.

Selected Bibliography and Further Reading

Asian Art. 'A Few Quotes on Zao or by Zao'. www.asianart.com/exhibitions/zao/quotes.html.

Bartlett, Djurdja. *FashionEast: The Spectre that Haunted Socialism* (Cambridge, MA: MIT Press, 2010).

Basant, Sarmistha Gupta, and Zhou Zheng. 'Women and the Media in China: A Survey of *Beijing Review* and *China Reconstructs* 1978–1990'. *China Report*, vol. 30, no. 4 (November 1994), 421–431. doi: 10.1177/000944559403000403.

Bolton, Andrew, et al., eds. *China: Through the Looking Glass*, exhib. cat. (New Haven, CT/London: Yale University Press, 2015).

Brownell, Susan. 'The Body and the Beautiful in Chinese Nationalism: Sportswomen and Fashion Models in the Reform Era'. *China Information*, vol. 13, no. 2–3 (September 1998), 36–58. doi: 10.1177/0920203X9801300203.

Cameron, Nigel. 'Art Review from Nigel Cameron: New Direction in Contemporary Chinese Tapestry'. Manuscript, 25 October 1988. aaa.org.hk/archive/223821.

Chen Tong and Song Huai-Kuei, eds. *Maryn Varbanov* (Hangzhou: China Academy of Art Press, 2001).

Chen Yifang. 'Clothing a Billion People'. *China Reconstructs*, vol. 30, no. 5 (May 1981), 5–7.

Cheng Min. 'China International Young Fashion Designers Contest', trans. Jane Shaw. *Women of China*, no. 8 (1996), 30–31.

Danzker, Jo-Anne Birnie, Ken Lum, and Sheng Tian Zheng, eds. *Shanghai Modern 1919–1945*, exhib. cat. (Ostfildern-Ruit: Hatje Cantz, 2004).

'Designers Invade China'. *Women's Wear Daily*, 21 May 1993.

Fashion, Style & Popular Culture, vol. 4, no. 2 (2017).

Finnane, Antonia. *Changing Clothes in China: Fashion, History, Nation* (New York: Columbia University Press, 2008).

———. 'China on the Catwalk: Between Economic Success and Nationalist Anxiety'. *The China Quarterly*, no. 183 (September 2005), 587–608. www.jstor.org/stable/20192510.

Forden, Sara Gay. 'China Embraces New Revolution: Designer Fashion'. *Women's Wear Daily*, 21 May 1993.

Gao Shiming. 'The Symphony of Histories, the Emancipation of People'. *Yishu: Journal of Contemporary Chinese Art*, vol. 13, no. 2 (March/April 2014), 32–39. yishu-online.com/browse-articles/?730.

Gao Shiming and Shi Hui, eds. *Maryn Varbanov and the Chinese Avant-Garde in the 1980s I* (Hangzhou: China Academy of Art Press, 2011).

———, eds. *Maryn Varbanov and the Chinese Avant-Garde in the 1980s II* (Hangzhou: China Academy of Art Press, 2011).

Gao Zhe and Liu Jing. 'From Thin Air: Stories of China's First Top Models'. Posted on Chinanarrative blog, 7 November 2019. https://chinarrative.substack.com/p/resend-the-stories-of-chinas-first?s=r.

Geczy, Adam. *Fashion and Orientalism: Dress, Textiles and Culture from the 17th to the 21st Century* (London: Bloomsbury, 2013).

Gong Yan, ed. *Decorum: Carpets and Tapestries by Artists* (Shanghai: Shanghai Literature & Art Publishing House, 2014).

Gu Wenda. Interview with Jane DeBevoise, Asia Art Archive, 4 November 2009. www.china1980s.org/files/interview/gwdftfinal_201405131320131373.pdf.

Gu Xin and Lu Min. 'Re-negotiating National Identity through Chinese Fashion'. *Fashion Theory*, vol. 25, no. 7 (2021), 901–915.

Guiducci, Mark. 'John Galliano on Why He Loves Chinese Motifs'. *Vogue*, 21 April 2015. www.vogue.com/article/met-china-catalog-costume-exhibit-john-galliano-interview.

Hesse, Jean-Pascal. *Pierre Cardin: 60 Years of Innovation* (New York: Assouline, 2010).

Hobsbawm, Eric J. 'Socialism and the Avantgarde in the Period of the Second International'. *Le Mouvement social*, no. 111 (April 1980), 189–199.

Jacobson, Dawn. *Chinoiserie* (London: Phaidon Press, 1999).

Jiang Jingjing. 'Facelift'. *China Daily*, 5 May 2008. www.chinadaily.com.cn/bw/2008-05/05/content_6660503.htm.

Jin Yating. 'A Mechanism of the Chinese Fashion System'. *Fashion Theory*, vol. 26, no. 5 (2020), 595–621.

Kazalarska, Svetla. 'Fashioning Fashion in Socialist Bulgaria'. *Centre for Advanced Study Sofia Working Paper Series*, no. 6 (2014), 1–25.

Längle, Elisabeth. *Pierre Cardin: Fifty Years of Fashion and Design* (New York: Vendome Press, 2005).

Li Xiaoping. 'Fashioning the Body in Post-Mao China'. In Anne Brydon and Sandra Niessen, eds, *Consuming Fashion: Adorning the Transnational Body* (Oxford/New York: Berg, 1998), 71–89.

Liu Qian. 'Song Huai-Kuei Never Accepts Defeat', trans. Chen Shanshan. *Women of China*, no. 2 (1995), 18–19.

Ma Qing. 'China International Fashion Contest'. *Women of China*, no. 8 (1996).

Markarov, Assadour, and Shi Hui, eds. *The Artist's Dream: 'Unrealized' Projects* (Hangzhou: China Academy of Art Press, 2017).

Morais, Richard. *Pierre Cardin: The Man Who Became a Label* (London: Bantam, 1991).

Ou Shuyi. 'Chic '97 Brings Beijing Fashionable Clothing'. *China Daily*, 15 April 1997.

Porter, David L. 'Monstrous Beauty: Eighteenth-Century Fashion and the Aesthetics of the Chinese Taste'. *Eighteenth-Century Studies*, vol. 35, no. 3 (Spring 2002), 395–411.

Pozzo, Barbara. 'Fashion between Inspiration and Appropriation'. *Laws*, vol. 9, no. 1 (February 2020), 5. doi: 10.3390/laws9010005.

Prial, Frank J. 'China Names Cardin as Fashion Consultant'. *New York Times*, 8 January 1979. www.nytimes.com/1979/01/08/archives/business-people-china-names-cardin-as-fashion-consultant-pattison.html.

Ramey, Joanna, and Lisa Lockwood. 'NEW YORK—Donna Karan Has Taken a Small First Step into What May Be Fashion's New Promised Land: China'. *Women's Wear Daily*, 26 May 1993.

Rayns, Tony. 'Model Citizen: Bernardo Bertolucci on Location in China'. *Film Comment*, vol. 23, no. 6 (November 1987), 31–36.

Relics: Maryn Varbanov (Shanghai: BANK, 2015).

Sampson, Catherine. 'Peking Luck Turns Sour'. *The Times*, 18 May 1991. https://link.gale.com/apps/doc/IF0503275928/TTDA?u=oxford&sid=TTDA&xid=cd91cf4e.

Samuel, Aurélie, ed. *Yves Saint Laurent: Dreams of the Orient* (London: Thames & Hudson, 2018).

Segre Reinach, Simona. 'The Identity of Fashion in Contemporary China and the New Relationships with the West'. *Fashion Practice*, vol. 4, no. 1 (2012), 57–70.

Steele, Valerie, and John S. Major. *China Chic: East Meets West* (New Haven, CT: Yale University Press, 1999).

Sterk, Beatrijs. 'Lausanne Tapestry Biennial: Nomad Tapestries 2016'. *Surface Design Journal* (Summer 2016), 34–39.

'The Bright Lights of Peking'. *The Economist*, 27 October 1984. https://link.gale.com/apps/doc/GP4100168289/ECON?u=oxford&sid=ECON&xid=987173d6.

'The 4th Chinese International Young Fashion Designers Brother Cup Contest (1996)'. *China Today*, no. 9 (September 1995), 47.

Til, Barbara, ed. *Pierre Cardin: Fashion Futurist* (Berlin/Bielefeld: Kerber Verlag, 2019).

Tsui, Christine. 'From Symbols to Spirit: Changing Conceptions of National Identity in Chinese Fashion'. *Fashion Theory*, vol. 17, no. 5 (2013), 597–604.

Varbanov Tapisseries (Paris: Galerie Hervé Odermatt, 1978).

Wei Liming. 'Chinese Clothing Catches Up with World Trend'. *Beijing Review*, vol. 32, no. 30 (July 1989), 20–24.

Wen Tiansheng. 'What They're Wearing in Beijing'. *China Reconstructs*, vol. 30, no. 5 (May 1981), 8–9.

Wiseman, Carter. *I. M. Pei: A Profile in American Architecture*, rev. edn (New York: Harry N. Abrams, 2001).

Wren, Christopher S. 'The Improbable in Peking: A Maxim's'. *New York Times*, 28 September 1983. www.nytimes.com/1983/09/28/garden/the-improbable-in-peking-a-maxim-s.html.

———. 'I. M. Pei's Peking Hotel Returns to China's Roots'. *New York Times*, 25 October 1982. www.nytimes.com/1982/10/25/arts/im-pei-s-peking-hotel-returns-to-china-s-roots.html.

Wu Juanjuan. *Chinese Fashion: From Mao to Now* (Oxford/New York: Berg, 2009).

Xu Lei and Ge Mingfu. 'Urban Feminine Fashion in China from 1987 to Now'. *International Journal of Arts and Commerce*, vol. 5, no. 7 (October 2016), 30–37.

Yan Keyu. 'Craft or Avant-Garde? Contemporary Chinese Fiber Art at the Thirteenth Lausanne International Tapestry Biennale'. Unpublished MA thesis, Ohio State University, 2020. https://etd.ohiolink.edu/apexprod/rws_olink/r/1501/10?clear=10&p10_accession_num=osu1595538262296012.

Zhao Jianhua. *The Chinese Fashion Industry: An Ethnographic Approach* (London: Bloomsbury, 2013).

Acknowledgements

This book, the first to explore the life and times of Madame Song, would not have been possible without the Song-Varbanov family's generous donation to M+ in 2013 of the Madame Song and Maryn Varbanov Archive, along with Song's vast collection of Pierre Cardin garments. My deepest gratitude goes to Boryana Varbanov and Phénix Varbanov, who trusted M+ to steward this remarkable legacy even before the museum had a permanent home. I am grateful to Dr Lars Nittve, former executive director of M+, and the first Interim Acquisition Committee, chaired by Victor Lo Chung-wing, for approving what represents M+'s first-ever archival collection. This archive straddles art and design, thereby constituting an important first step towards building the museum's visual culture collection. The acquisition was a close collaboration with Aric Chen, formerly of M+, who co-curated the first exhibition of Song's Pierre Cardin garments at the Central Academy of Fine Arts in Beijing in 2010. Veronica Castillo, Deputy Director of Collection and Exhibition, also went to Beijing with Aric and me to make the physical transfer of the family archive possible.

Throughout the research and writing process, we have interviewed and sought help from numerous individuals, many of whom were Song's family members, friends, or colleagues. They include Song Huaibing, Eddie Lau, Liu Heung Shing, Becky Zau, Jerry Zhang, Chen Juanhong, Fang Fang, Sylvie Zhang, Wu Anna, Zhang Youdai, Cui Jian, Zheng Shengtian, Hou Hanru, Shi Hui, Liang Shaoji, Assadour Markarov, Philippe Koutouzis, Dong Yisha, Lv Yue, Hung Huang, and Mi Jiashan. Their recollections and insights were essential to shaping our depiction of Song's fascinating life and character. This book is enriched by contributions from Boryana Varbanov, Liu Heung Shing, and Cui Jian, all of whom have elevated our narrative by highlighting different facets of Song and her legacy.

I am indebted to many of my colleagues, whose contributions to various stages and areas of the book's development and delivery have been indispensable. Dustin Cosentino, Senior Manager of Museum Publishing; Pauline J. Yao, Lead Curator, Visual Art; and William Smith, Head, Digital and Editorial Content, offered invaluable advice and expertise that helped shape this book from the start. Special acknowledgements go to members of my curatorial team—Dr Wu Mo, De Ying Associate Curator, Visual Art; Tanja Cunz, Associate Curator, Design and Architecture; Yeung Tin Ping, Curatorial Assistant; and research volunteers Christina Shen and Ethan Luk—for their exceptional contributions to the research, writing, and editorial and administrative coordination. I thank Lam Lap-wai, Zhong Yuling, Jacqueline Leung, Or Ka Uen, our editors at M+; and Piera Chen, Grace Lam, Alvin Li, Amy Li, and Andrea D. Lingenfelter, as well as Zoe Diao, for their work on the manuscript. Tom Morgan, Jacqueline Chan, and Crystal Yu from our Rights and Reproductions team managed the complex image sourcing and rights clearance with care and precision, ably aided by Lai Man Kit and Daphne Ng. Images from the Madame Song and Maryn Varbanov Archive and M+'s collection of Pierre Cardin garments were digitised by our in-house photo studio, led by Lok Cheng, and were expertly processed and managed by our Collections Database team, headed by Jim Whittome. I also thank Textile Conservator Isobel Harcourt for her research and conservation of the Pierre Cardin garments from Song's archive. In 'Dressing the Modern Woman: Madame Song's Wardrobe', she was instrumental in providing the technical and material details of the garments. Natalie Harding, Conservator, Objects, offered help with identifying and describing the jewellery pieces worn by Song in the archival photos. I wish to thank Lucas Dietrich and Julian Honer of Thames & Hudson for believing in this project, as well as Roger Fawcett-Tang for his inspiring design and Makkaihang Design for their sensitive execution of the Chinese edition of the book. Lastly, I thank Karen Wong, Exhibition Manager of *Madame Song: Pioneering Art and Fashion in China*.

Finally, I wish to thank my family, friends, and colleagues for their encouragement and support.

Dr Pi Li

Copyright and Image Credits

Index